SSSP

Springer
Series in
Social
Psychology

SSSP

Changing Conceptions of Leadership

Edited by
Carl F. Graumann and
Serge Moscovici

Springer-Verlag
New York Berlin Heidelberg Tokyo

Carl F. Graumann
Psychologisches Institut der
  Universität Heidelberg
D-6900 Heidelberg 1
Federal Republic of Germany

Serge Moscovici
École des Hautes Études en
  Sciences Sociales
Laboratoire de Psychologie Sociale
F-75016 Paris
France

With 17 Illustrations

Library of Congress Cataloging in Publication Data
Main entry under title:
Changing conceptions of leadership.
  (Springer series in social psychology)
  Based on contributions from symposia held by the
Study Group on Historical Change in Social Psychology.
  Bibliography: p.
  Includes index.
  1. Leadership—Congresses. 2. Leadership—History—
Congresses. I. Graumann, Carl F. (Carl Friedrich),
1923–   II. Moscovici, Serge. III. Study Group
on Historical Change in Social Psychology. IV. Series.
HM141.C367 1986   303.3′4   85-27809

Typeset by Ampersand Publisher Services, Inc., Rutland, Vermont.
Printed and bound by R.R. Donnelley & Sons, Harrisonburg, Virginia.
Printed in the United States of America.

9 8 7 6 5 4 3 2 1

ISBN 0-387-96222-0 Springer-Verlag New York Berlin Heidelberg Tokyo
ISBN 3-540-96222-0 Springer-Verlag Berlin Heidelberg New York Tokyo

Editorial Note

This volume is the second in a series of three dealing with changing conceptions in social psychology. The chapters contained in these volumes originated in symposia which were organized by the editors with the help of members and guests of the Study Group "Historical Change in Social Psychology." The work of this group has been made possible by a grant and the hospitality offered by the Werner–Reimers Foundation, Bad Homburg, Federal Republic of Germany, with the assistance of the Maison des Sciences de l'Homme, Paris, France.

Further volumes:

Changing Conceptions of Crowd Mind and Behavior
Changing Conceptions of Conspiracy

Acknowledgments

The editors are grateful for the exemplary editorial and production assistance given by the staff of Springer-Verlag, both in New York and Heidelberg. It was again Barbara Keller in the Psychology Department in Heidelberg who most efficiently assisted one of the editors and who, with the help of Sabine Dittrich and Ariane Hornung, finished off the editorial tasks by supplying the index. Their help is deeply appreciated.

Contents

Contributors

Joseph Agassi, Department of Philosophy, York University, Downsview, Ontario M3J IP3, Canada.

Erika Apfelbaum, Laboratoire de Psychologie Sociale, F-75005 Paris, France.

Luciano Cavalli, Istituto Di Sociologia, Dell'Università Di Firenze, 50121 Firenze, Italy.

Mario von Cranach, Psychologisches Institut der Universität Bern, CH-3012 Bern, Switzerland.

John H. Crook, Department of Psychology, University of Bristol, Bristol BS8 1HH, England.

Daniel Dayan, 16, rue de la Glacière, Paris 13me, France.

Fred E. Fiedler, Department of Psychology, University of Washington, Seattle, Washington 98195, U.S.A.

Carl F. Graumann, Psychologisches Institut der Universität Heidelberg, D-6900 Heidelberg 1, Federal Republic of Germany.

Dieter Groh, Fachbereich Philosophie und Geschichte, Universität Konstanz, 775 Konstanz, Federal Republic of Germany.

Martha Hadley, 60 East Eighth Street, New York, NY 10003, U.S.A.

Elihu Katz, The Communications Institute, Hebrew University of Jerusalem, Jerusalem, Israel.

Nadav Kennan, 60 East Eighth Street, New York, NY 10003, U.S.A.

Lenelis Kruse, Psychologisches Institut der Universität Heidelberg, D-6900 Heidelberg 1, Federal Republic of Germany.

M. Rainer Lepsius, Institut für Soziologie der Universität Heidelberg, D-6900 Heidelberg 1, Federal Republic of Germany.

Serge Moscovici, Laboratoire de Psychologie Sociale, École des Hautes Études en Sciences Sociale, F-75016 Paris, France.

Margret Wintermantel, Psychologisches Institut der Universität Heidelberg, D-6900 Heidelberg 1, Federal Republic of Germany.

Chapter 1

Changing Conceptions of Leadership: An Introduction

Carl F. Graumann

The present volume is a companion to *Changing Conceptions of Crowd Mind and Behavior* (Graumann & Moscovici, 1985). The order of the books reflects a historical sequence: When the crowd was discovered as a social problem for close scrutiny by the new sciences of psychology and sociology, leadership almost from the beginning became an essential topic, if not a significant feature, of mass psychology—although perhaps one should say leaders rather than leadership. Because the general and scientific interest in crowds—due to the "rise of the masses"—had a political origin, mainly in France, the prototypes were the historically decisive crowds of the French Revolution, of the Paris Commune, and of the strikes, the new weapon of an awakening working class or labor force. Hence, the question of who led the revolting or striking masses, or, at least, who might have been the agent or agents behind the "mob," was felt as most important, if not politically much more urgent than the inquiry into the nature of crowds.

Also theoretically the topic of leadership, albeit in different terms, became closely related to that of the mind of the crowd. It was customary in the nineteenth century (and for many has remained so), to regard crowds as primitive, instinct-driven, emotional, irrational, subconscious, and so on. The individual, however educated, rational, and disciplined he or she might be, once submerged in the crowd, took on all its attributes as a result of contagion and/or suggestion. Accordingly, it was to the fields of epidemiology and psychiatry that mass psychologists looked for models and theories. Animal magnetism (mesmerism) and hypnotism served as the first explanatory paradigms for the mental change individuals undergo when merging with a crowd. Hypnotism, however, requires a hypnotist, whose relationship with the subject or patient is transferred to the leader and the crowd. As the hypnotized (conventionally female) patient, half-conscious, half-awake, is open to the suggestions of the hypnotist, so the crowd was said to be in relation to a leader (for well-documented reviews of early crowd psychology see Barrows, 1981; Nye, 1975).

For Le Bon the suggestibility of crowds was the counterpart of the hypnotic or at least very persuasive power of prestigious leaders. Their power was mainly seen as executed in speeches—the highly suggestive, rhetorically artful addresses of political leaders, demagogues, or evangelists who were able to enthuse, enrage, madden, and mobilize crowds. This was one of the messages that mass psychology succeeded in getting across to the orator-leaders of the twentieth century, that to lead the masses is essentially to talk to them in mass assemblies or by radio and televised messages. Not only did leaders such as the *Duce* and the *Führer* learn this lesson well (although not always acknowledging the sources); the message is still widely acknowledged in mass democracies, revised and refined by mass communication experts who act as consultants and stage directors to many of those in power and those who aspire to be (cf. Chapters 9 and 10). Yet the study of leadership as we find it in the context of contemporary social psychology is no longer a study of the mighty, of the personalities and behaviors of the outstanding figures of modern society, but of the many minor heads, bosses, and superiors of everyday, mainly institutional, life.

This shift of interest from the Great Man to petty leadership is closely connected with the shift from crowd to group psychology. This lowering of aspiration and narrowing of focus has several reasons, the most conspicuous and debatable of which is methodological convenience. Experimentation is still the principal method of social psychology, and petty leaders and small groups are much more accessible to scientific research than are socially eminent leaders and large crowds. However, accessibility and availability are not the best heuristic of scientific procedure, nor should a method, however privileged, be crucial for the decision whether a problem should be treated or discarded. In the history of psychology it has happened that problems were abandoned for methodological reasons; so it was both after the behaviorist revolution, and in the wake of the cognitive turn. Yet despite today's research preferences and reluctances in social psychology, not only leadership and groups but also leaders and masses have remained crucial problems to be dealt with scientifically, and that, we believe, includes psychology.

The interdisciplinary Study Group on Historical Change in Social Psychology, from whose symposia the contributions to this volume are taken, inquires into the nature of this change. Is it the phenomena under investigation that have changed, or is it our conceptions, or is historical change a covariation of both? As we did with crowds we asked again whether leaders and leadership have changed from the late nineteenth to the late twentieth century: changed in character, in functions, in role, in the ways they emerge or are created. To answer such questions presupposes that our instruments are sharp enough to measure any differences. But are our concepts so well-defined and practicable that we are able to compare, say, Napoleon's charisma with Hitler's or de Gaulle's? Are they discriminative enough to decide whether it is legitimate to ascribe charismatic leadership to John F. Kennedy or Ronald Reagan?

A shift of focus of research interests in leadership has been noted before: from emphasis on theory to emphasis on research, from unidirectional to interactional or reciprocal conceptions, from individual-centered approaches to individual × group or person × situation conceptions (cf. Stogdill, 1974; Bass, 1981; Hare, 1976). These are general trends that may be found in other areas of psychological research as well.

If one is interested in the modern social psychology of leadership and examines the more recent theories or models, another narrowing of scope becomes evident. There is a preference for conceptualizing leadership as "a set of group functions which must occur in any group if it is to behave effectively to satisfy the needs of its members" (Gibb, 1969, p. 205). Although this proposal for conceiving of leadership psychologically is not a proper definition, it gives, mainly in its normative conditional clause, the direction of most recent theorizing and research: the parameters contributing to the *effectiveness of leadership* or of groups in general, part of which may be the *efficiency* of leaders. Most of the contingency approaches (cf. Fiedler, 1967), the path–goal theory (House, 1971), and the normative decision model (Vroom & Yetton, 1974) are primarily effectiveness oriented. Even when the focus is on leadership styles or patterns of interaction between leaders and subordinates, the overall perspective of such studies is with a view to the effectiveness of styles of interaction. This holds for the so-called Ohio and Michigan studies of leadership (e.g., Fleishman & Bass, 1974; Fleishman & Hunt, 1973; Hill & Hughes, 1974), for the managerial grid (Blake & Mouton, 1964), as well as for the four-factor theory of leadership (Bowers & Seashore, 1966). The field of application and validation of such models is the task-oriented group or organization, and the fostering disciplines are organizational and personnel psychology and business and administrative science rather than "pure" social psychology.

Because presentations and critical discussions of the various competing models of efficient leadership are offered in many places, on the handbook, the critical review, and the textbook level, they are not taken up here. The Study Group and, hence, this volume remain committed to the idea of historical change in social psychology. One recurrent phenomenon in the history of the social and behavioral sciences is the apparent "loss" and "recovery" of a problem. The problem may be a large one such as language or the crowd, or it may be relatively small such as the relation between intelligence and leadership performance. Loss and recovery may be terms at once too emphatic and too broad to cover the various forms of the disappearance and reappearance of theories, problems, and methods from professional journals, textbooks, or the minds of researchers. Disproof, invalidation, lack of progress, but also satiation due to overresearching an area are the most frequent motives for the discontinuous nature of historical change in the sciences. Their counterparts are the discovery that turns out to be a rediscovery, the belated insight that a disproof or invalidation in itself was invalid, the fresh look at an old problem, a new urgency to resume work in a deserted field, and, frequently, a new method enabling us to tackle problems formerly considered too complex for the instruments then available. Considering that science is always in a state of tension between risk and security, between exploration and proof, we sometimes observe and appreciate a return from the safer ground of multiply confirmed results to a still-uncharted area previously bypassed as unsafe. The new look then implies fresh courage. The reconsideration of Kurt Lewin's and the Lewinians' contribution to the topics of power and leadership (as in Chapter 6) was not undertaken in a merely historical attitude nor as a ritual homage to one of the pioneers of leadership and small-group research. It was rather the discontinuance of the Lewinian approach that motivated this retrospect and reassessment as an "interrupted task" in the Lewinian sense. Resuming this unfinished task does not mean merely picking up the thread where Lewin had to drop it, but reassessing an approach that in its factual research never quite matched the Galilean mode of thought in which it was undertaken. The field-theoretical key construct of *interdependence*, important as it is for the conception of leadership, requires that the mutual behaviors of leaders and followers be taken as seriously as their mental representations of one another and their mutual (social) knowledge. The present cognitive trend has, mainly in social psychology, strengthened the tendency to underrate real behavior and environment in favor of their representation. That this tendency also invigorates the theoretical and methodological *individualism* prevalent in social psychology (Graumann, 1986) may serve as a monitory signal, at least for those who like to view social psychology as a social science and to communicate more freely and profitably across the boundaries between the social sciences.

A growing faction of social psychologists in Europe and America has been working since the late sixties for a reintegration of their discipline into the social sciences (cf. Israel & Tajfel, 1972). Since our Study Group was founded as an instrument to promote and practice the dialogue among psychology, social history, and other social sciences, there has always been a strong interest in the social context in which disciplines, theories, and research topics emerge. We can really understand neither the crowd psychology of the *fin de siècle* nor its conception of mass leadership without knowing the political, social, economic, and partly even the military situation of France. The same holds for the rise of *Völkerpsychologie* in nineteenth-century Germany, or, for that matter, the dependence on the post–World War II intellectual climate of the Lewinian conception of group and leadership "climates." Nor is it mere happenstance that the attempts at liberalizing and "socializing" social psychology were begun in the very years when the wind of change rose in many fields. In the meantime the wind itself has changed, but the few changes brought about in social psychology are there to work with. Otherwise, we would experience another instance of discontinuity.

In a different sense Fred Fiedler tries to retrieve a topic that had been laid aside for a while: the role of intelligence in leadership performance (Chapter 7). Have we not heard repeatedly how little personality traits in general and intellectual traits in particular contribute to effective leadership? At least, the tests designed to measure intellectual differences have not been very predictive of the selection of leaders; experimental studies have yielded contradictory or inconclusive evidence. The fresh look presented in this volume is a differentiating reevaluation of parameters in both the leader and the group, accomplished by means of a new theoretical model.

A new theoretical approach is also offered by Mario von Cranach (Chapter 8). Whereas the idea that leadership is determined by the nature of the group and the problems it means to solve can be traced back at least to Bogardus (1918) and was central to all group-dynamic conceptions of leadership since Brown (1936), the fresh look von Cranach invites us to take is from a sociopsychologically adapted theory of action. Recalling what was said about continuities and discontinuities in the history of science, we have here a conceptual and methodological innovation emerging or construed from the convergence of two traditions.

Although it makes sense to analyze leadership in the context of groups and group actions and to understand group activities as always implying some kind and degree of leadership, we must not forget the lesson from history: There are leaders of the masses who are not primarily leaders of small groups (the favorite units of social psychological analysis). The leader of a nation or of a mass movement and the idol of a generation may be members of small groups, but their leadership role derives from the feelings and the responses of the masses. In full analogy with the group-psychological approach we are held to study mass leadership in its social context. There may be similarities, but there will also be differences. And who dares to generalize from small-group research to the study of crowds and mass movements? Although we know that some do, we preferred to look into some of the specifics of collective leadership.

One remarkable phenomenon is the patent contradiction that arises in social movements that, while resenting hierarchical structures, and above all dominating leader figures, are in urgent need of direction and structure. Leaders are needed but unwanted, or at best tolerated as necessary ills as was the case in the German socialist movement in late nineteenth century, as demonstrated by Groh in Chapter 3. This problem continues to be faced by contemporary grassroots movements like the West German Green Party, who resent the existence of those partisans to whom they owe a good part of their public appeal, prestige, and constituency. It is the figures against the more homogeneous ground of the masses that make up the public image of social movements, and the image may become an essential part of a social representation.

One of the modern means of creating, building up, shaping, and strengthening the prestige of leading figures is by the design and rehearsal of media events. Leadership at the top levels of modern mass society has become unthinkable without its regular or intermittent presentation to the public by means of the mass media. In Chapter 9 Katz and Dayan contribute a brief study on the different social functions served by the rehearsals of contests, conquests, and coronations. The questions behind this demonstration remains: What is the need for heroes in a democratic society? Is it the need to identify? to adore? to be carried away? Whatever the proper answers may be, we are back in the psychology of the crowd rather than the group. In any case, the media of modern mass communication are an integral part of the social context in which leadership is realized.

In a similar vein—partly more extreme, partly more down-to-earth—Nadav Kennan and Martha Hadley demonstrate how political leaders are made and marketed like other consumer goods with the help of modern marketing research and strategy (Chapter 10). This contribution was bound to receive more than mere praise. As perhaps the most prosaic text in our discourse on leadership it came closest to the ideal of experimental design: control all the variables but the ones you want to vary in accordance with your intention (hypothesis). On second look, however, it is less an experiment in conditioning than a well-designed training program. As such it is in line with a long tradition of training candidates to become political, ecclesiastical, business, or military leaders. At the far modern extreme from the original conception of the Great Man manipulating the masses, we have now the irony of a quasi-inversion: The leader-to-be is the leader to be manipulated according to the expectations and hopes of the masses who, in yet another aspect of the interactions, are regularly or intermittently being told what they may expect or at least hope for. The social context in which such leadership occurs is truly complex in its reciprocal nature and a challenge for better theory and methodology.

The present volume contains the revised papers presented to the Study Group. It does not reflect the group discussions except in a much digested form in this introduction and in the epilogue by Serge Moscovici. A few comments on the vicissitudes of our communication are in order. The Study Group is interdisciplinary as well as international; its lingua franca is English, the second language for the majority of speakers (and authors). It is in this language that we have tried, mostly with success, to communicate differences that sometimes were difficult to convey because of the need to translate into a common language. Only superficially can the difficulties be called linguistic, however. They were also cultural in many respects. I daresay that our exchange on the changing conceptions of leadership was as cross-cultural as it was cross-disciplinary. Cross-culturally we have several problems that make comparisons difficult. Most comparisons may involve differences in political culture and tradition, for example between France,

Germany, Great Britain, and the United States. If we assume different styles of political socialization, or at least a different distribution of such styles, then different conceptions of leadership should result. At least the ideas of good leadership should vary and differentially enter theoretical constructs. Although the Study Group did not engage in an explicit cross-national or cross-cultural comparison, the differences between the various national approaches to the problems of leadership—of leaders, *meneurs*, and *Führer*—were felt in many discussions and contributed to the emergence of the cross-gender issue.

Here, as elsewhere, while communicating in English, we had misgivings about the synonymy of the key words (to lead = *mener* = *führen*) and of their derivations. Is a leader *un meneur* or even *ein Führer*? Is leadership *Führung*? Are the words equipollent in all their common and scientific usages? The questions may be wrong, but in the textbooks these terms are often used as equivalents. On the other hand, *leader* is often treated as untranslatable (one finds *le leader* in French, *el líder* in Spanish); so is *der Führer*. Historical reminiscences of Hitler's *Führerstaat* and *Führerprinzip* seem to induce avoidance behavior.

We are already deep in the jungle of psychological semantics. It is true that the everyday German noun *der Führer* has been so negatively cathected through its Nazi use and misuse that for many years after 1945 the word was tacitly banned from scientific discourse, replaced by the related but neutral *Leiter*, which is still the official technical term in East German social psychology. So one would find *leadership* translated into East German as *Leitung* but into West German as *Führung* since the latter term has been (tacitly) readmitted to psychological discourse. After all, the verb and the noun are too common and too broad in meaning to be replaceable. The verb *führen* (to lead) originally was the causative of *fahren* (to drive). So its basic meaning was *to set in motion*, which implies the aspects of mobilization and direction. That is why most adult Germans nowadays possess a *Führerschein* instead of a *Fahrerschein* (driver's license). *Führen* is here to conduct (*conduire*) a vehicle. Hence, this license is not a permission to lead anybody but oneself. *Sich führen* (literally, to lead oneself in the sense of conduct) is also good German, and it may help to get another document, not a license but a testimonial, the *"Führungszeugnis,"* which is a certificate of good conduct. Thus, one who behaves properly shows *Führung*, and the *Führerschein* may be easier to get than the *Führungszeugnis*.

While *Führung*, like *leadership*, has a variety of interconnected meanings (the position or role of a leader, the quality or capacity to lead, the acts or behaviors of leading, as well as a group of leaders), many other usages require different translations, such as guidance, direction, control, management, command, conduct, morale. As always it is not a proper definition but only the context that determines that analogous problems arise between the French and the English or German usages. Political and industrial leaders in France would rather be labeled as *chefs, dirigeants*, or even *leaders* than as *meneurs*, a term that carries a historically explicable pejorative connotation.

These intricacies of the leadership discourse are, unfortunately, not confined to ordinary lay language. Almost the whole family of leadership terms, but definitely those referred to above, have entered scientific discourse. Whether this has happened autochthonously within each language and cultural community, or by way of adoption from and assimilation to the English or American usage, seems of secondary importance. The ubiquity of leadership, however, and the cultural variety of forms and styles of leadership, of learning how to deal with leadership, from the perception of leaders and followers to their evaluation, which pre-supposes learning how to talk about leading and being led, have become part and parcel of our common stock of social knowledge (in Schütz's sense) and cannot stay outside the social scientific universe of discourse. Nor will technical terminology remain confined to the scientific realm and com-munity. If it refers to issues of public interest it is easily popularized, as the studies of social representation have shown (Moscovici, 1976; Farr & Moscovici, 1984) and modern mass media demonstrate every day. As an example, the concept of *charisma* has become secularized from its originally theological usage (as a divinely inspired grace), through its introduction as a technical term in social science by Max Weber (see Chapters 4 and 5 by Lepsius and Cavalli, respectively) to any appeal or charm of a leading figure that captures the imagination and enthusiasm of a public. That charisma in the latter sense of a personal quality is not in accordance with Weber's technical term of charismatic domination does not prevent some social psychologists, who would not accept the concept as a theoretical construct, to use it nevertheless in its vulgarized form as a synonym for prestige (another term, originally nontechnical, but gradually incorporated into the terminology of social influence).

Among the subtle pitfalls of the leadership discourse is what the female symposium participants contributing to this volume identified as a (male or masculine) "gender bias" in leadership discourse, theorizing, and research. Evidently, it is less in the denotative, dictionary meanings of leadership, authority, and dominance, or the qualities attributed to leaders and managers than in the connotations of these symbols that associations with and habitual preferences for masculinity in leadership come to light. Language may only be the sediment of the age-old experience of male dominance and/or the social representation of men having the say (and the guts). However, language is also the organon of thought and communica-tion and as such the subtlest instrument of discrimination. The hypothesis brought up in the Study Group that this masculinity bias has also tinged our scientific conceptions of leadership has not been finally supported (cf. Chapter 11 by Kruse and Wintermantel and Chapter 12 by Apfelbaum and Hadley). That it could credibly be raised and preliminary evidence endorsing it could be collected is another indication of the entanglement into which the semantics of the leadership discourse can lead even the critical scholar. Although we should know better, the legacy of the "Latin" crowd psychology that, whereas crowds are feminine, leaders, be they male or female, are not, has still to be renounced.

The chapters in this volume are framed by two contributions that helped us to deepen our understanding of the *ethos* of leadership in the universe of social beings. The first one, by John Crook (Chapter 2), is ethological and refers us in a preliminary but very thoughtful way to the evolution of leadership, which for some seems to be a daring expression. Leadership is not normally a concept traded among biologists. The question of why biologists are reluctant to use this all-too-human term leads us to the familiar problem of theoretical and methodological individualism and to the group context of leadership, which has its analogues in the upper ranks of the animal realm. The most fascinating analogies for the human psychologist, however, are the attribution of leadership and its concomitant phenomena of male-female differentiation.

The concluding chapter by Joseph Agassi (Chapter 13), which deals with the ethics of scientific leadership, underlines one last time the ubiquity of leadership. Its unavoidability, even in the scientific community, poses problems similar to those of democratic control in politics. In science much more than in politics, the necessary control amounts to information control. The free access to and flow of information as well as open debates about controversial issues should be both the responsibility of leadership and of its democratic control—a change, not yet historical, but still to be brought about.

References

Barrows, S. (1981). *Distorting mirrors—Visions of the crowd in late nineteenth century France*. New Haven: Yale University Press.

Bass, B. M. (1981). *Stogdill's handbook of leadership research*. New York: Free Press.

Blake, R. R., & Mouton, J. S. (1964). *The managerial grid*. Houston: Gulf.

Bogardus, E. S. (1918). *Essentials of social psychology*. Los Angeles: University of Southern California Press.

Bowers, D. G., & Seashore, S. E. (1966). Predicting organizational effectiveness with a four-factor theory of leadership. *Administrative Science Quarterly, 11*, 238–263.

Brown, J. F. (1936). *Psychology and the social order*. New York: McGraw-Hill.

Farr, R. M., & Moscovici, S. (Eds.). (1984). *Social representations*. Cambridge, England: Cambridge University Press.

Fiedler, F. E. (1967). *A theory of leadership effectiveness*. New York: McGraw-Hill.

Fleishman, E. A., & Bass, A. (Eds.). (1974). *Studies in personnel and industrial psychology*. Homewood, IL: Dorsey.

Fleishman, E. A. & Hunt, J. G. (Eds.). (1973). *Current Developments in the study of leadership*. Carbondale, IL: Southern Illinois University Press.

Gibb, C. A. (1969). Leadership. In G. Lindzey & E. Aronson (Eds.), *Handbook of social psychology: Vol. 4*. (2nd ed., 205–282). Reading, MA: Addison-Wesley.

Graumann, C. F. (1986). The individualization of the social and the desocialization of the individual. In C. F. Graumann & S. Moscovici (Eds.), *Changing conceptions of crowd mind and behavior* (pp. 97–116). New York: Springer-Verlag.

Graumann, C. F., & Moscovici, S. (Eds.). (1985). *Changing conceptions of crowd mind and behavior*. New York: Springer-Verlag.

Hare, A. P. (1976). *Handbook of small group research* (2nd ed.). New York: Free Press.

Hill, W., & Hughes, D. (1974). Variations in leader behavior as a function of task type. *Organizational Behavior and Human Performance, 11*, 83–97.

House, R. J. (1971). A path-goal theory of leadership effectiveness. *Administrative Science Quarterly, 16*, 321–338.

Israel, J., & Tajfel, H. (Eds.). (1972). *The context of social psychology—a critical assessment*. London: Academic Press.

Moscovici, S. (1976). *La psychanalyse—Son image et son public* (2nd ed.). Paris: Presses Universitaires de France.

Nye, R. A. (1975). *The origins of crowd psychology. Gustave Le Bon and the crisis of mass democracy in the third republic*. London: Sage.

Stogdill, R. M. (1974). *Handbook of leadership*. New York: Free Press.

Vroom, V. H., & Yetton, P. W. (1974). *Leadership and decision-making*. New York: Wiley.

Chapter 2

The Evolution of Leadership:
A Preliminary Skirmish

John H. Crook

Leadership is so clearly an important aspect of human life that it comes as a surprise to find almost no literature concerned with its origins. In particular the excitements caused by new ideas about the origins and functions of several types of altruism—ideas that crystalized as the sociobiological approach within ethology (Hamilton, 1964; Trivers, 1971; Wilson, 1975)—do not seem to have led to more extended inquiries into other aspects of advanced sociability. Recent work on human social evolution is predominantly based on a paradigm that, in focusing exclusively on the inclusive fitness of individuals, tends to leave aside aspects of social life that are essentially group phenomena. Nonetheless, it seems strange that although recent textbooks (Wallace, 1979; Wittenberger, 1981; Barnard, 1983; Huntingford, 1984) contain detailed accounts of complex social activity in animal groups in which leaderlike behavior is often in evidence, actual discussion of leadership is absent and the term does not appear in their indexes. Even in Alexander's review *Darwinism and Human Affairs* (1980), the term receives a derisory one-page, one-paragraph citation.

The evolutionary theorist does in fact face difficulties where certain terms descriptive of social interaction are concerned. Evolutionary theory discusses the origins and transformations of anatomical and behavioral traits considered as properties of individual organisms, behavior being envisaged essentially as anatomy in action. Such properties, especially with regard to lower organisms, are treated as consequences of developmental processes the basis of which lies in the genetic constitution of the individual. Many arguments about natural selection are grounded in simplifying models of what is known to be an exceedingly complex process in population genetics (Alexander & Borgia, 1978). Such mathematically precise modeling has yielded massive fruit in the form of provocative hypotheses (e.g., Maynard Smith, 1976; Wilson & Lumsden, 1981), although the relation of these to actual natural history remains questionable and difficult to test.

It follows that in discussing interactional processes biologists focus on the performance of individuals and the advantages of behaviors to the actors concerned rather than on the group process itself. Indeed, some useful interpretations of the roles of individuals in the social processes of groups, showing how the performances of individuals contributed to the overall performance of the group (Bernstein, 1966; Gartlan, 1968; see also review by Crook and Goss-Custard, 1972), have been criticized for shifting attention away from the adaptive significance of individual behavior toward that of groups and thereby risking a heretical move toward the assumption of group selection. Wittenberger (1981) summarized this response:

> Social roles are functional consequences of each individual's behaviour on group dynamics and social organization, but these consequences do not necessarily reflect the adaptive significance of the behaviours involved. Thus the concept of social roles is useful for describing and analysing the functional organization of group processes, but it is inappropriate for studying the adaptive significance of individual behaviours within social groups. (p. 594)

To such thinkers the attribution of a property called leadership to an individual is problematic, for although an individual may indeed show leadership behavior or even leadership qualities, being a leader necessarily involves adopting a role that can only be defined within a group context. There are no leaders without followers. Furthermore, the quality of the leader–follower relationship may produce a differential effectiveness between groups in their pursuit of the need satisfactions of their memberships. To discuss leadership in the context of evolution it will thus be essential to transcend such theoretical difficulties. Most ethologists will probably agree that the relevant questions are: (i) Under what circumstances may an individual lead or follow? (ii) What is the effect of being a leader on an individual's fitness? (iii) What is the effect of being a follower on an individual's fitness? (iv) What is the effect of leadership on the efficiency of a group? The answers can be discussed using currencies of cost–benefit deriving either from an individual's behavior itself or from indirect effects derived from differentiated behavior between groups.

In contrast to sociobiologically oriented ethologists, social psychologists have tended to move away from questions concerning the qualities of individuals toward the view that contextual factors are the prime determinants of the form and function of leadership behavior (Gibb, 1958; Eiser, 1980, pp. 262–312). In attempting to discuss the evolution of leadership we are perforce engaged in an attempt to relate the fields of ethology and social psychology, which have an inbuilt tendency to adopt opposing theoretical directions. Even so, I believe an attempt at bridge building can be both useful and productive. We need to renew the presociobiological focus on group processes in animals as an important field of social ethology, to which, indeed, studies of developmental and interactional processes in populations of advanced animals necessarily lead (see Crook 1970, pp. 130–138; Crook & Goss-Custard, 1972, pp. 296–306). The neglect of this aspect of social behavior is at last receiving attention through the work of Wrangham

(1982), Dunbar (1983), Colvin (1983), and Hinde (1983) on the determinants of relationship in complex primate groups.

The Group Context of Leadership

A useful beginning is to consider the way in which the term *leader* is used in everyday language and the implications of such usage. Hollander and Julian (cited in Gibb, 1968) argue that any act of leading implies an interindividual influence in relation to some shared motivational intention, locational direction, or goal or task completion: Leader influence suggests a positive contribution towards the attainment of these goals. There are four basic elements in such a relationship: the leader, the follower, the context, and the goal (task). These four variables and their interaction provide a setting for the examination of our problem. More dynamically, we have two dimensions here in which properties of the leader–follower relationship however conceived, interact with degrees of goal satisfaction or task success or failure, the whole process being conceived as structurally related to contextual variables (Figure 2-1). In effect we have a cost–benefit problem expressible in terms of the differential effectiveness of individuals with respect to their contribution to the effectiveness of their groups. Individuals whose degrees of leadership or followership fall on different points on this dimension may also be more or less effective in achieving their individual goals. In biological terms, this may also be expressed as differential individual fitness in reproduction.

The relationship of leader with follower in itself presupposes a group with a minimum of two members, one in each reciprocally related social position. Individuals who enter into such relationships presumably do so because of some constitutional or acquired disposition to assume such roles in relation to one another. Individuals probably differ in constitutional factors that predispose them either to lead or to follow. Nonetheless, which behavior is expressed by individuals in a group will also be a function of the

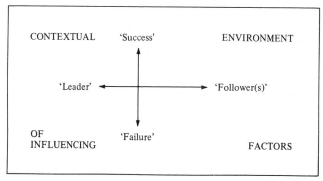

Figure 2-1. Dimensions of evaluation for leader–follower relations.

behavioral tendencies and motivational determination of their companions. Individuals share in common only the potential of developing a reciprocal relationship involving these two roles.

In an animal population, the capacity to express this type of reciprocity must be part of the adaptedness of individuals. We may assume that leading or following contributes normatively to the maintenance of the inclusive fitness of individuals living in both group and species populations. It must then follow that a group constituted by the behavioral expression of the dispositions of its members is primarily a mechanism for achieving individual satisfaction which often involves a degree of compromise. Furthermore, it appears as if individuals interact in groups in ways that may well optimize the accruing benefits to the group as a whole. This argument shows a striking similarity to the formal doctrine in which individual organisms are but the expression of the means whereby genes maintain their ability to replicate (Dawkins, 1979). The currency of group needs translates then into the currency of individual satisfaction, which is in turn geared to the optimization of the genetic fitness of individual members in each generation.

Such a viewpoint transcends the opposition between those arguments supportive of individual selection and those supportive of exclusive group selection. In fact, the opposition of these two, based in the contrasting arguments of Wynne-Edwards (1962) and Lack (1954, 1966) with respect to the function of social behavior in the natural regulation of animal numbers, is no longer so complete as it once was (Williams, 1966). Recent work suggests that selective processes may operate at several levels, each of which is concerned with rather different mechanisms of survival, reproduction, or need satisfaction but which mutually contribute to the fitness of individual organisms within their social and physical environments (Plotkin & Odling-Smee, 1981; Odling-Smee, 1983).

As far as human beings are concerned, it has long been recognized that groups that are differentially successful may also show differential survivorship of the group structures per se, and consequently of their members, and that leadership may play a signficant role in the evolution of more successful social systems from less effective ones. However, this has never been an argument for the exclusivity of selection to the group level through the existence of genetic barriers between groups, but has always constituted a process additional to individual selection as traditionally conceived. Contemporary thinkers (Odling-Smee, 1983) see no great difficulty in extending this viewpoint, at least to some socially elaborate populations of birds and mammals.

Leadership and Social Evolution

Populations showing the reciprocity of leader–follower relationships are necessarily socially structured into at least two moieties, and forms of hierarchy, however defined, will necessarily arise. This role differentiation is part and parcel of a group dynamic that allows benefits to accrue to both parties in the interactional system. Leader–follower differentiation is likely to appear when it is functionally effective in the mutual acquisition of benefits. The issue seems at first to be the same as for other problems in evolutionary biology concerned with the origins of types of collaborative behavior.

Yet the collaboration involved in the leader–follower relation cannot be simply mapped onto traditional discussions of altruism. In altruistic behavior there is a division into an apparent donor and an apparent recipient of benefits. Under kin selection, the donor, although making an apparent sacrifice in aiding a relative, can be shown to be maintaining his or her *inclusive* fitness by doing so. Altruism of this kind occurs primarily between relatives not much farther apart than cousins. In closely organized bands of small size and constant membership, the possibility of reciprocating altruism arises when donors receive returns of benefit (in the currency of fitness) that need not necessarily follow precisely in time the apparent sacrifice. Furthermore, this type of altruism is not necessarily restricted to categories of kin (Trivers, 1971). The leader–follower relation cannot be conceived necessarily as one in which one party is a donor of benefits and the other a recipient. The essence of the process is a mutuality of contrasting roles in which each receives benefit.

"Mutualistic relationships are defined as those by which two or more individuals gain greater reproductive potential (i.e. expected number of future offspring) than they would by acting alone" (Wrangham, 1982, p. 270). In its elementary forms at least, the leader–follower relationship is best classified under the category of mutualism, and Wrangham's thought on this subject is germane to our discussion here.

There are two sorts of mutualistic interaction: noninterference mutualism (NIM) and interference mutualism (IM). In NIM, collaboration increases the reproductive potential for both parties, but this gain is not achieved at the expense of other individuals. For example in a population of isolated pairs, those collaborating in a fishing expedition benefit one another but not necessarily at the expense of noncollaborators. In IM, by contrast, the benefit of cooperation is achieved at the direct expense of conspecifics in a population of competitors. Whenever two individuals deny a third access to some significant commodity, an IM situation has arisen. Such situations are well known in the cooperative defense of nest sites, food sources, territories, or mates.

Competition within populations is especially likely to arise when one or more key resources (Wrangham, 1982) are limited. When animals compete for key resources they develop key strategies related to the acquisition of resources that promote reproductive success. When alliance formation is a critical aspect of behavior ensuring access to key resources, it is predicted that the competition will result in IM. In particular, because support between kin rather than non-kin has a special value for the inclusive fitness of individuals, IM may be responsible for the evolution of at least some kinds of kin-groups.

In their analysis of the adaptive significance of group formations, most theorists today emphasize a difference in the socioecology of the sexes. The key strategies of female mammals and many female birds concern the acquisition of food resources for their young. Females distribute themselves in the environment in relationships that ensure the most effective exploitation of food resources. When resources are unlimited, NIM behaviors are likely to appear; however, when resources are in short supply, and especially when ecological conditions reduce the carrying capacity of the environment to produce so-called K. conditions of selection (see Pianka, 1974), IM is likely to evolve. Wrangham found a broad correlation between patchy food distribution, competition, and IM among primates. In many cases, then "breeding females who live in groups of female relatives do so specifically because of the advantages gained in competing mutualistically for access to key resources" (Wrangham, 1982, p. 279). Although group formation also produces direct or indirect competition between the members, the advantages of a key resource strategy involving alliances appears to outweigh the effects of increased intragroup competition.

Competitiveness among males in many mammal and bird species is less concerned with the exploitation of food than with their most important reproductive "resource": access to females. Male distribution and group formation is thus most often envisaged as contingent on the food-resource-related distribution and social structuring of the females. In a variety of primate species, male kin groups do in fact compete for access to females and therefore constitute an IM condition. As present, however, further research is needed to reveal the reasons for the contrasts between these kin groups and other male distributions showing different relations to female dispersal and social organization. IM also occurs in reciprocating actions involving individual males in their competition with third parties for access to females (Packer, 1977), but the importance of this process within large groups of primates needs further examination because the conditions determining the frequency of this behavior are not yet clearly established.

Intersex mutualism arises where members of each sex gain advantage from the presence and activities of the other. In particular, the behavior of males in guarding their mates against interference from other males may be reproductively significant for both sexes. Among mountain gorillas, for example, the presence of a group male who keeps off the aggressive attentions of other males reduces the high costs to females of such impositions. Females prefer males who protect them most effectively (Harcourt, 1978). In fact, male–female mutualism seems to be the prime determinant of the pattern of social grouping among gorillas. Research suggests that females in this type of group do not necessarily form alliances with one another as kin, but assemble essentially to relate with effective mates (Harcourt, 1978; Marsh, 1979). Female mobility between groups and populations is frequent in species that demonstrate intersex mutualistic associations of this kind, for females will move on if their male or males become less effective (see review by Harcourt & Stewart, 1983).

In primate alliances, complex hierarchical organization involving dominance and subordination and rankings of access to individuals is common and reflects the patterns of intragroup competition that alliance formation entails. These interactions are often relatively muted, however, suggesting that selection has favored means of reducing individual damage that would follow upon aggression within such groups. High-ranking partners are often preferred as companions in both male and female systems, although preferences in the latter also depend on whether the female concerned has a baby or not. Subordinate animals often associate with dominant ones through grooming, and competition for grooming access is frequent (Seyfarth, 1976).

Alliances in IM can thus lead to the evolution of relatively closed and stable groups containing complex hierarchically organized differentiation of social roles. Kin relations may be complex and female rather than male mobility common when female preferences among protector males are a key aspect of the intersex orientation.

Both Wrangham (1982) and Maynard-Smith (1982) point out that much of the social complexity of primate groups has been attributed to sexual selection, kin selection, and reciprocal altruism. An additional component of social selection (Crook, 1971) that has been neglected involves the patterns of mutualism discussed above. Research on mutualism is especially promising; not only developing further the study of contingencies between ecology and social selection but also bringing within the same argument the problem of origins of role complexity within groups.

The leader–follower relationship fits well into this picture as a role-differentiated mutualism with specially developed functions for situations in which competition with other alliances is likely. The behavioral properties, dispositions, and skills of individuals with respect to their common goals will, of course, vary, and their role differentiation may be a consequence of their differential contributions to key strategies in the context of competition. For example, it would be mutually advantageous to alliance members if the skills of members in relation to the performance of a key strategy could be identified in such a way that followers were defined as those who gain most by following, copying, replicating, and reciprocating the behaviors of a more skillful individual, who thus becomes an initiator or "leader." Furthermore, when competition between groups occurs in such a way that conflict results, some individuals may have strengths or qualities that when "followed" influence the outcome.

It will be clear at this point that we are not merely concerned with dominance relations. Differing types of influence will be related to the strategic behavior that is required in a particular situation. It follows that a whole range of dispositionally related roles may, under appropriate circumstances, acquire functions around which a leader–follower– relationship may develop on the basis of differences in skill (or other relevant behavior). The essence of the problem comes into focus around the question of what determines the attribution by followers of leadership to a fellow individual in such a way that the mutual benefits are greater than those to be obtained within an alliance without such differentials.

Leader-Follower Associations

A full survey of the range of leader–follower associations in animals is impossible here. It would certainly be a task well worth undertaking, for a better understanding of the circumstances under which complex group structuring develops could well emerge from an exhaustively comparative approach. In this chapter, I restrict myself to a brief look at some types of leader–follower relations that support the approach developed above and are provocative with respect to ideas concerning human evolution (Figure 2-2).

A consideration of four types of leader–follower relation produces contrasts in the extent to which leaders assume social roles and to which benefits accrue to followers or to both parties or become differentially distributed between them.

Leader–Follower Relation in *Quelea* Flocks

In the nonbreeding season, birds of many species form flocks that are organized as a dispersion system based on a night time roost from which they fly forth daily to forage. Ward and Zahavi (1973) suggested that the roost functioned as an information source at which birds that had not been adequately successful in a day's foraging could determine from an observation of others the direction in which areas of abundant food lay. In effect, food resources are located by following birds whose behavior indicates that they know where good food is to be found.

This hypothesis, at first based only on a comparative analysis of flocking systems, was subjected to experimental testing in our Bristol laboratories by de Groot (1980). He placed birds in aviaries that had a set of exits, some of which led to a food resource and some of which did not. The experimental subjects were *Quelea*, an exceedingly gregarious, sparrow-sized weaverbird (Ploceinae), that lives in vast numbers in the African savannah and that roosts in vast "conurbations" outside the breeding season (see Crook & Butterfield, 1970; Crook & Ward, 1968; Ward, 1965, 1970). When parties of birds, half of which knew which exits led to food, were placed in the experimental aviary and deprived of food, those who did not know which exits to use rapidly discovered them through observation of the knowledgeable birds. The mechanism whereby this effect is achieved depends on

Type of Leadership	Followers Attribute Leadership Qualities	Leaders Assume Roles	Long-Term Role Differentiation	Only Followers Benefit	Contrasting Benefits Accrue to Roles
Flocking in *Quelea*	+	−	−	+	−
Alpha animals in deer, sheep, elephants, etc.	+	+	$\pm$	−	−
Male or female leadership in hunting groups, wolves, hyenas, etc.	+	+	+	−	+
Protective leadership in primate communities	+	+	+	−	+

Figure 2-2. Preliminary categorization of leader–follower relations in animals.

the fact that birds lacking knowledge of the correct exits hang back and wait for more knowledgeable birds to move. The most parsimonious explanation for such a strategy requires (i) some kind of self-assessment of an individual's recent feeding experience in comparison with that which it might expect, and (ii) a means of gauging the quality of foraging experienced by companions. To a human observer careful observation discloses differences in behavior between hungry and satiated birds when perched in cages without food. Experiments showed that hungry birds could locate food by distinguishing the behavioral cues of satiation in potential companions. It was also found that by hanging back birds lacking knowledge of resources necessarily caused those with knowledge to move first and thus to disclose the direction to be taken. The knowledgeable birds were thus attributed a leadership function by those who by hanging back defined themselves as followers. Behavioral cues and past feeding experience both play roles in determining whether an individual holds back or flies first. Such a system could only work where there existed some synchrony of need states. Indeed, when the requirements of birds were not matched in time, birds tended to separate into motivationally distinct groups, and the communication effect did not then arise. Synchrony of need allows the behavior of other individuals to be interpreted in a meaningful way. The behavior enables individuals to live in a marginal habitat with patchy and unpredictable resources by assessing resource availability and quality over an area far in excess of the search capacity of a single bird.

Flocking in *Quelea* is interpretable in terms of NIM. The actual mechanism whereby the food resource strategy is made effective is the ability to differentiate between behavioral indicators of hungry and well-fed individuals and to respond differentially so that the latter lead or at least indicate directonality to the former. Because the luck of individuals will vary from day to day, no permanent roles are established here. The attribution of leader and follower is determined solely by the motivational needs of the moment and based on attentive behavior involving categorization of companions according to criteria of behavior appearance. The leader does nothing and receives no benefit by virtue of the attribution but will in turn perform as a benefit-receiving follower when hungry. Although at any one moment the knowledgeable bird seems to be altruistic, this has to be viewed in a temporal setting, which discloses the reciprocal and mutualistic balance between the two role designations. In Figure 2-2, therefore, *Quelea* are categorized as attributing leadership qualities to certain companions as part of a key resource strategy. These short-duration leaders do not assume roles, nor does a role differential of long-term duration develop within groups. Only the followers benefit directly from the behavior in the short term, but the system as a whole ensures a mutualistic distribution of benefits among all performers. This system seems to be the simplest leader–follower system but one with major contributions to offer in resource-acquisition strategies.

"Alpha" Animals (female) Among Ungulates

In several ungulate species in which females congregate collectively, certain females (referred to as *alphas*) acquire leadership roles in the sense that when they move other females follow. Here the attribution probably most usually arises among kin, the original follower group being the children of a particular female. A system may develop whereby an old animal is followed not only by immediate offspring, but also by their families and even distant relatives. In that such leadership is an extension of parental care, one can readily perceive the balanced advantages that accrue in terms of inclusive fitness to each of the moieties involved. It may be supposed that such advantages are a consequence of shared knowledge, as in the *Quelea* case, but here producing an enduring structured role relationship based on kinship links. Older animals, having experienced changing seasons of food supply variation and incidences of predation, retain a knowledge of many years' worth. It pays offspring to rely on such knowledge and sometimes to generalize their reliance to other knowledgeable animals who need not always be close kin. It seems likely here that the attribution of leadership roles is not merely a matter of kinship, but that certain individuals by virtue of traits such as assuredness, dominance without excessive aggression, and affiliativeness provide clues as to who would be a reliable (goal-predictable) animal to follow. Furthermore, the repeated positive reinforcements experienced in the company of such animals would lead to firm social structuring around them. In such groups male leadership is often absent; males merely travel with the females, competing with one another for access to them and occasionally gaining short-term control through dominance over small groups of mates.

Hunting Groups

In group-hunting carnivores (wolves, hunting dogs), either sex may play a predominant role in leading or coordinating the complex maneuvers of the chase and the transportation of food. Among hyenas the leader of a clan is female, owing, according to Kruuk (1972), to the insecure status of the young hyenas, the risk of cannibalization, and hence the need for a powerful mother. These females lead clans that may engage in battle when territorial rights are infringed. Hunting groups are highly collaborative, with the males commonly undertaking the riskier exploratory activities and the females the more reproductively conservative activities of nourishment and care (for example, see Rasa, 1977, on the dwarf mongoose). In many species, male collaboration is considerable and crude competitive interaction reduced. A more gradual transfer of power to influential males is apparent here than in the mateships discussed below. Intersex collaboration is of a high order.

Reproductive Units in Primates

Research on wild primate populations has recently focused on a contrast of major significance between female-resident and male-resident populations. In the former, a social group comprising female genealogical lineages or 'matrilines' occupies a range within which daughters replace mothers in intergenerational sequence and males compete for short-term sexual consortships with estrous females. Competition among males leads to the emigration of some of them from the natal population and their attempts to enter others. Examples are macaques and several species of *Papio* baboons (see Packer, 1979 and up-to-date reviews in Hinde, 1983).

Male-resident populations comprise "one male reproductive groups" (Kummer, 1968), in which males replace one another as the reproductive male in a harem of females. The females may, however, desert one male in favor of another or even leave a population of males in favor of a neighbouring one. Females in such cases are the mobile sex and males the residents. Males that are effective in attracting and retaining mates naturally show a high reproductive fitness. The development of these reproductive units implies a stabilization of sex roles within a group wherein the males' presence is a resource for the female and fulfills the males' reproductive requirements. The female's choice of a male is based on the protection he can provide against predators and, more importantly, against sexual interference by other males. Examples include the hamadryas and gelada baboons (Kummer, 1968; Dunbar, 1983) and the great apes (Harcourt & Stewart, 1983).

In female-resident populations, such as a baboon troop (*Papio ursinus*), subordinate females pay attention to more dominant ones, who tend to be their mothers or younger sisters acting in alliances. Members of matrilines acquire ranks that tend to pass intergenerationally to younger daughters (Datta, 1981). High-status females are the focus of attention in groups, and dominance confers preferential access to resources. Association with a dominant animal is for this reason commonly a preferred one. Among these females assertive individuals exercise great influence over the decision making of subordinates faced by choices of social action.

Female rank in a captive group of pigtail macaques was found to be independent of male rank, and an alpha female did not lose her social position when the dominant male in the group related preferentially with another female (Gouzoules, 1980). The female system seems largely independent of male influence, but dominant macaque and baboon males contribute to troop organization in a number of ways: acting as police to ensure relatively peaceable interactions among the females, supporting weaker individuals in interactions, and engaging in collaborative protective action against predators. Although dominant "alpha" males influence the structure of a group, some research suggests that female aggressiveness limits the number of males in it (Packer & Pusey, 1979). Clearly in such troops social situations may be influenced by the dispositions of individuals, causing them to limit or be limited by the choices of others. Dominant animals are often leaders in the sense that they have the greatest influence on the social decisions of others and are themselves relatively unlimited by the behavior of others.

During group marches dominant male baboons tend to move in the vanguard, females in the center, and subordinate males in the rear. When the rear of the troop is the more open to danger, the more dominant males move back. This behavior is believed to be due to the less timid dispositions of males who have a greater experience of the troop periphery and solitary life beyond the troop bounds (Rhine & Westlund, 1981). Troop progressions provide evidence for cognitive mapping of the range, movements are based on knowledge and not on here-and-now responses to stimulation (Sigg & Stolba, 1981). Dominant animals, whether female or male, exert considerable influence on the directions of march taken by more timid and hence socially dependent animals.

In male-resident populations the variety of male relationships and their influence on other animals is still being researched. In the hamadryas baboon (Abbeglen, 1976), males in reproductive units are kin; males coordinate band movement during foraging and communicate decisions about direction of movement and timing of rests and act to prevent too great a scattering of reproductive units. Complex signaling called *notifying* is used in the transmission of these intentions. A high degree of coordination of behavior results, and some males are more influential than others.

The gelada baboon has a superficially similar social structure, but Dunbar (1983) has shown this to be due to underlying dispositions that contrast strongly with those shown by hamadryas. Although young gelada males with harems tend to direct female movement, older animals are preoccupied with attempting to maintain viable links with increasing numbers of females and chasing off the approaches of potential rivals. Their control over the females progressively decreases as the harems enlarge, and no effective collaborative control develops. The gelada harems are closed groups of female kin that accept the presence of a male. Although they maintain contact with their male, they are prone to join other, more attractive males if an effective challenger appears. The dominant female exerts considerable influence over the movements of the group. Dunbar (1983) argues that the contrasts between these two superficially similar primates are due to convergence in societal structure from differing social origins; this convergence becomes apparent as soon as the deep structure of their interactions is analyzed.

Male residence also characterizes the population dispersion of great apes although specific social structures show considerable contrasts in adaptation to differing ecologies. Harcourt and Stewart (1983) point out that frequent affiliative and agonistic interactions, linear dominance hierarchies, and the servicing of status via grooming are typical of females in female-resident species and of males in male-resident species. Competition among males for females means, however, that male hierarchies are less stable than female ones.

Subtle differences among species require much further analysis, but in general it seems safe to agree with Wrangham (1982) that female-resident populations arise primarily as a consequence of benefits derived from cooperation among females in competition for economically defendable and clumped food sources. Male residence arises when females receive benefits from close associations with powerful males and move to areas where preferred males are to be found.

Clearly, patterns of interindividual influence (both intra- and intersex) vary greatly in relation to societal contrasts such as the above. That these primates are capable of complex relationships, communication of affect and intention, behavioral reciprocity, and partnering is well established. The analysis of how influential animals acquire and exert their control over the behavior of companions is still in its infancy.

From Animals to Humans: Natural
and Institutional Attention Control

Human populations have marital systems predominantly of the male-resident type. Females in simple societies are exchanged traditionally between intermarrying moieties within complex systems of kinship. Female residence is a relatively rare phenomenon attributable to distinct ecological and historical circumstances (see Maitland-Bradfield, 1973, on the Plains Indians, for example). It is likely, therefore, that protohominid populations were organized socially somewhat in the manner of primates such as gorillas or baboons such as the hamadryas and gelada. The highly affiliative, internally agonistic, hierarchically ranked associations of human males with their complex servicing of relationships through cultural conventions (Tiger, 1969) certainly bear comparison with those of other male-resident species. The less-formalized relationship style of women also fits this pattern. It seems likely that at least some aspects of human social interaction resemble those of these other primates and that this resemblance may extend to the socially controlling behavior of individuals and to contrasts in style shown by the two sexes.

In both avian and mammalian groups the attribution of leadership to certain individuals is, as we have seen, closely associated with the ways in which they receive the attention of others or attract it through advertence. In situations of social collaboration where one party may cheat on the other, the need for social attention is especially enhanced. This is likely to be the case in all examples of alliance formation, although the style will vary with differing types and functions of alliances.

Where the leader–follower relationship involves reciprocating collaboration, the situation may be so complex that the calculus needed for estimating degrees of trust is considerable. Crook (1980) and Humphrey (1983) have both emphasized that a need for cognitive appraisal of another's intentions in small interactive groups of long-term membership carries powerful implications for the evolution of consciousness that involves an objective self-awareness (Duval & Wicklund, 1972). The ability to experience consciously evaluated feelings in an empathic understanding of another's intentions emerges in these accounts as an essential part of cognitive enhancement in groups in which social cheating is a built-in probability. The attribution of leadership at this level of cognitive complexity begins to involve objectivized thought, in which acts of trust are related to the feeling an individual may have for another as competent for a leadership task.

Chance (1967) pointed out that the study of the attention structure of primate groups would reveal an important concomitant of social action significant for ethological theory. The attention structure of a group is the pattern of interindividual gaze and attention in terms of who looks at whom, under what circumstances, and in relation to what need or motivation. Studies confirm the importance of social acts of attending and advertence in both nonhuman primate and human groups (see Chance & Larsen, 1976). Attending in itself does not, however, cause behavior; rather, in my view, attention structure expresses the moment-to-moment motivational tendencies of group members. Although attending is an important aspect of group life, the focus of attention may be determined by many aspects of a group's internal dynamics and not by dominance rank alone (see Assumpção & Deag, 1979). Influence is not necessarily a simple function of dominance.

Awareness of attentional patterning in groups is likely to be an important source of information regarding the intentions of individuals in relation to one another (i.e., intentional structure). Attentional behavior is thus highly communicative of both the overall social activity in a group—the "atmosphere"—and the motivational states of members. "Attention structure is a way of understanding social organization in terms of the structure of communication rather than solely in terms of its contents or behavioural effects" (Barkow, 1976, p.: 203). Who looks at whom, the information about his or her intentionality, prediction of action, and calculation of an optimizing individual response (in terms of commodity acquisition or status or asset preservation) in the context of a key strategy are all interdependent aspects of the tactics of individuals in influencing one another in groups.

We may guess that at some early stage in human evolution reproductive-age males in families began to interact in ways that caused a rapid development of both interfamilial competition and cooperation. Competitive and cooperative social skills involve cognitive abilities of a high order, and some individuals would have shown more than others. Benefits achieved through associating with such individuals, especially if they were of high rank, would have soon led to elementary politics, made even more complex in kinship networks regulating the exchange of women as spouses (Sahlins, 1968).

An individual who acquires a following also receives benefits in both material and reproductive terms (Chagnon & Irons, 1979), and it will become as advantageous to that individual to retain these as it will be to others to displace him or her. Social influence rapidly becomes a process of social manipulation for the material and reproductive advantage of lineages and factions.

In human culture a competitive leader may make a claim of omnicompetence. This high-risk claim may yield very great personal benefits in terms of assets, which in traditional societies have also entailed an especially high reproductive success for male leaders. The competition for assets will be on many levels and assumes cognitive skills in personal evaluation in the service of interpersonal competition. Attribution by the people of charismatic qualities to a leader who succeeds in substantiating his or her claim then becomes predictable, owing to the satisfaction of social psychological needs the leader provides.

Research with humans (Stogdill, 1948; Gibb, 1958; Secord & Backman, 1964; Bales, 1953; Fiedler, 1967; and this volume) suggests that where social situations call for contrasting abilities in a leader, individuals demonstrate appropriate choices. In situations of group distress involving risk to survival, leaders appropriate to the task are also chosen and changed as circumstances alter (Bennet, 1983). Research on children also reveals the differential attention with which companions are regarded in the choices made prior to forming an association (see Chance & Larson, 1976). In humans it is thus the awareness of a situation and its appraisal in relation to the dispositions and abilities of individuals that produce collective decisions leading to attributions of leadership.

This natural and partially unconscious process presumably operates continuously in human groups. Early in human history it was recognized that control over the process of leadership choice might be made in several ways: by influence, by manipulation of perception, or by coercion.

Advertence presented for public consumption (Callan, 1976) in modern life comprises all those devices that make full use of media control and manipulation to maintain social leadership by ensuring that public attention focuses on the more satisfying activities, real or imaginary, of the leader. The leader is commonly a personification of an institutionalized stance taken by a political faction which is carefully orchestrated "theatrically" through public presentations of an individual and his media image (see Beck, 1976; Kennan & Hadley, this volume).

In modern life, therefore, natural social psychological processes of leadership attribution have fallen to a considerable degree under the control of institutions. Institutional manipulation through over-control of the media could thus in a Western democracy cause a mass population to exercise choices based on presentations of individuals whose appearance differs greatly from their real character, their true intentions, or their actual abilities. It seems unlikely that choices made in such a manner could increase the sum of happiness for anyone except the manipulators of society.

This process may seem far removed from the innocent jockeyings for social or reproductive advantage seen in birds, baboons, or chimpanzees, yet it can be viewed quite clearly as an evolutionary emergence from animal behavior consequent upon the dynamics of social selection in mammalian groups (Crook, 1980). We need no longer think of leadership among humans as a social psychological topic without ethological reference. Our perspective can, I believe, be greatly deepened by opening up the discussion of origins in this area. Evolutionary theory, like history, is, after all, not concerned with novelty but rather with transformations.

Some Conclusions

This all-too-brief survey suggests that mutualism and sexual selection are the main evolutionary sources of social systems in which one moiety attributes leadership to another. The advantages to leader and led may be mutual or may involve contrasting gains; however, these are presumed to produce balanced benefits when translated into the currency of inclusive fitness. Some leadership roles in animals, especially perhaps those attributed to males, may provide exceptional reproductive advantages to the leading individual. Competition for the occupancy of such roles will occur, and a role-holder may then be an exceptionally dominant individual who holds his or her position not so much by attribution but, at least for a time, by his or her skills at social coercion. The risks of conflict will now be high, however, and a subtle calculus of the outcome probabilities rules the decisions that individuals make as to whether fighting or withdrawal is the wisest tactic in an overall strategy determining their social positions. Assertion–withdrawal thus becomes a dimension of behavior on which an individual varies in responsiveness to variables such as group composition, intergroup relations, relative ages of group–outgroup leaders, and the kinship network. This dimension is then superimposable on a more basic one in which attribution of leadership to others is at one pole and action as a leader at the other (see Figure 2-3). The possibility that behavior in complex social groups of advanced mammals may be determined by some such interaction of dimensions is interesting, because similar inter-dimensional relations have been proposed for human relationship dif-

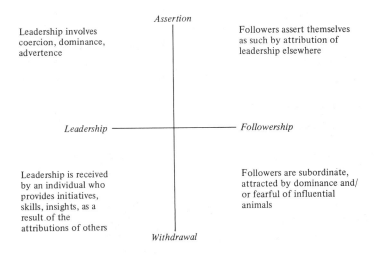

Figure 2-3. The dimension of leadership–followership related to that of assertion or withdrawal.

ferentiation (Leary, 1957; Carson, 1969) and applied to primates (Crook, 1980, p. 236).

In nonhuman animals we can recognize a series of increasingly complex yet overlapping conditions in the emergence of the leader–follower relationship. In a very rough-and-ready manner, these are as follows:

i. Leadership attributed to those possessing information needed by other individuals (e.g., among *Quelea*)
ii. Leadership by knowledgeable and usually older female kin (common in female-resident populations)
iii. Leadership attributed to individuals, usually male, that afford protection (common in male-resident populations)
iv. Leadership acquired by competition but accepted by less-confident followers because of its protective or other advantages (occurs in both male- and female-resident populations)
v. Leadership maintained by forms of coercion, including dominance, stealth, reciprocal collaboration, and misrepresentation (occurs in some primate groups and human societies)
vi. Leadership attributed in relation to specific goals, where both intra- and intersex collaboration is a prime feature of the interaction; attribution is based on *assessment*, varies in *task-specific* ways, and utilizes *criteria concerned with trust* as well as relevent skills (occurs in group-hunting carivores, some primates, and human societies).

In ethology research on leadership is likely to involve detailed quantification of cost–benefit relations arising from the preference for either leading or following roles. Inference from such studies to the effects of such costs or benefits on the reproductive fitness of individuals may then spur further modeling of the complex evolutionary scenarios plausibly responsible for the emergence of complex role-differentiating societies.

Renewed awareness of the multiple nature and systematic interaction of factors responsible for social action is, moreover, likely to return the focus to field studies at several levels. Recent demonstrations of the importance of demographic factors as controllers of social structure and of the widespread effects of social learning on social behavior will become increasingly influential, as will the need to understand how animals make cognitively controlled decisions that tend toward their advantage.

These approaches will have much to offer the social psychologist interested in the processes of leadership creation open to manipulation by institutional control. The clear exposition of such processes and their systemic interrelation will be all to the public good. Individuals about to choose a leader need authentic information with which to make an unalienating choice.

References

Abbeglen, J-J. (1976). *On socialization in hamadryas baboons*. Unpublished doctoral Ph.D. thesis, University of Zürich.

Alexander, R.D. (1980) *Darwinism and human affairs*. London: Pitman.

Alexander, R.D., & Borgia, G. (1978). Group selection, altruism and the levels of organization of life. *Annual Review of Ecology and Systematics, 9*, 449–474.

Assumpção, T. de, & Deag, J.M. (1979). Attention structure in monkeys. A search for a common trend. *Folia Primatologica, 31*(4), 285–300.

Bales, R.F. (1953). The equilibrium problem in small groups. In T. Parsons (Ed.), *Working papers in the theory of action* (pp. 111–161). Glencoe, IL: Free Press.

Barkow, J. (1976). Attention structure and the evolution of human psychological characteristics. In M.R.A. Chance & R. Larsen (Eds.), The social structure of attention (pp. 203–220). New York: Wiley.

Barnard, C.T. (1983). *Animal behavior: Ecology and evolution*. London: Croom Helm.

Beck, H. (1976). Attentional struggles and silencing strategies in a human political conflict: The case of the Vietnam moratoria. In M.R.A. Chance & R. Larsen (Eds.), *The social structure of attention* (pp. 273–314). New York: Wiley.

Bennet, G. (1983). *Beyond endurance*. London: Secker and Warburg.

Bernstein, I.S. (1966). Analysis of a key role in a capuchin (*Cebus albifrons*) group. *Tulane Studies in Zoology, 13*, 49–54.

Callan, N.M.W. (1976). Attention, advertance and social control. In M.R.A. Chance & R. Larsen (Eds.), *The social structure of attention* (pp. 221–234). New York: Wiley.

Carson, R.C. (1969). *Interaction concepts of personality*. London: Allen and Unwin.

Chagnon, N.A., & Irons, W. (Eds.). (1979). *Evolutionary biology and human social behaviour: An anthropological perspective*. Boston: Duxbury Press.

Chance, M. (1967). Attention structure as the basis of primate rank orders. *Man, 2*, 503–518.

Chance, M.R.A., Larsen, R. (1976). *The social structure of attention*. New York: Wiley.

Colvin, J. (1983). Description of sibling and peer relationships among immature male rhesus monkeys. In R.A. Hinde (Ed.), *Primate social relationships*. Oxford: Blackwell.

Crook, J.H. (1970). The socio-ecology of primates. In J.H. Crook (Ed.), *Social behaviour in birds and mammals* (pp. 103–166). London: Academic Press.

Crook, J.H. (1971). Sexual selection, dimorphism and social organisation in the primates. In B. Campbell (Ed.), *Sexual selection and the descent of man 1871–1971* (pp. 231–281). Chicago: Aldine.

Crook, J.H. (1980). *The evolution of human consciousness*. Oxford: Oxford University Press.

Crook, J.H., & Butterfield, P. (1970). Gender role in the social system of *Quelea*. In J. Crook (Ed.), *Social behaviour in birds and mammals* (pp. 211–248). New York: Academic Press.

Crook, J.H., & Goss-Custard, J.D. (1972). Social ethology. *Annual Review of Psychology, 23*, 277–312.

Crook, J.H. & Ward, P. (1968). The *Quelea* problem in Africa. In R.K. Murton & E.N. Wright (Eds.), *The problem of birds as pests* (pp. 211–229). London: Academic Press.

Datta, S.B. (1981). *Dynamics of dominance among Rhesus females*. Unpublished doctoral thesis, University of Cambridge.

Dawkins, R. (1979). *The extended phenotype*. Oxford: Oxford University Press.

Dunbar, R. (1983). Relationships and social structures in gelada and hamadryas baboons. In R.A. Hinde (Ed.), *Primate social relationships* (pp. 299-306). Oxford: Blackwell.

Duval, S. & Wicklund, R. (1972). *A theory of objective self-awareness.* New York: Academic Press.

Eiser, J.R. (1980). *Cognitive social psychology.* New York: McGraw-Hill.

Fiedler, F.E. (1967). *A theory of leadership effectiveness.* New York: McGraw-Hill.

Gartlan, J.S. (1968). Structure and function in primate society. *Folia Primatologica, 8,* 89-120.

Gibb, C.A. (1958). An interactional view of the emergence of leadership. *Australian Journal of Psychology, 10,* 101-110.

Gibb, C.A. (1968). Leadership: Psychological aspects. In D.L. Sills (Ed.), *International Encyclopedia of the Social Sciences: Vol. 9.* (p. 91). New York: Macmillan.

Gouzoules, H. (1980). The alpha female: Observations on captive pigtail monkeys. *Folia Primatologica, 33*(1-2), 46-56.

Groot, P. de (1980). Information transfer in a socially roosting weaver bird *(Quelea quelea. Ploceinae)*: An experimental study. *Animal Behaviour 28,* 1249-1254.

Hamilton, W.D. (1964). The genetical evolution of social behaviour. I, II. *Journal of Theoretical Biology, 7,* 1-52.

Harcourt, A.H. (1978). Strategies of emigration and transfer by primates, with particular reference to gorillas. *Zeitschrift für Tierpsychologie, 48,* 401-420.

Harcourt, A.H. & Stewart, K.J. (1983). Interactions, relationships and social structure: The great apes. In R.A. Hinde (Ed.), *Primate social relationships* 307-313. Oxford: Blackwell.

Hinde, R.A. (Ed.). (1983) *Primate social relationships: an integrated approach.* Oxford: Blackwell.

Humphrey, M. (1983). *Consciousness regained.* Oxford: Oxford University Press.

Huntingford, F. (1984). *The study of animal behaviour.* London: Chapman and Hall.

Kruuk, H. (1972). *The spotted hyaena.* Chicago: University of Chicago Press.

Kummer, H. (1968). *Social organization of hamadryas baboons.* Chicago: University of Chicago Press.

Lack, D. (1954). *The natural regulation of animal numbers.* Oxford: Oxford University Press.

Lack, D. (1966). *Population studies of birds.* Oxford: Oxford University Press.

Leary, T. (1957). *Interpersonal diagnosis of personality.* New York: Norton.

Maitland-Bradfield, R. (1973). *A natural history of associations: A study in the meaning of community.* London: Duckworth.

Marsh, C.W. (1979). Female transference and mate choice among Tana River red colobus. *Nature, 281,* 568-569.

Maynard Smith, J. (1976). Evolution and the theory of games. *Scientific American, 64*(1), 41-45.

Maynard Smith J. (1982). The evolution of social behaviour—classification of models. In King's College Sociobiology Group (Ed.), *Current problems in sociobiology* (pp. 29-44). Cambridge: Cambridge University Press.

Odling-Smee, F.J. (1983). Multiple levels in evolution: An approach to the nature-nurture issue via applied epistemology. In G. Davey (Ed.), *Animal models of human behavior* (pp. 135-158). Chichester, England: Wiley.

Packer, C. (1977). Reciprocal altruism in *Papio anubis. Nature* (London), *265,* 441-443.

Packer, C. (1979). Intertroop transfer and in breeding avoidance in *Papio auubis. Animal Behavior, 27,* 1-36.

Packer, C., & Pusey, A.E. (1979). Female aggression and male membership in troops of Japanese macaques and olive baboons. *Folia Primatologica, 31,* 212-218.

Pianka, E. (1974). *Evolutionary ecology*. New York: Harper and Row.

Plotkin, H.C., & Odling-Smee, F.J. (1981). A multiple level model of evolution and its implications for sociobiology. *The Behavioural and Brain Sciences, 4*(2), 225–268.

Rasa, O. (1977). The ethology and sociology of the dwarf mongoose (*Helogale undulata rufala*) *Zeitschrift für Tierpsychologie, 43*, 337–406.

Rhine, R.J., and Westlund, B.J. (1981). Adult male positioning in progressions: Order and Chaos revisited. *Folia Primatologica, 35* (2–3), 77–116.

Sahlins, M.D. (1968). *Tribesmen*. Englewood Cliffs, NJ: Prentice-Hall.

Secord, P.F. & Backman, C.W. (1964). *Social psychology*. New York: McGraw-Hill.

Seyfarth, R.M. (1976). Social relations among adult female baboons. *Animal Behaviour, 24*, 917–938.

Sigg, H., & Stolba, A. (1981). Home range and daily march in a hamadryas baboon troop. *Folia Primatologica, 36* (1–2), 40–75.

Stogdill, R.M. (1948). Personal factors associated with leadership. *Journal of Psychology, 25*, 35–71.

Tiger, L. (1969). *Men in groups*. London: Nelson.

Trivers, R.L. (1971). The evolution of reciprocal altruism. *Quarterly Review of Biology, 46*, 35–57.

Wallace, R.A. (1979). *Animal behavior: Its development, ecology and evolution*. New York: Goodyear.

Ward, P.A. (1965). Feeding behaviour of the black-faced dioch *Quelea quelea* in Nigeria. *Ibis, 107*, 173–214.

Ward, P. (1970). Synchronisation of the communal cycle within populations of *Quelea quelea* in E. Africa. *Proceedings of the XVth International Ornithological Congress* (pp. 702–703).

Ward, P.A., & Zahavi, A. (1973). The importance of certain assemblages of birds as 'information centres' for food finding. *Ibis, 115*, 517–534.

Williams, G.C. (1966). *Adaptation and natural selection*. Princeton: Princeton University Press.

Wilson, E.O. (1975). *Sociobiology: The new synthesis*. Cambridge, MA: Belknap Press of Harvard University.

Wilson, E.O., & Lumsden, C. (1981). *Genes, mind and culture*. Cambridge, MA: Harvard University Press.

Wittenberger, J.F. (1981). *Animal social behavior*. Boston: Duxbury Press.

Wrangham, R.W. (1982). Mutualism, kinship and social evolution. In King's College Sociobiology Group (Eds.), *Current Problems in Sociobiology* 269–290. Cambridge: Cambridge University Press.

Wynne-Edwards, V.C. (1962). *Animal dispersion in relation to social behaviour*. Edinburgh: Oliver and Boyd.

Chapter 3

The Dilemma of Unwanted Leadership in Social Movements: The German Example Before 1914

Dieter Groh

In Germany, those grass-roots movements that can at all be qualified as democratic, and which made their appearance at the beginning of the sixteenth century, had as a rule no leader in an institutional form or in a form modern typologies would identify as such. This statement is partly valid for the "Revolution of the Ordinary Man," as the Peasants' War of 1525 has recently been termed (Blickle, 1981). It is above all valid for the numerous peasant revolts, above all in Southern Germany, that began at the end of the sixteenth century and extended in an uninterrupted tradition up to the peasants' liberation at the beginning of the nineteenth century, (Blickle, 1979, 1980, 1982; Elbs, 1987; Schulze, 1980, 1983; Trossbach, 1986); it is equally valid for the journeymen's strikes during the eighteenth century (Griessinger 1981, 1983; Griessinger & Reith, 1983) and the first half of the nineteenth (Eggers, 1987). The revolts of the burghers and peasants in the first half of the nineteenth century, which came to a head during the revolutionary events of 1830 and 1848, are no exception (Volkmann, 1975; Wirtz, 1981; Reith, 1982).

Only with the emerging workers' movement, borne primarily by the journeymen and apprentices in the Paris "exile" in the 1830s (Schieder, 1963) and in Prussia in the 1860s, do definite leader figures such as Wilhelm Weitling and Ferdinand Lassalle appear, who more or less successfully placed themselves at the head of existing social movements and worked out explicit ideologies which, in the case of Lassalle, marked the emerging and fast-growing German workers' movements for decades. During the revolution years 1848–49 there arose for the first time something like a German workers' movement as a mass movement of some political significance—the Workers' Fraternity (Quarck, 1924; Balser, 1962) Despite the influence of Stefan Born and others, this movement belonged more to the traditional type of leaderless grass-roots movement defined above. The eccentric figure of Lassalle, who created the tenacious myth that he had founded the German workers' movement in 1863, became the center of bitter controversy surrounding the organizational structure of the early movement (Na'aman, 1975; Engelhardt, 1977) immediately after his romantic death in 1864 in a duel concerning a woman of the nobility. In the course of this controversy, the term "personality cult" came into currency, directed against Lassalle's style of leadership and that of his successor but also against its cultish features—pictures, songs, poems, and festivities. In the short period of his effectiveness, Lassalle laid claim in his whole habitus to being a leader of the German workers' movement in both its organization and its ideology. This role was also attributed to him by his followers. For the next several decades up to 1914, however, his personality was seen as more a negative than a positive example: The tendencies of party and union officials toward an authoritarian style of leadership were consistently blocked with references to Lasalle.

Generally, however, the development of the Social Democratic Party and the trade unions after the Gotha Unification Party Congress in 1875, during which the Allgemeine Deutsche Arbeiterverein founded by Lassalle joined together with the Sozialdemokratischen Arbeiterpartei led by August Bebel and Wilhelm Liebknecht and known as the Eisenachers, offered no further reason for grass-roots discussions about the relationship between leaders and supporters. The fact that Marx's works, especially the first volume of *Das Kapital*, were so highly respected as the "bible of the working class," mainly because of their unintelligibility to workers (Groh, 1985a); that Bebel was honored to the extent of being referred to by German workers as "our emperor"; that an American colleague could give his political biography of Bebel the subtitle "Shadow Emperor of the German Workers" (Maehl, 1980)—all these facts are highly significant of the specific authority structures of the working-class movements. Bebel and to a lesser extent Liebknecht were charismatic leaders according to the Weberian typology, but their charisma was, so to speak, bound or embedded in a highly democratic or egalitarian organizational structure, so that the authoritarian components of charismatic leadership could never develop. Bebel was, to use another typology, a sort of prototype of the organized German workers of the time with their strong artisanal background.

However, the key to Bebel's role and that of other workers' leaders in the psychological makeup of Protestant, class-conscious German workers should be sought less in specific characteristics or in the charisma of the particular person as in the fact that all were equipped with a specific knowledge supplied by the texts of Marx and others. This knowledge can be described as insight into the historical process that would lead by way of class struggles to the decline of capitalism, the elimination of exploitation and war, and thus the emancipation of the working class. In this role, leadership was seen more as a mediator of directive knowledge and specific interpretation patterns than as organizational talent. Workers' leaders like Bebel or Liebknecht were called "one of us" or "soldiers of the revolution" and not seen as distancing themselves from their class comrades or facing the mass as its leader.

The German workers of the time were not in a position to conceive of the irrational and asymmetric tendencies present in the relationship between the leader and the led, let alone verbalize them. However, they did sense and even articulate that leaders, in the strict sense, of social movements such as theirs (as opposed to other contemporary mass movements of the right) were, to use a catch phrase, as foreign bodies.

Given the leader–masses problem as it was being discussed in the international workers' movement until shortly before the First World War, and indeed during and after the war, the emancipation movement of the working class was confronted with an unsolved problem that had been on the agenda of the Enlightenment. With the words, "les lumiéres ne sont pas pour les faubourgs," Diderot had coined a handy phrase for the antidemocratic prejudices of many of the Enlightenment philosophers. The Enlightenment, as later the workers' movement which saw itself as its heir, had had as its motto that it was better for the further development of mankind—whether by revolution or reform—to enlighten heads rather than chop them off. The workers' movement, which like the self-aware Enlightenment philosophers, perceived itself as an elite, the vanguard of the working class, was faced with the problem of what role in the historical process those class comrades played who for moral, ideological, or other reasons would not allow themselves to agitate or be organized—that is, into whose heads the socialist doctrine would not penetrate. The aspiration was structurally similar to that of the Enlightenment; it was merely that the problem had been transferred to another sociological level.

In this emancipation movement, in full knowledge of the historical process, there could not be a leader–masses problem—not as the movement defined itself. Furthermore, the organizational structure was not built hierarchically from top to bottom, but vice versa: Only that person could hold a post as trade union or party functionary who had won a mandate from the grass-roots by means of a strictly democratic majority vote. The grass-roots, at least at the beginning of the development of party and trade unions, could revoke that mandate by means of strict voting procedures. Thus, the point presented here is different from the later one about organizational models within the socialist and communist movements revolving around the problems of cadre versus party (Lenin) or of "correct consciousness" (Lukacś). Only when correct class consciousness becomes the monopoly of leader elites, of small, self-appointed advant-gardes, and the consciousness of all other members of the working class is put aside as false consciousness, does a fundamental asymmetry arise in the process of enlightenment and organization. An analogy can be made between this process of enlightenment of false consciousness and its direction toward correct class consciousness (if one takes it seriously and believes that cadres or elites will in the long run become of themselves superfluous) and the psychoanalytical process (Habermas, 1968). However, here we are not dealing with such an *ideological* asymmetry between leaders of the workers' movement and its members—an ideology understood as correct consciousness from which proceeds insight into the historical process and the choice of correct strategy.

According to the self-definition and self-understanding of the socialistically organized workers, there existed an asymmetry between them and their unenlightened class comrades, whereby socialism in the German Empire of the turn of the century is to be defined as the dominance of Marxist discourse and its inherent definitions; however, this should not be confused with the dominance of Marxist theory and Engels' strategy in the exact sense. In this sense, the German workers' movement was never Marxist (Groh, 1985b). Unenlightened class comrades were relegated to the "one reactionary mass" (to use an ideological and strategic catchphrase of Lassalle's) which, in the event of conflict, would be on the other side of the barricades.

After the 1890s (Groh, 1978, 1981, 1983), above all in the trade unions and later in the party, there appeared a group of functionaries with quite specific features: They were permanently appointed, paid correspondingly, and lived locally but had functions at the district, state, or national level. They could no longer be removed by democratic voting procedures—the less so the further away from the grass-roots they were. The only possibility of dismissing them was to convince the respective leaders by word and deed that they were a potential danger to the organizations. The emergence of these bureaucracies cannot simply be attributed to the "iron law of the oligarchy" to which the workers' movement had finally to succumb (Michels, 1911/1969). In view of the large increase in voting and membership after the fall of the "Socialist Law" in 1890, both trade unions and party had to face the problem of how to adapt to the growth in membership, both quantitatively and qualitatively. The establishment of an organization administered by permanently appointed and regularly paid functionaries was at the time imperative for two reasons.

First, fluctuation among organized trade union and party workers was particularly high, as these were mainly specialized craftsmen at the age most ripe for agitation (20 to 40 years old). In many trades this fluctuation was well over 100%, meaning that statistically every position was refilled every 12 months. The problem for the organizations resulting from such a constant fluctuation could only be solved by the creation of a group of paid functionaries.

Second, most of the companies had begun to join together in class-struggle organizations in the face of the swiftly increasing strike activity after the abolition of the "Socialist Law." One of their first steps was to draw up and exchange blacklists of the names of workers who were known to be party and trade union members, or who held posts in the local or regional organizations, or who had been particularly active in strikes. These workers quickly met the fate of dismissal and unemployment, which in a short time became a type of professional prohibition when communication between the entrepreneurs was functioning well and they were not being forced by the economic situation to lure workers from each other. What was more obvious than to remove these endangered comrades and those who were already suffering the fate of permanent unemployment from the line of fire of the entrepreneurs and to make them functionaries, especially when such cases became frequent?

Two other factors help to explain the increasing tension between functionaries and members. The first can be seen in the development of the working process. The establishment and expansion of the organizations, and thus of the functionaries, ran parallel in time with another process. With the beginning of the economic boom around the middle of the 1890s (the new Kondratieff cycle, which extended to the threshold of the First World War), technological and organizational innovations in work procedures began to take effect; these were first perceived by workers as an intensification of work. As a result of these innovations the experience of those who had become trade union or party officials and thus automatically left the working world became obsolete much more quickly than had been the case before in the history of the industrial system. This swift aging of experience led to a widening discrepancy between the perceptions of the effects of the work process on the part of the functionaries and on the part of the workers in the factories. This difference and even contradiction in perception furthered conflicts.

A second factor was the paradoxical strengthening of the workers' organizations in a context alien to them. During the journeymen's strikes in the eighteenth century and the workers' strikes in the nineteenth, public opinion and the public authorities always formed an important factor in the calculations of the strikers, almost to the point of their becoming a third party in the game. Thus, one could reckon on either pressure from public opinion on the authorities, which these in turn would pass on to the employers, or pressure from both directly on the employers. In the political and economic situation in Wilhelmine Germany this traditional strike strategy gained more and more importance (Groh, 1978, 1983).

The Beginning—An "Impossible" Discussion

In the German workers' movement, as with any topic in history, words and terms, their origins, spread, and disappearance, are closely connected with actual historical development. To ask when the terms *mass* and *leader* were being discussed in the German workers' movement is at the same time to ask why such a linguistic innovation occurred.

The idea that persons (that is, leaders) make history contradicted, as already indicated, the historical-materialist self-understanding of the movement, which in principle found a consensus from the right to the left wings on this point. Thus, Robert Schmid, chairman of the Woodworkers

Association and on the right wing of the Social Democratic Party spoke
ironically against those who tried to place responsibility for unsuccessful
strikes on individual trade union officials (*Protokolle Verbandstag* 1906, p.
163):

> We, who represent a materialist understanding of history, who are of the
> opinion that individual persons cannot direct such a movement but rather
> that the whole social milieu gives the direction, we the great theoreticians of
> a materialist understanding of history are suddenly talking about the
> disastrous influence of individual trade union officials.

Clara Zetkin, friend and comrade of Rosa Luxemburg and like her a
member of the party's left wing, wrote to her magazine *Die Gleichheit* on the
occasion of Bebel's birthday, in an article entitled "The Political Leader of
the German Working Class" (1910, no. 10, pp. 146ff.):

> Social Democracy as a conscious supporter and spiritual child of a
> materialist understanding of history recognizes no hero-cult in history. Not
> even in regard to itself as a part of the historical development of society in
> general. Social Democracy is a product of an objective development in the
> womb of our modern class state. On the other hand Social Democracy is
> the product of the conscious influence of the working idealism of the
> Innumerable and Unnamed, of many generations of men and women; it is
> a product of mass actions. Without these Innumerable and Unnamed,
> without the conscious work of the masses, even the most gifted leaders
> could not form Social Democracy into that which it is: a power of the first
> order in the public life of modern society.
>
> However, within this framework the role of leader in Social Democracy
> receives, due to the particular character of this party, a historically definite
> context with definite limitations. The bourgeois parties are condemned by
> their very own interests to realize their goals, their policy in the broadest
> sense, against the interests of the mass of the people. But since the support
> of the masses is to a certain extent indispensible for the existence and
> effectiveness of every bourgeois party the following comes about: the more
> bourgeois leaders are powerful and influential, the more their actions
> adventurous, large in scale, and effective, the more these leaders are in a
> position to deceive themselves and the masses following them about the
> true character of their goals, about the historical limitations of their
> task . . . .
>
> Social Democracy is nothing more than the embodiment of the class
> struggle of the modern proletariat borne on by the consciousness of its
> historical consequences. Its real leader is in fact the masses themselves,
> understood dialectically in its process of development. The more Social
> Democracy develops, grows, and strengthens, the more the enlightened
> working masses can take into their own hands their fate, the leadership of
> their movement, the determination of its directives. And as Social
> Democracy as a whole is only the conscious vanguard of the proletarian
> class movement, so the leaders within Social Democracy are more
> powerful, more influential, the more clearly and consciously they make
> themselves the mouthpiece of the will and striving of the enlightened,
> fighting masses, the bearers of the objective laws of the class movement.

How is it that despite this agreement from right to left that leaders should
not emerge within the socialist movement, the discussion of the problem of

leader and masses should become more vehement from year to year? According to my very preliminary investigation (I have not examined closely the respective word families) the word *mass* first appears in 1904, above all in connection with the *political mass strike*, which up until 1903 had always been called a *general strike*. The Russian revolution of 1905 and the miners' strike in the Ruhr in January 1905, in which more than 200,000 miners (more than 70% of the mine workers) participated, as well as the discussion arising out of these events about the political mass strike, led in February 1905 to an explosive increase in the use of the words *mass* and *leader*. The Russian revolution brought about the first political mass strike, and it was hotly debated whether or not the Ruhr workers' movement had a strong political dimension. To understand why *mass strike, mass*, and *leader* could become provocative words in the discussions within the party and the unions one should know that the discussion regarding the pros and cons of the mass strike as a political weapon of the working class became the most debated point of strategy in the German workers' movement from the beginning of 1905 and up to 1918. Even when problems of leaders and masses were not debated specifically, this special context was constantly in an explicit or implicit relationship to the strategy discussion.

High Tide in Discussions of the Political Mass Strike

The discussion of the mass strike is the transformation into a strategy debate of the feeling about, and insight into, the fact that the policy of the party and the unions was not adequate to improve the situation of the working class. The aims of a possible mass strike were, according to one's party leaning, a change in voting eligibility and thus a strengthening of the tendencies toward parliamentarism, or an exercise of system-transcending behavior toward a revolution. Karl Kautsky had been pointing out to the unions since the turn of the century that the economic wage movement was condemned to become a lost cause if they did not succeed in influencing the legislators through economic and political actions. The climax in the mass strike discussion coincides with the strikes and demonstrations against the class franchise: 1905/6, 1910, 1913/4 mass-strike discussion and mass-strike agitation; Voting rights demonstrations: 1905/6 in Prussia, Saxony, Hamburg, Lübeck, 1908, 1910, 1914 in Prussia.

The attentistic policy of waiting for and avoiding revolution (Groh, 1973b), derived from the party's official concept of revolution, facilitated at least the rejection of actions beyond the traditional framework. The attentistic ideology enveloped with the solemnity of insight into historical necessity all that was the result of concrete historical structures, both events as well as the actions of persons and groups, and thus all that in principle was changeable.

The political mass strike demanded agitation and organizational measures as it was, however, above all an action—and as such different from all other traditional forms of action of the (social democratic) workers' movement at that time, such as election campaigns, demonstrations, protests, participation in representative bodies—that had to lead to direct confrontation with state power in one form or the other.

When the left as well as some revisionists and reformists demanded the mass strike as a new weapon at that time, it had for them two functions, one direct and one indirect. On the one hand this new weapon was aimed at the final goal; on the other it was intended to initiate here-and-now learning processes.

The direct function of the mass strike was to pave the way for an as-yet-undefined socialist society or social democracy. Regarding this final aim, however, the strategic ideas of the radical revisionists and reformists on the one side and of the left on the other differed fundamentally. For the radical revisionists and reformists the mass strike was an extraparliamentary means of forcing concessions, for example, better voting eligibility rules in the different states, or of opposing any attack on already-existing rights, for example, the right to vote in the Reichstag's elections or the right of coalition. In other words the mass strike was made a function of the process toward gaining parliamentary power.

It was just this concept of the mass strike as an instrument of parliamentary strategy that was rejected by the left wing. The latter placed the mass strike at the center of a revolutionary strategy which in the age of imperialism appeared to be the only appropriate strategy. Their strategy of mass struggle was conceived so as to cover a longer period of time. Rosa Luxemburg once spoke of a period of a few decades. The bastions of the opponents were to be gradually undermined by continual mass strikes and thus finally brought down. All possible opportunities, any given fuel in the economic or political realm should be availed of to win over an ever-growing part of the population to the goals of socialism. This cumulative process should then at an unspecified point in time give rise to the social revolution.

The indirect function of the political mass strike was to learn to carry out specific forms of action and to intensify the learning processes. These processes should take place within the total realm of social cognition. Through the mass strike, which could also be carried out on a local or regional scale, actions of solidarity were to be practiced and insight into economic, social, and political connections accelerated, indeed made possible for many. One argument even claimed that one such action, through its enlightening effect regarding the nature of the class struggle, outdid agitation and traditional demonstrations. Furthermore, the supporters of the mass strike pointed to the importance of the shared memory of common struggles, which provide a feeling of solidarity and of group identity, and in this way facilitate future actions.

As both a political weapon and a learning process, the mass strike was the unique means of achieving three things: gradually luring the social democratically organized workers out of their passive stance, testing the power of the state, and sounding out the possibilities for solidarity among the non–social democratic workers and among the liberal burghers with leanings to the left—in other words a means of gathering common experience among these groups.

Since 1896 there had existed a debate about the political mass strike as a defensive or offensive weapon, but only in 1903, after this new strategy had been realized in other countries, above all in Belgium, was the proposal made to discuss the mass strike at the Party Congress. However, the Party leadership managed to postpone inclusion of the mass strike on the Party Congress agenda until 1905.

The faintheartedness and caution among German Social Democrats faded away, however, as soon as the first reports about the revolutionary events in Russia in January 1905 reached Germany. The revolution in Russia obviously overtook the revolutionaries, that is to say the Social Democrats; revolutionary practice overtook theory. Through the enthusiasm for the Russian revolution energies were released within the German workers' movement calling for action that went further than the "legal" tactics to date.

The impression of a prerevolutionary situation was conveyed by three phenomena: First, the discussion of the mass strike, given rise to and encouraged by the Russian revolution, led to a mood for such a strike. Second, the strikes of 1905 exceeded in scale and intensity all that had been experienced before. Special mention should be made of the spontaneous miners' strikes in mid-January in the Ruhr; then the lockouts in the building industry in the Rheinland and Westphalia, in the Bavarian metal industry, in the Dresden tobacco industry, in the Berlin electrical industry, and in the Saxon and Thuringian weaving industry. The third phenomenon was the franchise movements in Saxony and Prussia for general and equal voting rights as well as the opposition to the undermining of voting rights in Hamburg and elsewhere.

The decisive question for the future strategy and tactics of the Social Democrats, namely, whether the Russian revolution was a forerunner of the proletarian revolution or a latecomer in the bourgeois revolution in Europe, was answered in favor of the former by the growing left wing in the Social Democratic Party. They drew the conclusion that the course and methods of the Russian revolution, above all the political mass strike as an offensive weapon, should act as a model for Western Europe. This conclusion was decisive for their behavior in the debate on mass strikes and during the franchise protests.

Rosa Luxemburg went farthest of all. For her the mass strikes in Russia were *the* new weapon of the proletariat. In her theory of spontaneity based on the model of Russian practice in 1905 she changed the question of class consciousness and the organization of the workers from a pre- into a postrevolutionary problem; revolution, consciousness of the class situation, and organization of the proletariat merge into one. It was this that made Rosa Luxemburg's theory so attractive for movements to the left of the communist parties, which lacked an established mass base.

The Leader–Mass–Problem in 1905

In the *Leipziger Volkszeitung* (1905, nos. 41–44, 61–63, 18.,20. -22.2.,14. -16.6.), a paper belonging to the left wing of the party, Konrad Haenisch, himself editor of the *Dortmunder Arbeiterzeitung*, in two series of articles—"Some Critical Remarks on the Workers' Struggle" and "Practical Revisionism"— broached the theme of leader and mass from the new point of view of the left that the leaders had failed in the Ruhr mine workers strike.

The trade union leaders of the strike were not informed about the mood in the district even up to shortly before the strike broke out. They may have threatened to strike, but they had never really considered it seriously and were thus completely surprised by its outbreak. The leadership also showed itself incapable by breaking off the strike to the complete surprise of the strikers: "Just as the struggle had begun totally 'wildly' in the psychologically weak eyes of the leaders, so too it ended . . . in complete disorganization and confusion as a result of the same lack of foreseeing leadership." "With their own hands the union leaders have undermined the confidence of the masses in their political honesty." These weaknesses could be attributed not to "the personal inefficiency or even ill-will" of individual leaders but "to inadequate mastery of mass psychology," which both at the outbreak of the movement and "at its tragic end played a most disastrous role." The origins of these inadequacies are stated as follows: "Politics is not an arithmetic problem" where one has to deal with exactly calculable quantities, but rather something in which "as elsewhere in life one has to reckon with imponderables." "Living masses are not chess figures that one can push around at will on a board." One cannot "commandeer" and "tame passions." "Such commandeering from above . . . in a struggle of such political, cultural, and ethical qualities, was something worse than a crime—it was *stupidity*."

On the other hand "the masses were taken over by an indescribable enthusiasm more magnificent and infectious than I have ever before experienced." They were in a "splendid ecstasy," which "in the practice of this movement was perhaps the most important moment." There was a "general mood of elation and festivity such as has never been seen in the proletarian movement, at least in Germany." "With the working masses of the Ruhr district, half of which were completely unorganized and only a quarter organized [i.e., in social democratically oriented unions] and who were literally thirsting for social-democratic mass propaganda, *the leadership failed totally*." The whole "mood of unanimity that reigned among the masses during the struggle" came about "despite the tactics" of the union leadership.

It was not only during the Ruhr miners strike in 1905 that it became clear that in the case of decisive action by the workers one could no longer speak of leadership in the sense of guiding actions, but rather of leaders who placed themselves at the head of movements that had come about without them, with the intention of putting a stop to them or chanelling them in keeping with their own tactics. The union leaders would have preferred to obstruct discussion of the general or mass strike before the events of early 1905 forced it on the agenda and kept it there until 1914. Already in November 1904, during preparations for the Trade Union Congress of May 1905, the combined managing committees of the various unions had decided to force if possible a resolution to prohibit discussion of the mass strike. In May 1905 in Cologne just such a resolution was passed by a large majority. In the preparation phase of the congress this met with opposition from the organizations and the press. Thus Emil Kloth, a "genuine practitioner," said in the *Neue Zeit* (1904–05, 23, Vol.2, p. 217):

> Lax opportunism and a too considerate notion of the possible have replaced fresh daring, and an agonizing fear of victory for the "still so immature" workers' movement is deterring action. . . . Are stronger interests forcing [the unions] to oppose all notions of a general strike? No! For in Germany the notion of a general strike does not function as explosive powder against the constant union spadework. And the last general strike by the miners is the best evidence for this, demonstrating better than a hundred speeches the value of trade union organization and calling for mass intervention in the latter.

Heinrich Ströbel, a representative of the left wing of the party, did not view the masses as optimistically as did Kloth. Not only the leaders, he said, but the unions in general were lacking "socialist spirit." Their whole development was "independent of the well-meant private intentions of a handful of leaders" who declared emphatically that "unions and party are one!" What was important was to "recognize the weaknesses in the system" and not to allocate personal guilt to some leaders for these weaknesses in the system, for (*Neue Zeit*, p. 564):

> without the confidence of the masses the union officials could not survive. At least we do not believe that the majority of the union members desire a different tactic than that represented by their officials. The situation is such that the mass of unionists, as a result of the "neutrality" they have been observing for years, have become *politically indifferent* and judge the union movement from the point of view of the pettiest professional or momentary interest.

The answer from the union leadership to attacks about principles of this sort or criticism of the events in the Ruhr district was defensive. The old theses, that the workers' movement needed composure for its organizational expansion, that successful large-scale strikes were unthinkable as long as the largest groups—for example, the miners—were not yet organized, and other such theses came into their own again. However, new tones were also to be heard arising out of the leader-masses discussion. Thus, for example, the union leader Adolph von Elm, himself an opponent of the Cologne resolution preventing the mass strike discussion, countered in the *Sozialistische Monatshefte* (1905, p. 733) before the September 1905 Jena Party Congress during which the great discussion about the political mass strike was supposed to take place:

> Unfortunately statements from one section of the party press lead us to believe that some comrades are inclined to push the matter onto a personal level. It would probably comply with the intentions of these critics if in Jena an inquisition were held against a number of union leaders and a call made to the *grass-roots*. The *union bureaucrats*, the *people of a higher position in life* were obviously being thought about most kindly; they were accused of being *narrow-minded scorners of theory*. The leaders were responsible for the theoretical demoralization of the union members!

During the demonstrations of November and December 1905 in Saxony against the class franchise there, a primarily politically and not economically motivated action, interesting phenomena were observed. In the *Sächsische Arbeiterzeitung* (January 4, 1905) the following events were reported in Dresden:

> Battalions of workers who fell into formation without an order, without a leader. A movement born spontaneously out of the masses. None of the speakers at the meeting had called for a demonstration; no leader, no spokesman gave the word. Driven by a mighty impulse the workers took to the streets.

That in this situation the "masses"—whatever that might mean—or organized and unorganized workers led the movement on can be observed clearly in the negotiations and discussions between party and unions in the years 1905 and 1906 (Groh, 1974). Only under the pressure exerted by the mass strike discussion did the party committee include the political mass strike among the weapons to be used at a given time in the struggle, and in taking this decisive step fed the conflict with the General Committee, the leaders' body of the unions, which smouldered up to the outbreak of the First World War.

In the situation of the winter of 1905–06, which can be characterized as one of pressure from below, from the masses upon the leaders, for the first time an objective identity of interests developed between the government bureaucracy and the leadership of the workers' movement, one that was probably scarcely perceived subjectively. Until the outbreak of the war this would occur a few times more. All these situations were marked by at least partial agreement between the *raison* of the state and of the organizations. The leaders of both were afraid of each other yet at the same time convinced that they could not destroy each other. On both sides were groups agitating for action, be it a strike against class franchise, antimilitarist agitation, or violent destruction of the workers' movement and an ensuing legal suppression. Both the government and the union leadership were interested in restraining these radical elements who were endangering the stability of the state by a *coup d'état* or the existence of the workers' organizations by actions with no clearly calculable chances of success.

The security measure of the government against possible action by the Social Democrats objectively contributed to the fact that the party leadership managed to channel the radical mood for action and the radical theoretical tendencies extending far beyond their formulated goals—this in accordance with their policy—without endangering the existence of the workers' movement. For the authorities directed their preparations not against peaceful demonstrations planned by the party committee but against the possibility of "street rallies" by the "radical elements." Thus the Prussian Minister for the Interior, later Chancellor, Bethmann Hollweg wrote in a circular letter to the Chief Superintendents of Police, "The party committee does not plan to hold street rallies, as we have it from reliable sources; but we must reckon with such a possibility. Any attempt to move through public streets in a demonstration must be hindered by police intervention and all other means."

One can go a step beyond the objectively existing partial identity of interests in the political situation in question. It can scarcely be denied that the party committee was not at all against the government knowing about its intentions in advance. Indeed the party committee did all in its power to prevent street demonstrations. Those who curbed activities in November, December, and January in Prussia., Saxony, and Hamburg were not the leaders of the unions but the leaders of the party. Thus the first political mass strike in Germany, which took place on January 17, 1906, in Hamburg against the deterioration of the voting rights situation there remained without a sequel untill 1918.

High-points in the Discussion: Luxemburg versus Kautsky and the Organizational Crisis of 1913

The discussion of the leader–masses problem constantly accompanied the strategy debate that began in 1905. In *Massenstreik, Partei und Gewerkschaften* (1906) Rosa Luxemburg developed for the first time her falsely named "theory of spontaneity" with reference to the leader-masses problem during a mass strike:

> The idea of a "made mass strike," shot out of a pistol by a simple decree of the party one fine morning, is childish, anarchist madness. However, a mass strike occurring after months of escalating demonstrations by the working masses, out of a situation in which a 3-million-member party confronts the dilemma of whether to go on at all costs or to let the already-moving mass action fall apart, such a mass strike, born out of the inner

needs and decisions of the shaken masses and out of the aggravated political situation, bears within itself its justification, the guarantee of its effectiveness....

The mass strike should not be seen as an artificial mechanical means of exerting political pressure according to rules and under conscious command. The mass strike is the outward form of an action that has its own inner development, its own logic, its own intensification, its own consequences, in close association with the political situation and its further advancement.

... yet one may not expect that one fine day the order for a mass strike will come from the top leaders of the movement, from the party committee and the General Commission of the unions.

The strategy debate begun in 1905 reached its next stage in the discussion between Rosa Luxemburg and Karl Kautsky, the chief theoretician of the German party, in 1910 over the strategy of exhaustion versus overthrow, *Ermattungsstrategie* versus *Niederwerfungsstrategie* (Groh, 1973a; Walther, 1982). Rosa Luxemburg further developed her idea of 1906 that mass strikes cannot be organized. She confronted "masses" and "leaders" and claimed that the whole discussion about the mass strike and the demonstrations against the three-class franchise in Prussia showed "how much the leaders, in their feelings and their thoughts, were lagging behind the masses" (*Neue Zeit*, 1909–10, 28, Vol. 2, pp. 257ff.).

On the occasion of the large strikes and lockouts above all in the building industry and on the docks in 1910, which once again demonstrated to the social democratic workers' movement the strength of the class war associations of the entrepreneurs, there appeared an article by Adolph von Elm under the title "Masses and Leaders" (*Neue Zeit*, 1910–11, 29, Vol. 1, pp. 521–526). Elm claimed correctly that the time for locally started strikes in many branches of industry was over: "The large central workers' associations now being faced with the central organizations of the capitalists." However, he drew conclusions totally opposed to those of Rosa Luxemburg. For in such a situation where the intervention of the opponents is determined by supraregional considerations, "the democratic lack of confidence in the leaders so often discussed of late could have disastrous results." The unions were faced with a real dilemma, for on the one hand "without the cooperation of the masses large economic struggles against capital were impossible," yet on the other hand "to show your plans openly to the enemy during a war is no strategy." Therefore in the last instance one had to leave the decision regarding the beginning and end of a strike to the union committees (p. 523ff.):

Disagreement with the "leaders," as the confidently elected union officials are now suddenly being called in certain workers' circles, is unavoidable. "Democratic lack of confidence" need not even be preached in such situations; it grows out of the bitter mood of the workers, out of their unfulfilled hopes. There is no union leader who has not under such circumstances either through ignorance or demagogy been accused by some of betrayal of workers' interests.... The referendum has never proved

> itself in union organizations useful for decisions about strikes. ... It is a
> false understanding of the essence of democracy to believe that anything
> that affects everyone must also be directly decided upon by everyone. It is
> more in the interests of the working people to allow its will to be expressed
> through its elected representatives.

Von Elm then made a case for the extension of the representative system in the unions to intensify contact between leaders and masses and to strengthen "the voluntary discipline of the masses" (p. 526):

> Then all this talk about the leaders having lost touch with the masses would
> be over at last. For in the struggle one needs to exchange confidence for
> confidence: Leaders who do not have the confidence of the masses cannot
> lead a struggle to a successful conclusion. The masses must be taught to
> subordinate themselves in the struggle to the decisions of those they have
> elected; an army that does not follow a unified plan of battle will only
> experience defeat after defeat and never victory.

The next high point in the discussion of this theme came with the party crisis of 1913 and the discussion of the mass strike closely associated with it (Groh, 1973a, pp. 461–476). At the root of this crisis lay a structural phenomenon, namely, the ever-growing discrepancy between the political potential of the workers' movement and its realization in concrete achievements, be they in the political or the economic realm. This discrepancy worsened with the growth of the organizations and parliamentary groups. The crisis was heigthened by both economic and political events. On the economic side, the beginnings of the recession and the sinking real wage level made it clear to the workers that the improvement of their living and working conditions had not only come to a standstill but in some cases was even regressing. As regards the political factors, there was disappointment about the result of the Landtag elections in Prussia and in some southern German states, above all about the outcome in the Reichstag elections of 1912 where the Social Democrats with 34.8% of the votes had won 27.7% of the seats. Despite 110 delegates in the Reichstag, "nothing had happened" that could be presented to supporters and members as a success, at least not without generous interpretation and explanation. Since the summer of 1910 the party leadership had channeled almost all the party's energies into the election campaign, so that one section of the members, blinded by confused notions, actually expected the realization of the future state to begin after such successful results. Another section expected at least a decisive influence on policy and legislation by the Social Democratic Party.

A short article by Johannes Meerfeld entitled "Nachdenkliche Betrachtungen" ("Thoughtful Observations") appeared in June 1913 and focused on all these annoyances, made conscious the widespread uneasiness, and aggravated the crisis. He spoke of the "danger of the leaders becoming bourgeois," of the bureaucracy of the party and the union organizations. "The revolutionary spirit has had its wings clipped," he said. However, Meerfeld could not prescribe any promising cure for this ailment.

He warned on the one hand against the belief that the union leaders would lead a mass strike in defense of political rights, while on the other against judging "the mood of the masses out there from its fighting spirit, a spirit which takes hold of a social democratic city gathering after a provocative speech." He meant, of course, above all Rosa Luxemburg.

The reactions to the article in the party and union press, from Karl Kautsky to comrades whose names no one had ever read (for examples see *Neue Zeit*, 1912–13, 31, Vol. 2, from no. 40), showed clearly that Meerfeld had verbalized and even found impressive terms for something that many were feeling. In the ensuing discussion the whole spectrum of opinions in party and unions was expressed. In blunt opposition to each other stood hopes that the "political mass strike" was an effective weapon and at some time a cure for the faintheartedness, the bourgeois tendencies, the fear, and the bureaucracy, and appeals that "our well-tested tactic be maintained, heads revolutionized, our organizations strengthened and put in a position to protect us from rash steps." "Organization issues," "organization problems"—thus the titles of many of the articles centered over and over again and with increasing intensity around the problem of leaders and masses. Before Lenin's concept of a cadre-organization was even known among German Social Democrats, the *form* of which brought him alongside most German union leaders, vehement criticism was being expressed of such an organization model (*Neue Zeit*, pp. 752f.):

> All depends not so much on the ability and effectiveness of the leaders as on the conviction, dedication, and passion of the masses. Thus it is a vital point for us to find useful organization forms that comply with the democratic sense of the masses!...
>
> Social Democracy was born of the idea that the liberation of the working class must be the task of that working class. One cannot speak of self-liberation when a handful of enlightened leaders leads the fettered proletariat into the Promised Land and there removes its chains. Furthermore, one cannot speak of self-liberation when the leaders draw up the plan of action and the workers display faith in their greater insight. Even if the leaders were ingenious enough to determine in advance with absolute accuracy the most successful weapons for the struggle, they would still notice that it is not the insight and confidence in victory of the leaders that count but that of the masses, if the struggle is to succeed. Confidence in victory among the masses is only possible when they themselves have discussed, examined, and chosen the weapons, that is to say when the tactics have been decided on democratically, and this is only possible in a democratic organization. Thus even the most ingenious leaders cannot take the responsibility away from the masses: shining genius cannot replace the forms of democratic organization.
>
> And it is these that we are missing in our large organization. The latter can be characterized as an official apparatus minutely subdivided and expanded. This apparatus not only administers, it rules the organizations. It takes decisions above the heads of the masses yet in their name. It excludes the masses more and more as if its motto were "I am the Organization."

Finally the voices of Karl Kautsky and Rosa Luxemburg were heard. In his "Nachgedanken zu den nachdenklichen Betrachtungen" ("Reflections on Some Reflections") Kautsky stated ex cathedra, as the leading theoretician, his position (*Neue Zeit*, pp. 560–563). He conceded to the left wing that the "spontaneity of the passion is a basic-prerequisite for a victorious mass strike" but accused them of demanding that the party "artificially create this spontaneity by means of a daring initiative."

> Münchhausen pulling himself out of the mire by his own ponytail! . . . This contradiction can be explained by the fact that behind the Marxist discussion the mass of the people can only be moved by great social changes there still lurks the blanquistic putsch-tactic claim that it is a small minority that makes history in such a way as to draw along the masses by its daring actions, a tactic that German Social Democracy has rejected from the very beginning.
>
> The mass strike is dependent on the masses and not on the leaders. It can only arise out of the striving of the masses and not out of the phrases coming from above. If the German masses have not yet pressed for an immediate mass strike then that is because these masses do not estimate the chances for an offensive in this area very highly at the moment.
>
> When the masses actually demand a mass strike, that is, its immediate realization and not just its propagation, then all the curbing tactics of the leaders will be of no avail. Belgium demonstrated this to us clearly. It is not the masses who are being influenced by the leaders but the latter by the masses. Daring, active masses produce daring leaders. But even the most willingly active leader loses all his enthusiasm when he has apathetic masses behind him.

Thus at least in his articles Kautsky managed to bring back the discussion fired by the organization crisis and the mass strike debate to the realm of revolutionary attentism whose theoretician he was. For the necessary prerequisites sketched out by him for a successful mass strike, it was merely necessary to wait.

Rosa Luxemburg made this weakness the kernel of her reply, "Das Offiziösentum der Theorie" ("The Officiousness of Theory") (*Neue Zeit*, pp. 842f.):

> Just as his theory aims at an officious dampening of all scruples and justifications of all that is present in the party, so too his tactics aim at the slowing of the movement along its old worn track of pure parliamentarism, the hope that history will provide the revolutionary development and when the time is ripe the masses will storm on ahead of the impeding leaders. Impeding leaders will no doubt be pushed aside in the end by the storming masses. But simply to wait for this happy result as a sure sign that "the time is ripe" may be appropriate for a lonely philosopher. For the political leaders of a revolutionary party it would be a declaration of weakness and moral bankruptcy. The task of Social Democracy and its leaders is not to be worn down by events but to march ahead of them consciously to comprehend the direction of the development and to shorten this by action, to speed up its course. A theory that serves to curb and not spur on the

masses can only discover that it will be overrun by practice, pushed aside without regard.

The mood and debate about the mass strike did not bring about the learning process that the most active elements inside the party from left to right had demanded with regard to behavior in political crisis situations. Only the exercise of new forms of action as well as concrete experience in the course of such actions would have altered the set behavior patterns of the political wait-and-see attitude. Instead of a learning process that might have been suitable for actualizing the political potential of the German workers' movement, another was introduced, which was to channel the spontaneity of the grassroots. This involved above all the relationship between members and leaders and was to be extremely important for the future of social democracy.

Members and supporters accustomed themselves to having their needs for political action curbed by the party leadership and channeled into the traditional paths of the organization and the agitation tactic, at best the election campaigns. At the same time the party leadership gradually acquainted itself with the idea of one day having to lead a political, active movement that it had neither initiated nor desired and with whose motives and aims it could not therefore fully identify. One can clearly observe how, after the first widespread discussion of the possibility of a political mass strike to obtain democratic voting rights in Prussia and Saxony in 1905–06, this learning process, which can be characterized as negative or pathological, was carried on. The next stages were the struggles for improvement of the Prussian three-class franchise in 1908 and 1910, the demonstrations against German imperialism at the time of the Morocco crisis in 1911, and the agitation for a mass strike from the summer of 1913 until the summer of 1914. Here again the issues were the Prussian franchise, later the avoidance of a possible *coup e'état*, as well as avoidance of intensification of the penal code and limitation of the right of coalition, all measures obviously directed against the workers' movement. The general rehearsal for November 1918 took place at the time of the January strike in 1918. The Social Democratic leaders took up positions at the head of the strike only out of solidarity with the striking workers but against their own will and conviction. Something similar happened at the time of the collapse of the German Empire in November 1918 (see Groh, 1985a).

Acknowledgment. I wish to thank Michael Josipović for his help in researching the source material.

References

Balser, F. (1962). *Sozial-Demokratie 1848/49–1963. Die erste deutsche Arbeiterorganisation "Allgemeine deutsche Arbeiterverbrüderung" nach der Revolution* (2 Vols.) Stuttgart: Klett.

Blickle, P. (1979). Peasant revolts in the German empire in the late Middle Ages. *Social History, 4*, 223–240.

Blickle, P. (Ed.). (1980). *Aufruhr und Empörung. Studien zum bäuerlichen Widerstand im alten Reich*. Munich: Beck.

Blickle, P. (1981). *Die Revolution von 1525* (2nd ed.). Munich: Oldenbourg.

Blickle, P. (1982). *Die Reformation im Reich*. Stuttgart: Kohlhammer.

Eggers, P. (1987). *Arbeits-und Lebenswelt Hamburger Handwerksgesellen im Wandel vom 18. zum 19. Jahrhundert*. Ph.D. Thesis, Konstanz, 1987.

Elbs, E. (1987). "Die von seculis her angewohnte Rebellionsseuche". Bäuerliche Aufstandsbewegungen in der Grafschaft Hohenzollern 1584–1740, Weingarten: Drumlin.

Engelhardt, U. (1977). *"Nur vereinigt sind wir stark." Die Anfänge der deutschen Gewerkschaftsbewegung 1862/63 bis 1869/70* (2 Vols.). Stuttgart: Klett-Cotta.

Griessinger, A. (1981). *Das symbolische Kapital der Ehre. Streikbewegungen und kollektives Bewusstsein deutscher Handwerksgesellen im 18. Jahrhundert*. Berlin: Ullstein.

Griessinger, A. (1983). Handwerkerstreiks in Deutschland während des 18. Jahrhunderts. Begriff, Organisationsformen, Ursachenkonstellation. In W. Conze & U. Engelhardt (Eds.), *Handwerkerschaft und Industrialisierung in Deutschland. Lage, Kultur und Politik vom späten 18. bis ins frühe 20. Jahrhundert* (pp. 407–434). Stuttgart: Klett.

Griessinger, A., & Reith, R. (1983). Obrigkeitliche Ordnungskonzeptionen und handwerkliches Konfliktverhalten im 18. Jahrhundert. Nürnberg and Würzburg im Vergleich. In R.S. Elkar (Ed.), *Deutsches Handwerk in Spätmittelalter und Früher Neuzeit*. (pp. 117–180). Göttingen.

Groh, D. (1973a). *Negative Integration und revolutionärer Attentismus. Die deutsche Sozialdemokratie am Vorabend des Ersten Weltkrieges*. Berlin: Propyäen-Ullstein.

Groh, D. (1973b). Waiting for an avoiding revolution. The Social Democracy and the Reich, Laurentian University Review 5, pp. 83–110.

Groh, D. (1974). La grève de masse, arme politique de la socialdémocratie allemande en 1905/06? *Revue Belge d'Histoire Contemporaine, 5*, pp. 339–359.

Groh, D. (1978). Intensification of work and industrial conflict in Germany, 1896–1914. *Politics and Society, 8*, pp. 349–397.

Groh, D. (1981). Osservazioni preliminari sulla formazione della class operaia tedesca. In F. Piro & P. Pombeni (Eds.), *Movimento operaio e societá industriale in Europa, 1870-1970* (pp. 75–132). Bologna: Marsilio.

Groh, D. (1983). Einige Überlegungen zur Herausbildung des Reformismus in der deutschen Arbeiterbewegung vor 1914. In F. Dreyfus (Ed.), *Socialisme, révisionnisme et réformisme en France, Allemagne et Autriche 1880-1980* (pp. 57–74). Paris: Ed. de la MSH.

Groh, D. (1985a). Collective behaviour from the 17th to the 20th century: Change of phenomena, change of perception or no change at all? In C.F. Graumann & S. Moscovici (Eds.). *Crowd mind and behaviour. A historical analysis* (pp. 143–162). New York: Springer.

Groh, D. (1985b). Le mouvement ouvrier "marxiste" allemand: Un malentendu historique. In Marx en perspective. Ecole des Hautes Etudes en Sciences Sociales, Dec. 1983 (pp. 585–608). Paris. EHESS Press.

Habermas, J. (1968). *Erkenntnis und Interesse*. Frankfurt am Main: Suhrkamp.

Maehl, W.H. (1980). *August Bebel: Shadow emperor of the German workers*. Philadelphia: American Philosophical Society.

Michels, R. (1969). *Zur Soziologie des Parteiwesens in der modernen Demokratie* (W. Conze, Ed.), Stuttgart: Kröner (Original work published 1911).

Na'aman, S. (1975). *Die Konstituierung der deutschen Arbeiterbewegung 1862/63. Darstellung und Dokumentation.* Assen: Campus.

Quarck, M. (1924). *Die erste deutsche Arbeiterbewegung. Geschichte der Arbeiterverbrüderung 1848/1849.* Leipzig: Hirschfeld.

Reith, R. (1982). *Der Aprilaufstand von 1848 in Konstanz. Zur biographischen Dimension von "Hochverrath und Aufruhr." Versuch einer historischen Protestanalyse.* Sigmaringen: Thorbecke.

Schieder, W. (1963). *Anfänge der deutschen Arbeiterbewegung. Die Auslandsvereine im Jahrzehnt nach der Julirevolution von 1830.* Stuttgart: Klett-Cotta.

Schulze, W. (1980). *Bäuerlicher Widerstand und feudale Herrschaft in der frühen Neuzeit.* Stuttgart: Frommann-Holzboog.

Schulze, W. (1983). *Aufstände, Revolten, Prozesse. Beiträge zu bäuerlichen Widerstandsbewegungen im frühneuzeitlichen Europa.* Stuttgart: Klett-Cotta.

Trossbach, W. (1986). *Bauernbewegungen im Wetterau-Vogelsberg-Gebiet 1648-1806: Soziale Bewegung und politische Erfahrung.* Weingarten: Drumlin.

Volkmann, H. (1975). *Die Krise von 1830. Form, Ursache und Funktion des sozialen Protestes im deutschen Vormärz.* Unpublished manuscript.

Walther, R. (1982). *"...aber nach der Sündflut kommen wir und nur wir." Zusammenbruchstheorie und politisches Defizit der deutschen Sozialdemokratie, 1890-1914.* Berlin: Ullstein.

Wirtz, R. (1981). *"Widersetzlichkeiten, Excesse, Crawalle, Tumulte und Skandale." Soziale Bewegung und gewalthafter sozialer Protest in Baden 1815-1848.* Berlin: Ullstein.

Chapter 4

Charismatic Leadership: Max Weber's Model and Its Applicability to the Rule of Hitler

M. Rainer Lepsius

Lately the word *charisma* has become widely used and to a large extent trivialized. Even in sports reports one comes across statements that a soccer player has charisma in his left foot. If charisma has no other meaning than personal excellence, superb performance of a task, or unexpected success in a difficult situation, there are other words like *esteem, influence,* and *idolization* that are more appropriate. We should in that case drop *charisma*, as it covers too many phenomena for which we have more precise concepts. If we retain the word *charisma*, it should be used as a defined concept, not as a trivialized expression.

Originally, a theological concept, *charisma* means a gift of God's grace that enables a human being to perform exceptional tasks. The cause for such an exceptional performance is believed to rest in an otherworldly power. It is in reference to this power that a person who is endowed by it is treated as a leader, whose authority is to be obeyed as if it were the divine authority itself. The charisma bestowed upon a person is considered a legitimate representation of God's grace.

Max Weber introduced the concept of charisma into the social sciences, thereby cutting it off from its original theological meaning. Charisma is now conceived as any quality of a person that is regarded as supernatural, superhuman, or at least specifically exceptional (*ausseralltäglich*) and inaccessible to ordinary people. Charisma thus becomes a specific quality attributed to an individual by which his or her perception as a leader, mode of behavior, the organization of social relations, the character of domination, and the form of obedience are influenced in a particular way. Charisma, therefore, is both a specific quality believed to be possessed by an individual and a specific pattern of social relations.

Weber's Model

Weber elaborated some properties of charismatic social relations and their structure. The first property is absolute trust in the leader that is unquestionably the duty of the followers. The leader demands this duty and claims ultimate authority; the followers accept this duty and obey the leader's orders. It is the interaction of leader and followers that constitutes this special relationship. The leader has to have the will to demand ultimate authority and must have a position or create a new position for himself by which to exercise ultimate authority. The followers must have a propensity to surrender to the will of the leader and must be in a position or accept a position by which they become dependent on the ultimate authority of the leader.

The second property is the dissolution of normative standards by which the behavior of a person is usually controlled and the acceptance by the followers that such normative standards are to be dissolved. The more a charismatic leader aspires toward ultimate authority, the less he or she can accept normative regulations and procedural controls. A charismatic social relationship, therefore, is characterized by deinstitutionalization of norms and by opposition to traditional values. As Weber states:

> There is no system of formal rules, of abstract legal principles, and hence no process of rational judicial decision oriented to them. Formally concrete judgments are newly created from case to case and are originally regarded as divine judgments and revelations. From a substantive point of view, every charismatic authority would have to subscribe to the proposition, 'It is written ... but I say unto you ....'" The genuine prophet ... preaches, creates, or demands *new* obligations. (Weber, 1968, p. 243)

The third property is the result of the former two. The social group formed around charismatic leadership is an emotional community bound by personal devotion toward the leader and organized by his or her agents, whom the leader chooses according to charismatic qualities:

> There is only a call at the instance of the leader on the basis of the charismatic qualification of those he summons. There is no hierarchy; the leader merely intervenes in general or in individual cases when he considers the members of his staff lacking in charismatic qualification for a given task. (Weber, 1968, p. 243)

The internal group structure imposes the pattern of strict command and obedience, as they exist between the leader and his or her agents, on the group members in their relations with the agents. This rigidity is characteristically combined with a fluidity of the realms of authority of the agents. There is no hierarchy and no definite sphere of competence, and hence a weakness of coordination and internal conflict management. Ad hoc interventions by the leader and in the name of the leader replace collective decision making and procedures of conflict resolution. In its internal structure the charismatic community is simultaneously rigid and loose, authoritarian and anarchic, unified and fragmented, centralized and uncoordinated.

Weber finally stresses the indifference of a charismatic community toward rational economic activities. A charismatic leadership "repudiates any sort of involvement in the everyday routine world.... Booty and extortion, whether by force or by other means, is the typical form of charismatic provision for needs" (Weber, 1968, p. 245). This can be generalized into an attitude of indifference to any systematic rationalization of action, whether economic or noneconomic. Charisma "may then result in a radical alteration of the central attitudes and directions of actions with a completely new orientation of all attitudes toward the different problems of the 'world' " (Weber, 1968, p. 245).

The fourth property of the charismatic model is the necessity of its proof and success. If the charismatic leader "appears deserted by his god or his magical or heroic powers, above all, if his leadership fails to benefit his followers, it is likely that his charismatic authority will disappear" (Weber, 1968, p. 242). This is the crucial boundary to the charismatic claim: the need to be proved. However, we know how prophecies that have failed are still believed, how tests are likely to be subsequently reinterpreted, and how cognitive dissonance can be resolved without altering the existence of a dissonance (Festinger et al., 1956; Festinger, 1957). This holds true particularly in the short run when emotional enthusiasm is still aroused or an alternative course of action seems too difficult to be pursued.

Charisma is not just another word for prestige, esteem, popularity, or personal excellence. A charismatic relation fundamentally restructures the social situation. Charisma is, as Weber says, a revolutionary force that deinstitutionalizes social relations and personalizes social structures until the charismatic claim by the leader is abolished by the routinization of charisma and the reinstitution of traditional or rational patterns of action and organization of social communities. A charismatic situation is characterized by a break with ordinary behavior, by the development of new modes and criteria for social relations. A charismatic leader is not only a person who gains trust, toward whom great expectations are directed, or to whom special qualifications are attributed: A charismatic leader creates a new pattern of social relations. Such a leader creates his or her own position, the structure of social organization, and the definition of the situation in general. As long as a highly esteemed leader does not alter the social pattern of the system but acts within the limits of the position, conforms to the traditional role expectations, observes procedures that limit his or her own course of action, allows independent institutions to control his or her actions, that leader is not charismatic, regardless of his or her excellence, prestige, and idolization.

It may be difficult to distinguish between the idolization of a leader and being considered charismatic. There is a fluidity in the degree of charismatization of a leader. However, charismatic leadership is always a new type of social relationship with specific properties, which are manifested in the structure of the social situation. A charismatic social situation is brought about by a charismatic leader, but the leader is only one element in it. For example, John Kennedy may have been a charismatic president, but he did not establish charismatic leadership; Martin Luther refuted all expectations of becoming a charismatic leader; Otto von Bismarck became charismatized after his successes but remained in a predefined position even when he extended his prerogatives and tried to weaken the position of parliament and the parties. Charismatic leadership, on the other hand, is not simply tyranny or military dictatorship. It is legitimate domination insofar as the followers believe in the virtues of the leader and the value of his or her leadership. Napoleon was a charismatic leader in this sense, and so was Hitler. Charisma as a sociological term thus defines not only a particular quality of an individual but a complex social structure.

The Latent Charismatic Situation

We will elaborate the Weberian model by applying it to the rule of Hitler. It will, of course, be impossible to give a systematic analysis of the historical events, the personality of Hitler, the structure of the Nazi party, the changing character of the German state, the strategies of repression, the perception of the population in the Third Reich, the international constellations, the conduct of the war, the motivation for and techniques of violence and crimes against humanity so closely connected with the Third Reich. For all that, we have to refer to the vast literature. Only a few general references which provide basic information and further bibliographical references will be given: K.D. Bracher (1970), M. Broszat (1969), and K. Hildebrand (1979) give a general analysis of the Nazi regime. J.C. Fest (1973), S. Haffner (1978), and J.P. Stern (1975) are excellent interpretors of Hitler himself. E. Jäckel (1981) gives a short overview on Hitler's belief system. W. Horn (1972), I. Kershaw (1980), J. Nyomarky (1967), and A. Tyrell (1975), and the contributions of K. Hildebrand, L. Kettenacker, and H. Mommsen in G. Hirschfeld and L. Kettenacker (1981) develop different aspects of the rule of Hitler and the political structure of Germany. For the present purpose, we cannot reproduce the historical evidence, but can only select indicators for the application of the concept of charismatic leadership.

The precondition for the establishment of charismatic leadership is the existence of a latent charismatic situation. Such a situation has two dimensions, cultural and social. "The propensity to impute charisma is a potentiality of the moral, cognitive, and expressive orientation of human beings" (Shils, 1975, p. 127). Its intensity varies with the content of the culture. This culture has to include the idea that transcendent powers directly influence human fate and that these powers may be represented by the actions of an individual. Both intensify the propensity to impute charismatic qualities to a person. In the German situation we find a comparatively high propensity for belief in charismatic leadership in the political culture. This is exemplified by the idolization of Frederick II of Prussia, whose unlikely success in the Silesian War was attributed to his uncompromising belief in his mission and his personal qualities. The unification of Germany was attributed to the genius of Bismarck. The expression "men make history" implicitly deflated the values attributed to institutions. German political culture had great trust in the notion of an "open-yet-authoritarian elite" (Struve, 1973). This latent propensity for charismatic leadership expressed itself after the defeat in the First World War in a distrust in the new constitution, parliamentarism, party government, and interest-group politics, which were all denounced as un-German, inefficient, and not serving the common good of the German people. The war experience also contributed to the growing propensity to surrender to the heroic genius.

The social precondition for a latent charismatic situation is the perception and experience of a crisis. The awareness of the incapacity to overcome the crisis delegitimizes the existing political institutions. The expectation arises that a powerful leader will alter the situation. In Germany the crisis in national identity, the weakness of the new democratic institutions, and the severe economic depression after 1929 contributed to the perception of a fundamental political crisis that seemed unsolvable under the existing political order. The authoritarian camp sought to establish a state of emergency based on the military with the goal of reinstalling the monarchy; the communists saw the chance for a dictatorship of the proletariat; and the democratic center lost its parliamentary majority, felt paralyzed, and had neither a program to deal with the crisis nor a convincing definition of the situation (Bracher, 1971; Matthias & Morsey, 1960).

There was thus a latent charismatic situation in Germany. The political and economic crisis and the political culture strengthened the propensity for charismatic leadership. Both had to interact. A cultural affinity for charismatic leadership alone will not gain dominance as long as the institutionalized political order is legitimized by its perceived efficiency; and the awareness of a political and economic crisis will not automatically lead to a propensity for charismatic leadership unless this is a plausible option, legitimized by the political culture.

The Manifest Charismatic Situation

A latent charismatic situation becomes manifest only if there is a claimant for charismatic leadership whose promise of salvation is perceived as appropriate to the solution of the crisis. Not just any charismatic claim will work; it must be one that fits the perception of the crisis. Whether a latent charismatic situation develops into a manifest charismatic situation depends, therefore, on the activities of the claimant for charismatic leadership. There may be many potentially charismatic leaders who cannot capitalize on the latent charismatic situation. In the case of Germany there was a successful claimant. Hitler offered a definition of the situation and means to overcome the crisis: The political order as such was corrupt, its inability to master the crisis the result of a conspiracy of evil powers whose aim it was to destroy and enslave Germany. The means to overcome the crisis were the destruction of the political order and the replacement of the forces of evil by the forces of good. Then Germany would be reborn. The mythical generality of his definition of the situation kept Hitler aloof from any technical debate about his program. It seems important that a claimant for charismatic leadership address ultimate values like survival, honor, self-respect, and justice and not the technical problems of concrete programs and their implementation. Only in the pursuit of ultimate values can charisma be claimed and will it be granted. However, the ultimate values chosen must be considered directly pertinent to the solution of the crisis. Here again political culture plays an important role: It has to make plausible the causal relation between the magic formula and the concrete experience. Hitler did not succeed by arguing for a concrete program but by persuading the German people that something completely new had to happen, whatever it may be. The battle cry, "Germany awake!" (*Deutschland erwache!*) quite properly represents this simultaneous emptiness and resoluteness.

Hitler's tactics deliberately sharpened the awareness of the crisis. His highly organized and mobile storm troopers provoked a situation of public disorder, thereby once more proving the incapacity of the political system to control the situation. The threat of a civil war was produced, polarizing public opinion and artificially creating the perception that there were only two alternatives: Hitler or the communists. Friend or foe, right or wrong, survival or death—this world view of a Manichaean dualism, for which Hitler himself felt great affinity, was dramatized in everyday life. The definition of the situation became real in the staging of election campaigns, street battles, demonstrations, beatings, magic formulas, and death rituals. The burning of the Reichstag in 1933 was skillfully used to exploit the Manichaean definition of the situation once more and to issue a decree by which civil liberties were suspended until the end of the Nazi regime. The presentation of seemingly unavoidable alternatives leads to the acceptance of ultimate values as frames of reference. The more abstract these ultimate values are, the less specific interests and particular goals serve as references. If the perception of reality is directly oriented toward ultimate values, the chances grow for an acceptance of the claim to ultimate authority. A process of circular stimulation sets in by which the definition of the crisis as provoked by the charismatic leader makes him or her the only person able to overcome the crisis. Indeed, when Hitler came to power, he ended public disorder by demobilizing his militia and in 1934 by destroying their leadership. Hitler proved himself a very successful claimant for charismatic leadership by using a crisis to turn latent into manifest charismatic expectations.

However, the claimant's bid for charismatic leadership must be supported by evidence of extraordinary qualities. Before Hitler came to power, it was his success in elections that was used as empirical proof. In 1928, the National Socialists polled 2.6% of the national vote; in 1930, its vote grew to 18.3%; in 1932, it won 37.3% and became the strongest party in the Reichstag. At the second Reichstag elections in November 1932, the party's share declined to 33% of the vote, and this was seen as a challenge to Hitler's charismatic qualities. Members and functionaries of the party became doubtful, but they had no means to oppose Hitler. The party had no procedures for collective decision making and for representation of its members. Charismatic qualities are not voted upon: They have to be proved. The internal crisis of the Nazi movement had to be solved by a test of Hitler's charisma. The local elections in Lippe were chosen for this test. This election was fought with disproportionate intensity, and the results were favorable. Unimportant as it was at the national level, this campaign proved Hitler's charisma and his claim to ultimate authority was secured.

By 1932, the latent charismatic situation had turned into a manifest one. An acknowledged claimant for charismatic leadership had organized his followers into a charismatic community, which he could use as an instrument for his claim. Backed by about 40% of the population and taking advantage of a situation that had already delegitmated the existing order, the moment of seizure of power was near.

The Establishment of Charismatic Leadership

The transition from a manifest charismatic situation to charismatic leadership occurs if the claim of the charismatic person to ultimate authority is accepted by the followers, if pretension is met by ascription of charisma. The process of charismatization of an individual has structural repercussions. The establishment of charismatic leadership is achieved with the fundamental restructuring of social relations. The leader not only claims but commands ultimate authority; the followers not only acknowledge the leader's extraordinary qualities but surrender to the leader's will, and consider obedience a duty.

Hitler succeeded three times in establishing himself as a charismatic leader. In 1921, he forced the then-tiny sectarian party to acknowledge him as its leader, unbound by any formal regulations. It was his demagogical talent that had just brought the party to public attention, and he threatened to resign unless he was granted ultimate and unrestricted authority. In 1925–26, after the abortive putsch on November 9, 1923, and upon his release from prison, he founded the party anew, again forcing the leaders who had established themselves in the meantime to grant him absolute authority and to obey his orders without question. At a meeting in Bamberg on February 14, 1926, he summoned the district chiefs on short notice, and after a 5-hour speech by Hitler, the spokesmen for the dissenters, among them Gregor Strasser and Joseph Goebbels, expressed their personal loyalty without discussion. In 1933–34 the third seizure of power took place, now with Hitler as Chancellor of the Reich (Bracher, et al., 1960). Again he succeeded in claiming ultimate authority unbound by a constitution. The same process thus took place in three different settings: first, within a small group of individuals interacting directly with each other in Munich; second, in an organization with divergent vested interests and intellectual orientations; and third, within the context of an institutionally differentiated, highly organized nation fragmented by interests and ideological orientations. The establishment of charismatic leadership on the micro and the macro level shows striking similarities.

The first common element is the destruction of formal rules and institutional differentiations. Just as within the Nazi party Hitler willfully suppressed procedural regulations and institutionalized representation of its members, so the very beginning of Hitler's rule as Chancellor of the Reich was marked by the dissolution of the constitution. On February 28, 1933, just 4 weeks after his appointment, he issued the Emergency Decree for the Protection of Nation and State (*Verordnung zum Schutz von Volk und Reich*), claiming that the burning of the Reichstag was the beacon light of a communist upheaval. Thereby all civil liberties of the constitution were suspended. On March 23, 1933, at the first session of the newly elected Reichstag, the parliament passed a law by which all legislative powers were transferred to the administration (*Ermächtigungsgesetz*). Thereby Hitler achieved at the level of the state what he had achieved within the party: dissolution of procedures and institutions that would limit his ultimate authority. Without being formally abolished, the constitution was simply suspended. It was not only the Weimar constitution that Hitler opposed, but any constitution seemed incompatible with his claim to ultimate authority. Therefore, Hitler never was interested in creating a National Socialist constitution, as he opposed all comprehensive legislative codifications, even when they were proposed by his followers as a means of furthering National Socialist ideals. A new penal law, which was to represent the new values of National Socialist *Volksgemeinschaft*, was not enacted in 1936 because of Hitler's opposition to any such codification.

The second element of charismatic leadership is the replacement of structurally organized leadership by personal leadership. Under Hitler collective decision making was abolished, as were procedures of institutionalized coordination and conflict resolution. Within the party there was no collective decision making at any level nor even a council of the district chiefs (*Gauleiter*). Hitler was very explicit that without his consent no more than three *Gauleiter* were to meet on their own initiative. His model of leadership was adopted from the strict command structure of the army, the only organization he knew from personal experience. Within the state this model was not easy to realize, and it took Hitler time to achieve the situation he preferred. It was upon the death of the President of the Republic on August 2, 1934 that he saw the chance to combine the positions of Chancellor, President, supreme commander of the armed forces, and leader of the Nazi party into the new position of *Führer*. This meant the definite establishment of charismatic leadership, a position created by the will of the leader and unbound by any other legitimated agency or institution. *Führer* was not just a title like Mussolini's *Duce*; it signalled the replacement of the organized leadership structure of a nation by personal rulership. Hitler's position as a charismatic leader of the party became fused with his position as President and Chancellor of the state into a new position of leader of the German people. The state structure was penetrated by the ultimate authority of the *Führer*, which no longer rested on the constitution or the organization of the state but on Hitler's claim to fulfill the historical mission of the nation. His will was the *volonté général*, the true will of the nation (Buchheim, 1967, pp. 15–29). The establishment of charismatic leadership was a revolutionary break with all former political organization since the development of the constitutional monarchy.

Charismatic leadership thus is the result of the transition from the claim to ultimate authority to the execution of ultimate authority. It can be controlled only by providence and will be judged only by history. It can be overcome only if the belief in the charisma of the leader is falsified. However, the more the authority of the leader is unbound, the greater are the chances that the leader will be able to define the situation such that his or her actions will be perceived as successful.

The chance to define a situation in terms of the leader's interest is greatly enlarged if the leader is in possession of ultimate authority and can suppress or prohibit alternative definitions of the situation. People under his or her domination then will have no other source of information about the situation. This opportunity is greatly enhanced if there is no official body of doctrine. Then the leader is able to alter *ex post facto* the criteria of success according to the outcome of his actions. In the case of Hitler this was the case. National Socialism never developed a codified body of doctrine according to which Hitler's actions could be legitimately evaluated or criticized by standards to which Hitler himself would have had to comply. The doctrine was not separated from Hitler's interpretation thereof and he never allowed the codification of a program to which he would have had to conform. He discouraged all attempts to formulate a National Socialist doctrine and thereby remained in a position to control ideological positions, so that even faithful National Socialists could not criticize Hitler in terms of an official ideology. Hitler was in a position to define means and ends, to execute ultimate power, and to control the ideological categories which he used to justify his power.

How is this transition accepted by those who consent to ultimate authority? Why do they agree to the surrender and dissolution of procedures and institutions that would serve their own rights? There are different elements to be considered. Weber assumes that a situation of despair, helplessness, hope, and enthusiasm gives rise to a feeling of personal devotion. This may be the case with those who are personally converted into true believers in the charisma of the leader. However, they are usually a minority. The majority may not be able or willing to grant such exalted status. They may have great expectations in the charismatic leader, but this is not yet enough to convince them to surrender. They must be deceived and forced to surrender. Hitler threatened in 1921 to resign from the party and push it back into obscurity. Hitler dramatized the burning of the Reichstag in 1933 as a threat of civil war, thereby getting the emergency decree accepted. Finally, by starting the war Hitler made himself appear to be the only alternative to defeat and destruction.

Acceptance of charismatic leadership thus does not only depend on the true believers of charisma; it can be induced simply by the perception that there is no alternative. The charismatic leader has to define the situation in such a way that nonbelievers will be induced to accept his or her claim. Still, it seems unbelievable that the German conservative elites in politics, big business, the military, and the churches did not recognize their own deprivation of rights in 1933–34. They should have known better, but they did not realize what was happening. All the discriminations and persecutions that occurred were directed toward citizens whom the elites did not care about because of their political conviction or racial descent: communists, socialists, liberals, Jews. It seemed as if only minorities and adversaries were being outlawed, but in reality the entire German people had lost its civil liberties unnoticed. Although one can employ the notion of moral indifference (Baum, 1981) on the part of the German elites in regard to their attitudes toward the discrimination of communists, socialists, and Jews, it still remains to be explained why they were so short-sighted in regard to their own position. The consequences of charismatic leadership, once established, were apparently not taken seriously. They could not be believed even when Hitler was announcing them. The strategy of taming Hitler, which the conservative elites thought they would be able to do in 1933, was abortive the moment the same elites granted Hitler charismatic leadership. It was, therefore, not only the true believers who accepted the claim to charismatic leadership, it also was the nonbelievers, who reluctantly, for opportunistic reasons, and morally indifferent to standards of humanity, supported the claim to ultimate authority and brought about the transition to charismatic leadership.

The dissolution of norms, procedures, and institutions enlarges the capacity to enforce conformity by the leader and decreases the capacity to resist. There is a fundamental shift in the distribution of power within a group or a society after the establishment of charismatic leadership. There is no legitimate opposition, there is no tolerance for deviant behavior, there are no institutional means to defend independence from the orders of the charismatic leader. Conformity becomes duty, nonconformity treason, and opposition rebellion.

The Properties of Charismatic Leadership

Once charismatic leadership is established, the structure of domination is altered. The administrative staff of the leader is recruited from among personally loyal followers, who have no other basis for their position than the trust of the leader. They are completely dependent on the leader and therefore can be induced to obey without question. Among these agents there exists an atmosphere of competition and suspicion; no solidarity arises, but all try to defend their authority and their realm of competence against each other. The leader has direct control over the administrative staff and can at any time commission a new loyal follower with a new task. It is a task-oriented administration, unbound by lines of jurisdiction and competence. Such an administrative staff will be suited for mobilization of resources and quick, ad hoc decisions. It conveys the impression of activity, forcefulness, and rapid implementation of decisions, without bureaucratic delay, endless negotiations, and lame compromises.

For the mobilization of the Nazi movement, such an administrative structure was suited. But what about the administration of a complex state? Here we see the interesting mixture of a prevailing bureaucratic structure and a number of newly created agencies with undefined competence for a specific task. Two types of administrative structures worked side by side. The one was reduced to ordinary routine tasks, the other designated for accomplishing the goals of the leader. A "dual state" (Fraenkel, 1941) was the result. Weber sharply contrasted the administrative organizations of charismatic domination and legal domination. Bureaucracy was to him the typical form of administration of legal domination, whereas the staff of the charismatic leader was to consist of agents who were personally summoned by the leader on the basis of their loyalty.

The Nazi state seems to have been a mixture of bureaucracy and charismatic rule. However, charismatic leadership in large organizations or entire nations has to employ the procedural advantages of bureaucracies; it does not necessarily lose its specific charismatic character thereby. It is enough to have the will of the leader implemented without formal restrictions. If this can be achieved by special agents bypassing the bureaucratic structure or by weakening the coordination of the fragmented jurisdictions of the bureaucracy, bureaucratic structures may prevail without interfering with the ultimate authority of the leader. The ordinary state administration, the military, and industry retained their internal bureaucratic structures, but they did not endanger the charismatic leadership as long as they remained fragmented and the top positions were occupied by loyal followers of Hitler. During his rule Hitler successfully tamed the bureaucracy, not the other way around, as many expected. The effect was a curious overall disorganization despite vigorous attempts to organize. However, irrational decision making and the uncoordinated implementation of decisions are tenable only for a short period, as they exploit the basic fabric of society and uphold its functioning by draconian suppression. Terror thus becomes a functional prerequisite of charismatic leadership, to counteract the growing disorganization of the system. Charismatic leadership within large organizations does not become bureaucratized as long as it can act by emissaries cutting across the sphere of jurisdiction. Bureaucracies then become mere technical instruments; they do not execute an important influence of their own. The most powerful staff created by Hitler, the SS, was internally bureaucratically structured; nevertheless, it remained an instrument of direct rule for Hitler, unbound by general legislation and spheres of jurisdiction.

Charismatic leadership is required to demonstrate proof and success. An established charismatic leadership must seek to prove itself. There are a number of mechanisms by which this proof can be influenced and partly manufactured by the leader. The first is the leader's capacity to decide what shall be attributed to him or her and what is to be attributed to others, for whose actions the leader cannot be held responsible. Positive events should be attributed to the leader's qualifications; negative events should be excluded from his or her responsibility. The phrase, "If the Führer only knew this," shows quite clearly the importance of mechanisms of exclusion. Many negative aspects of the Third Reich were therefore attributed to the party and its functionaries rather than to Hitler himself; it was believed they would not have occurred if Hitler had known. On the other hand, events that were evaluated positively were to be attributed to Hitler personally—for example, the building of the *Autobahn*—despite the fact that they were not originated by Hitler. The manipulation of public opinion therefore plays an important role in manipulating the perception of success of the charismatic leader. Second, the criteria of success have to be controlled. Whereas before the war the exceptional qualifications of Hitler were proved by his unexpected successes in peacefully abolishing the provisions of the Versailles Treaty, in the years 1939 to 1941 it was the military victories and later the hope that his ingenuity would prevent a total defeat that sustained his charismatic leadership. To control the criteria of success and their alteration, it is necessary that only one definition of the situation be allowed. The manipulation of public opinion and the merciless persecution of anyone who dares to give another definition of the situation are therefore prerequisites for the manufacturing of the proof of charismatic qualities. However, signs of charismatic qualifications that were not manipulated occurred many times. All the failed attempts to assassinate Hitler strengthened the attribution of charisma. In particular, the abortive putsch on July 20, 1944, had the result of reinforcing in many people their propensity to believe the providential role Hitler claimed for himself.

Of course, the leader must be prepared to act according to the role prerequisites of a charismatic leader. The leader must present himself as a charismatic person and must defend this claim. Hitler did so by personal qualifications and by deliberate actions. He presented himself as a man of providence, secluding his trivial personal life. He was able to win over adversaries in personal conversation and in public speeches. He used all means of suppression, violence, and terror. He created situations that seemingly presented no alternatives to his actions. He was prepared to take the greatest risks personally and for the people who followed him. Like a gambler he played hazard first with the party he had founded and later with the nation he commanded. His irresponsibility, however, led to a catastrophe. The basic irrationality Weber saw in the revolutionary force of charismatic domination finally prevailed.

References

Baum, R.C. (1981). *The holocaust and the German elite.* Totowa and London: Rowman and Littlefield and Croom Helm.

Bracher, K.D., Sauer, W., & Schulz, G. (1960). *Die nationalsozialistische Machtergreifung.* Cologne: Westdeutscher Verlag.

Bracher, K.D. (1970). *The German dictatorship.* New York: Praeger.

Bracher, K.D. (1971). *Die Auflösung der Weimarer Republik* (5th rev. ed.). Villingen: Ring Verlag.

Broszat, M. (1969). *Der Staat Hitlers.* Munich: Deutscher Taschenbuch Verlag.

Buchheim, H. (1967). *Die SS—das Herrschaftsinstrument. Anatomie des SS-Staates: Vol. 1.* Munich: Deutscher Taschenbuch Verlag.

Fest, J.C. (1973). *Hitler.* Frankfurt: Propyläen.

Festinger, L., Riecken, H.W., & Schachter, S. (1956). *When prophecy fails.* Minneapolis: University of Minnesota Press.

Festinger, L. (1957). *A theory of cognitive dissonance.* Stanford: Stanford University Press.

Fraenkel, E. (1941). *The dual state: A contribution to the theory of dictatorship.* London: Oxford University Press.

Haffner, S. (1978). *Anmerkungen zu Hitler.* Munich: Kindler.

Hildebrand, K. (1979). *Das Dritte Reich.* Munich: Oldenbourg.

Hirschfeld, F., & Kettenacker, L. (Ed.). (1981). *The "Führer State": Myth and reality.* Stuttgart: Klett-Cotta.

Horn, W. (1972). *Führerideologie und Parteiorganisation in der NSDAP (1919–1933).* Düsseldorf: Droste.

Jäckel, E. (1981). *Hitlers Weltanschauung.* Stuttgart: Deutsche Verlagsanstalt.

Kershaw, I. (1980). *Der Hitler-Mythos.* Stuttgart: Deutsche Verlagsanstalt.

Matthias, E., & Morsey, R. (1960). *Das Ende der Parteien 1933.* Düsseldorf: Droste.

Nyomarky, J. (1967). *Charisma and factionalism within the Nazi Party.* Minneapolis: University of Minnesota Press.

Shils, E. (1975). *Center and periphery. Essays in macrosociology.* Chicago and London: University of Chicago Press.

Stern, J.P. (1975). *Hitler: The Führer and the people.* London: Fontana and Collins.
Struve, W. (1973). *Elites against democracy. Leadership ideals in bourgeois political thought in Germany 1890–1933.* Princeton: Princeton University Press.
Tyrell, A. (1975). *Vom "Trommler" zum "Führer".* Munich: Fink.
Weber, M. (1968). *Economy and society.* (G. Roth and C. Wittich, Eds.). New York: Bedminster Press (Original work published 1922).

Chapter 5

Charismatic Domination, Totalitarian Dictatorship, and Plebiscitary Democracy in the Twentieth Century

Luciano Cavalli

Toward a Theory of Charismatic Domination

This chapter is based on my recent study (1981) of Weber's work on charisma and subsequent research in the field. I introduce an outline of a theory of charismatic domination which is not in agreement with current formulations on several points. (Weber himself, of course, always spoke of an "ideal type" rather than a theory.) In fact this theory has been influenced by a stream of thought chiefly developed by Durkheim (1912, 1924, 1925) and Parsons (1937, 1951). I shall then discuss the topic of charismatic domination in the twentieth century, with a special regard to so-called totalitarian dictatorships and to plebiscitary democracy.

In his treatment of charismatic domination (*Herrschaft*) as an ideal type, Weber made it clear that obedience is given to a "charismatically qualified" leader by his or her followers, and, mostly because of their personal trust in the leader, to the order revealed or created by him or her (1922/1980). Charisma is defined by Weber as a person's extraordinary quality, because of which that person is believed to be endowed with powers and properties equally extraordinary, and therefore obeyed as a leader. The possession of this (no better defined) quality may appear insufficient to command obedience from others, but this difficulty can probably be solved by introducing and employing in a somewhat independent way two other ideas of Weber's: the calling and the extraordinary situation. He wrote that charismatic domination arises in extraordinary situations of any kind, whether political, economic, or religious, and that charisma constitutes a calling in a strong sense, a mission or an interior task.

These concepts may be further developed by reference to a historical context common to the would-be leader and his or her future followers, which, after the introduction of elements of change, they see as having become problematic at least in certain aspects, with danger for both personal and social integration. This development therefore implies the existence of a cultural code common at least in part to all the people involved. On this theoretical basis it is also possible to exploit fully the idea of a calling. In the new and problematic (extraordinary) situation, one individual feels called (in our century, usually in the lay sense) to lead the others toward a solution, which, given a common cultural background, can be felt by potential followers as a common cause, defining ends to be pursued as a gratifying duty.

However, a complex development of this kind also presupposes an uncommon trust in the leader which lends to a charismatic social process its peculiar character. Weber gave great relevance to this point, but he never examined it in depth. Nevertheless he suggested a useful distinction between the premodern era and the modern one, the first being primarily influenced by magic or religion. In our modern era the people's trust seems to derive mostly from the leader's personality, and principally from the strength of the leader's own conviction. This gives the leader that power of suggestion, of which Weber (1922/1980) spoke somewhat occasionally, giving the term a double meaning already developed by Hellpach and leaving aside (as I too will do here) the philosophical and psychological problems related to such a stand. As a consequence, for the average person the cause itself does not exist independently from the leader. The leader embodies it, together with the hope of its future implementation. Therefore trust in the leader tends to become total dedication, or "dedition." According to Weber, a general condition of this development is the irrationality and emotionality that characterize the masses—two qualities in obvious connection also with the phenomenon of suggestion, even though Weber did not deal with them in that context. Of course Weber did not speak of identification, but he was deeply interested in the leader as a source of new values for his or her followers.

Strangely enough, Weber did not draw from his premises the logical conclusion that only through a charismatic leader does the mass following elevate itself to a sphere of common ideals and values in a relatively stable way that ensures a society its moral basis. He pointed out insistently, however, that only such a leader may cause in his or her following a "change of mind" in the radical Christian sense of *metanoia*, although this should obviously be regarded as an extreme case, to be found rarely and principally in the premodern era.

I have lingered over my reconstruction of certain moments of a charismatic process because of their superior theoretical relevance, but such a process in all its manifold parts must be considered of the greatest importance for research purposes. It is basically with this process that historical cases with supposedly charismatic aspects must be compared—a point that seems to have been understood by very few social scientists. Given the importance of this process, I shall transform it into a paradigm, as far as possible following Weber and employing his language. The paradigm consists of twelve points: (1) an extraordinary situation (crisis) arises for people with a common cultural code; (2) one of them with a solution to the critical situation and a sense of calling about it asks for obedience as his or her due; (3) the others recognize this individual as their leader, thus becoming a following (and beginning a new process of social and personal integration), but psychologically they need confirmation (success, in their cultural terms); (4) when the leader gives such confirmation, he or she embodies the cause and enjoys dedition from the following; (5) the following structures itself as a leader-centered group, either as a self-contained community or as a movement for changing the social setting—which of the two depends on the leader's calling and the nature of the crisis; (6) the leader calls on some of the most dedicated followers to assist as emissaries in ruling the movement (or community)—they constitute a charismatic elite entirely dependent on the leader; (7) as the principal source of law, the leader imparts his or her rules to the movement (or community); (8) a change of mind caused by the leader takes place in the followers individually and in the following as a collective entity—in a charismatic movement (and even in a political regime born from such a movement) the change is displayed in an exhibition of "we"-feelings, self-confidence, enthusiasm, pugnacity, and a tendency to leave key responsibilities, mainly the moral one, to the leader; (9) this change brings about a greater collective effort to attain the ends stated by the leader in relationship with the cause—with a charismatic movement, this means effective action on the environment; (10) repeated lack of success in the cultural terms of the group causes the repudiation of the leader by the group and perhaps the dissolution of the latter, unless a new leader arises; (11) the same development may follow the leader's death, unless there is succession in one of six typical forms, the most relevant here being the institutionalization of charisma, by which charisma becomes inherent in an office, as in the Catholic Church and perhaps in political movements and regimes based on doctrines of salvation in this world, or secular religions; (12) within these institutions personal charismatic domination may appear in extraordinary situations, developing itself in a complex dialectic with institutionalized charisma.

As is well known, Weber conceived personal charismatic domination as ephemeral, though powerfully revolutionary. Western rationalization was moreover destroying faith in the extraordinary, the very basis of any charismatic phenomenon. Therefore charisma was doomed to lose its role as protagonist in history. However, Weber did seemingly allow for a partial exception in the political sphere. He believed that democracy had evolved from charismatic domination over the centuries, and that this was especially evident in plebiscitary democracy, or democracy "with" a leader. This kind of democracy, he wrote emphatically, is a kind of charismatic domination concealed under a legitimation derived from the subjects' will (1922/1980). In Weber's opinion, it always developed as a consequence of mass democracy. Weber thought that Athenian democracy in Pericles' era, and in his own day the British prime ministry and the American presidency, were good specimens of plebiscitary democracy. He seemed to believe that this variety of democracy might prevail in Germany as well. Its principal characteristics are a leader chosen directly by the masses as their trustee, and, correlatively, a decisive concentration of power in one role, the leader's role, whether formally defined or not.

The leader might also be a charismatic one, whose personality and life were built on a calling. In *Politik als Beruf*, Weber (1919/1971) points out the main internal charismatic qualities of such a leader: dedication to a cause, a sense of responsibility for its implementation, farsightedness implying distance from people and events—all of these relevant aspects of a properly developed calling.

The meditation on plebiscitary democracy belongs to the last years of Weber's life, and it was never fully developed. It has received scarce attention since Weber's death. I believe, however, that it offers a basically valid intuition from which to move for an adequate understanding of very important changes taking place in Western democracy. Some criticisms must be taken into account, however. Loewenstein (1965) and others have called our attention to the point that *charismatic* and *plebiscitary* cannot be considered synonyms, because the second term refers primarily to the electoral procedure, or even to the way an election developed de facto. That is certainly true. De facto, though, a relationship of trust and even the attribution of charismatic qualities to the leader by the masses are often implied in a plebiscitary choice. Such an attribution is, of course, no equal to the actual possession of charismatic qualities, especially the internal ones discussed in *Politik als Beruf*. Sometimes, however, the qualities are there, as the rare gift of the gods to one people. Another criticism was suggested by Weber himself. He seems to have believed that charismatic domination in Western democracy can develop only in a weak, lay form and within definite limits. This judgment concerns, however, not the quality but only the intensity of a phenomenon, and as such it can be easily accepted. Of course the leader of a plebiscitary democracy cannot be the author of mass *metanoia* in the radical Christian sense, nor the only source of law as in ancient times (or today in a totalitarian regime).

Within his theoretical frame, Weber also considered occasionally the development of political parties. According to him, charismatic phenomena had suddenly arisen in mass parties as soon as these had been confronted by extraordinary situations. He thought that the growth of party machines would favor in a decisive way the political ascent of strong personalities and possibly of truly charismatic leaders, as those capable of obtaining first the masses' trust, consequently power, and finally the means for rewarding the avid members of the party machine. Plebiscitary democracy would triumph in modern states because of this development within parties in a pre-disposed constitutional setting. The latter seemed to be, in Weber's view, a necessary condition. As I shall try to show, Weber was not completely right on this point and, in any case, other changes in modern society make for the development of plebiscitary democracy both in the state and in political parties.

Types of Extraordinary Situations

For decades there has been an open debate on whether the concept of charisma and the theory built on it are really useful to the social scientist working on contemporary society. Some scholars, such as Friedrich (1961), did not think so. Others, such as Tucker (1968), considered Weber's tools quite indispensable. Obviously I find myself closer to the second point of view. Weber's concept and theory of charisma provide us with a unique understanding of the dynamic process linking leader, elite, and masses in certain historical cases, on condition that the theory is properly developed in the light of subsequent sociological work. It must be said, however, that approval and disapproval of the theory seem also to depend on one's general attitudes toward human beings and society. Those in favor are more frequently scholars inclined to grant individual action prominence in the historical process; those not in favor usually give pride of place to collective subjects, such as social classes.

Not all research based on the concept of charisma may be described as altogether persuasive. However, it can be maintained with sound arguments that valid results have been obtained by employing the concept and the theory of charisma in research on twentieth-century movements, parties, and regimes, especially when a country is in a *statu nascendi* or in a state of crisis. At the nation-state level, it seems possible to develop a useful typology of these situations. Some can be outlined here: (a) the foundation of a nation-state, (b) a change of regime, (c) a change from parliamentary democracy to plebiscitary democracy, and (d) danger threatening the regime or the nation-state itself, from within and/or from without. These typical situations are certainly not unknown to Western history itself. Of course, the first was experienced only be relatively minor European nation-states in this century, but the three others have occurred, with important consequences, in the principal Western countries and in the Soviet Union, and to these we will limit our attention here.

Totalitarian Dictatorship

Changes of regime are especially important for contemporary Europe. Two groups of cases are worthy of attention here: change from a democratic to a totalitarian or authoritarian regime and change the other way around.

There is no agreement on the usefulness of the concept and theory of charisma in studying changes of regime and the subsequent totalitarian dictatorships in Russia, Italy, and Germany between the two world wars. Nevertheless certain research has revealed that the correspondence between models and phenomena is impressive and at times enlightening. In my opinion, the primary reference to the charisma theory in analyzing the dictator's personality and role has brought rewarding results.

Of course the usefulness of the concept of *personal* charisma is more evident insofar as Fascism and Nazism are concerned. Hitler's role seems especially worthy of being qualified as charismatic (Lepsius, 1978; Nyomarkay, 1967). Certain research seems to show that a charismatic process can be traced step by step (Cavalli, 1982). Hitler's party revealed charismatic characteristics after 1921. After seizing power in 1933, Hitler became the plenipotentiary of the German people in every sphere; as such he held all power, and the members of the Nazi elite acted only as his emissaries. Hitler himself took all the decisions that mattered, and he was— a decisive trait—the only source of law. Before and after the seizure of power (*Machtergreifung*), the attitudes of the elite and the masses were shaped by their recognition of an extraordinary quality and a calling of general interest (of the entire nation) in Hitler, which he himself firmly believed to possess, thereby exacting full submission from all Germans. Under his spell, new values spread among the people. "We"-feelings, self-confidence, enthusiasm, and pugnacity became typical features of the Nazi following, together with a renunciation of independent moral judgment.

Contrary to Weber's expectations, with Hitler charismatic domination did seem to revive in a full, strong sense. However, one should take into account the distorting intervention of Nazi coercion and manipulation in the charismatic process. In this respect it seems useful to draw a parallel with Lenin, who never had, either in his party or in the Soviet state, an institutional role that allowed him to enforce his will on others. In Tucker's (1974) studies especially, Lenin appears to have prevailed in decision making thanks to his great personal prestige and intellectual superiority, often at the price of delays and deviations due to the unfettered opposition of other members of the communist elite, which was, however, increasingly prone to make Lenin the object of a personal cult, quite against his will. In this as in other cases, however, the study of power in the Soviet Union is complicated by the presence of *institutional* party charisma and its dialectic with personal charisma. The strength of this institutional charisma also contributes to explaining the full totalitarian development of the Soviet regime, whereas such a thing was hindered by the tension between personal charisma and bureaucratic rationalization in Hitler's Germany. Both in Nazi Germany and in the Soviet Union, however, the source of inspiration and legitimation for charismatic phenomena was provided by secular religions promising salvation in this life (Cavalli, 1981, 1982).

Plebiscitary Democracy

The third and fourth types of situation, which bring about only weak charismatic phenomena, obviously occur also in Western contemporary democracies. The fourth type is a recurrent one. Now and then a danger arises from within or from without which threatens the regime or the nation-state itself, and a charismatic process may develop at least in part as an answer to it. Franklin D. Roosevelt's presidency was surrounded by a charismatic nimbus in 1933, during the great economic crisis, as was Churchill's prime ministry in 1940, the most crucial period of the war for the British (Tucker, 1981). Rejection of the theory of charisma by certain scholars seems to depend on a narrow interpretation of Weber's work (Kavanagh, 1974).

The pattern for the third type of situation is different in contemporary democracies. As we already saw in discussing Weber, the development of mass democracy (as opposed to elite democracy, without mass participation) has brought about a transition in some countries from one variety of democracy to another, that is, from the leaderless variety to one with a leader, or plebiscitary democracy. Such a change could also take place elsewhere. Weber pointed to the party machine as the main factor of that change in a predetermined constitutional setting. He did not discuss the relevance of an extraordinary situation of crisis, notwithstanding his theory and even though his sociological analysis allowed one to foresee those situations—with the exception perhaps of those deriving from the bipolar international order following World War II.

As I have already said, postwar developments in the West seem to show a tendency toward plebiscitary democracy, even though change has generally been recorded by means of other concepts and terms, for instance as a trend towards personalization of power. This tendency is observable in democracies characterized by a strong premiership, such as the United Kingdom, or by a strong presidency, such as the United States—especially in the latter (Ceaser, 1979). Leaderless democracy seems to exist at present in very few countries, among them Italy, with a multiparty system, proportional representation, parliamentary preponderance, weak governments, and a weak premiership. Precisely the country that once exhibited the most conspicuous specimen of leaderless democracy, France, has experienced the most radical transition to the opposite variety of democracy; moreover, this change was made possible by the charisma of one man, de Gaulle. For at least one of his successors, the socialist President Mitterrand, reference to charisma also seems at times appropriate.

In this context, the cases of three other European countries—Spain, Portugal, and Greece—which experienced a transition from authoritarian to democratic regimes in the 1970s are also particularly interesting. The new constitutional and electoral laws were not planned in order to give life to new specimens of leaderless democracy. In Greece and in Spain they did even allow for plebiscitary developments, which eventually took place with Papandreou and Gonzales, respectively, the two socialist leaders now in power. Since 1982, even the new military dictatorship in Turkey, erected on the ruins of a leaderless democracy, has been trying to build up a strong democracy on a two-party base, and plebiscitary elements already have shown up in the first presidential elections.

Of course a change to plebiscitary democracy in these countries posed new problems for scholars drawing on the theory of charisma (Panebianco, 1983). Some even seem to reject completely recourse to that theory. Skepticism has also been aroused by the application of that theory to the seemingly obvious case of de Gaulle, the founder and protagonist of the Fifth Republic. Some valid researches based on the concept of charisma did not suffice to persuade all the critics as to the value of that operation (Dogan, 1965; Tuchhändler, 1977). Doubts appear to be better founded in other cases, but sound research should rather concentrate on the question: Under what circumstances does the leadership selected by a plebiscitary democracy possess characteristics that may be properly defined as charismatic?

Plebiscitary Democracy and Political Parties

One must also consider the consequences for political parties of a change to plebiscitary democracy. However, this is only one aspect of the relationship between charisma and parties, which therefore requires a brief, preliminary discussion. After Weber, other scholars such as Michels (1911/1925, 1933) observed in mass parties elements of a charismatic process, or at least episodes of a cult of the leader that presumably could be ascribed to that process. At the end of World War I, the fascist movements developed from a composite social base and with clear-cut charismatic traits. New experiences of this kind were recorded after World War II. In the communist parties a charismatic process appeared to be artificially stimulated by the systematic cult of the leader, following Stalin's model. However, some socialist parties did not remain untouched by such phenomena, in spite of their libertarian traditions and statutes, and new charismatic movements of a political nature grew up from a very broad social base, even though middle-class people were overrepresented in them.

A case in point is de Gaulle's Rassemblement du Peuple Français (Rally of the French People) as it developed after 1947. Here, indeed, we encounter the consequences of a transition from democracy without to democracy with a leader. The French case shows that such a constitutional change and the president's election by the people in particular bring about a corresponding transformation of parties as well, from parties without to parties with a leader. As Schonfeld (1980a, 1980b) and others have shown, even parties with quite antiauthoritarian traditions, such as the French Socialist Party, conformed to the trend. In Greece and Spain also the constitutional and electoral laws have favored the development of parties with a leader, at least as far as the two leading parties, the Pasok in Greece and the Psoe in Spain, are concerned.

All these developments, and especially that in France, did however favor a diffuse overestimation of the constitutional context as a factor of party change in the manner specified above (Cavalli, 1983, 1984). Important factors have generally been underrated or even forgotten, such as an extraordinary situation of crisis and the leader's personality. One should stress the role of such men as Papandreou and of the charismatic processes that developed with him (Lyrintzis, 1983) and other socialist leaders (Caciagli, 1982), though to a different extent. Other relevant conditions of a trend toward plebiscitary democracy in the state and in the party are represented by some new characteristics of Western society: the dominance of the urban setting, social intercourse in a mass society, mass schooling, the preponderance of the middle classes, the growth of secularization (with destructive effects on secular religions as well), and, finally, the outstanding role of the mass media.

A more balanced view on party change is suggested by studying the evolution of the Italian Socialist Party (PSI) since 1976 (Cavalli, 1984). In the Italian context of a leaderless democracy and in a party context characterized by warring factions and libertarian moods, Bettino Craxi took over the leadership during a sudden and dramatic crisis, which might have caused the political annihilation of the PSI. Thus Craxi, an "innerly called leader," came to embody the socialist hope in the eyes of party members and voters.

The situation itself had endowed the new leader with a sort of charismatic nimbus. However, Craxi exploited this fortune by an unremitting struggle for party identity and success, cleverly taking advantage of the social and cultural conditions mentioned above (which were already fully developed in Italy), and especially of the mass media. Thanks to a series of political and electoral confirmations, Craxi's leadership has acquired clear-cut plebiscitary and charismatic traits, which were already evident in his election as party secretary directly by the national congress in 1981, for the first time in the history of the PSI. Craxi's election as party secretary finally assumed a pure and complete plebiscitary form in the 1984 national congress, where it was carried by acclamation. Other points of conformity to my general paradigm of the charismatic process deserve to be underlined, however. Craxi enjoys a sort of autocratic power. He governs the party with the assistance of a small elite of trusted friends and advisers. The spirit of the party is changing even more rapidly than its form. Self-confidence, enthusiasm, and pugnacity characterize the new militancy of a noticeably rejuvenated following. Craxi's will to dominate and reshape the socio-political environment has become the will of the following and was crowned with success on Craxi's being chosen as premier, a position never before held by a Socialist.

Contemporary Italy seems to offer other developments worthy of consideration in this context. Two other democratic parties, the Christian Democrats and the Social Democrats, have their secretaries elected by the party congress directly. This suggests that there is a tendency to change within the party in order to obviate, in part at least, the central weakness of this variety of democracy, namely, a lack of leadership at all levels of power. In turn, this development seems to confirm that more general tendency toward democracy with a leader that I, taking the hint from Weber, have predicted as gradually prevailing in this part of the century, as a consequence of the new character of society and of a protracted state of at least partial crisis in national as well as international affairs.

Toward a Systematic Study of Charismatic Phenomena

Against the theory of charisma some scholars have advanced prejudicial objections, asking whether the charismatic leader is really a creator of new values and ends, or simply the spokesperson of the masses with mature even if not verbalized needs. I think that I have furnished some elements for an answer in my research as well as in this chapter, but the task of confronting this and similar questions seems to lie beyond the limits of this chapter. I shall examine here only the critical debate on the principal conditions that favor the growth of charismatic processes, together with some psychological aspects of these processes. A brief review of this debate will show that not a great deal of progress has been made on these points, especially with regard to charismatic processes that may occur in our time.

1. The primary task in the field is certainly that of giving a contemporary meaning to Weber's extraordinary situation. In this connection, sociologists have stressed unanimously the relevance of social change. During this century millions of people moved from a peasant civilization to an urban and industrial context. That migration involved social and cultural transformations which seem to shape a truly extraordinary situation favorable to charismatic developments such as those experienced in Russia, Germany, and elsewhere after the World War I crisis. Charismatic processes in past centuries (such as the chiliastic movements in medieval Europe) seem to confirm the central relevance of social change (Cohn, 1961). However, the study of social change in relationship to charismatic movements has not been developed analytically, especially as far as contemporary society and plebiscitary democracy are concerned, although some authors (Germani, 1980; Mannheim, 1940; Michels, 1927) have made a contribution to the understanding of the crises of democracy in mass society that is relevant also to this study.

In the present context it must be remembered that a most interesting line of sociological reflection on the extraordinary situation has developed from Durkheim to Parsons and other contemporaries. These authors have tried to demonstrate, by such concepts as *anomie*, the fundamental relationship between social and personal integration. This relationship seems to offer us a primary reference for the study of phenomena experienced in this century, such as Fascism and Nazism (Cavalli, 1982; Mannheim, 1940). The centrality of the "community of blood" in Nazi ideology and propaganda is proof of this.

2. A second task is to study the cultural setting. What cultural conditions favor (or hinder) the growth of charismatic phenomena? Of course, Weber himself had already shown the relevance of religious traditions to these effects, and much of what he said is probably still valid today. Cohn (1961) made an important new contribution by linking Marxist communism and Nazism to Judaeo-Christian millenarianism, through the medieval movements. In this connection, the concept of secular religion also shows its great usefulness. Following Weber and going beyond him, other authors underscore how the whole Judaeo-Christian tradition extols the ideas of miracle, mission, calling, and charisma, and some Christian confessions have helped considerably to keep sensitivity to charisma alive in the common people, by such means as the cult of miracle-working saints (Cavalli, 1981). However, even the analogy between certain descriptions of mystic experiences on the one hand, and of charismatic ones on the other, probably merits more attention.

In this connection one must also mention politico-religious traditions, and even traditions of an apparently lay nature. Examples are the popular conception of the Russian czar as a father endowed with extraordinary powers, and the idea of a national mission once found in different versions among the peoples of Europe. This point has been treated systematically by such scholars as Poliakov (1974), without connecting it with charisma, whereas it has rarely been dealt with in research based on the charismatic theory.

Again, it must be underlined that the above-mentioned work on the cultural setting is especially, even if by no means exclusively, relevant to the study of charismatic processes in a strong form, such as those to be found in the history of Nazi Germany and communist Russia. For the study of plebiscitary democracy and its charismatic traits, the researcher should give particular attention to the crisis of secular religions (such as Marxism) that superseded traditional religions among Western masses. Other cultural traits of contemporary society should, of course, be taken into careful consideration. We do not yet possess many contributions of relevance, not even on how mass media condition society. No attempt has been made to pursue this second task systematically in contemporary terms, as far as I know.

3. The third task is, of course, to explain the psychological aspects of charismatic processes. The first problem is the sense of calling or mission, which is at the very origin of the charismatic process and constitutes perhaps its driving force. Weber traced the leader's sense of mission back to his passionate dedication to a cause, on the one hand, and to ecstatic states on the other. A very particular personality was presupposed. Some scholars, such as Marcus (1961) and Moscovici (1981), have thrown new theoretical light on this problem. Others have developed case studies of reputed charismatic leaders such as Hitler, adding, perhaps, new elements also to our general knowledge on the subject (Langer, 1972; Cavalli, 1982). However, no systematic work has yet been done on the sense of mission in connection with the theory of charisma.

Much has been written on the relationship between leader and followers. Weber seems to have followed Hellpach's theories faithfully. Apparently Weber thought that people were drawn into a charismatic process, even to the point of changing their values, by the suggestion exercised by the leader in two forms theorized by that author (Hellpach, 1906). Of course, this choice depends largely on Weber's opinion that the masses were by their very nature irrational and emotional. It is noteworthy that Weber, perhaps out of excessive attachment to his theory, exploited the contributions of Le Bon and Tarde in a reductive way, that is, only for mass situations without a leader (Weber, 1917–1919/1966, 1922/1980). Thus Weber gave up a chance of deepening his comprehension of charismatic phenomena.

Freud (1940) developed, of course, a new and penetrating insight into the leader–follower relationship, and contemporary psychoanalysts such as Schiffer (1973) have elaborated it in interesting ways with reference to the theory of charisma. Building on Freud, but also on Tarde and Le Bon, Moscovici (1981) has offered a new and stimulating approach to the relationship between the charismatic leader and those who follow him or her. The main task for present scholars is perhaps that of establishing a tighter integration between psychological and sociological research on this problem. Some research already suggests, for example, that the extraordinary situation, although it must be defined primarily in sociocultural terms, can be better understood as the basic condition of the charismatic process by employing psychoanalytical concepts such as that of regression.

Of course, in these three points I have touched on only a few relevant themes and problems. Among others one should mention at least the so-called personality cult, which was hinted at in discussing totalitarian dictatorships. The cult of personality has a very long and complex history in the Western world. It has also accompanied great twentieth-century charismatic leaders, sometimes even after their death, as in the case of Lenin, possibly echoing specific traditions of orthodox Christianity (Tucker, 1974).

On the other hand, the cult of personality may well appear as a typical, genuine aspect of a charismatic process. On the other hand, it may be at times the product of the gigantic manipulatory power inherent in modern mass media, which has not injustly been defined as a factor of pseudo-charisma (Bensman & Givant, 1975; Glassman, 1975). These reflections, in turn, open the way to a many-sided discussion of the controversial relationship between charismatic domination and mass media, as already mentioned in connection with plebiscitary democracy.

Following in the wake of Loewenstein (1965), several authors have commented that mass media work against charisma, at least in a free and pluralistic world. However, a large part of humanity is still living within states in which democracy does not exist, except perhaps as a façade. Even in some European countries and in the United States, mass media work in favor of plebiscitary and charismatic phenomena, already facilitated by general sociocultural developments, as we noted previously. Few political leaders take full advantage of the mass media. A great leader can appear simultaneously to millions of people spread sometimes over a very large territory, entering their homes, as if by magic, and acting on them with a direct seduction, magnified by technical and psychological devices. As president or premier of a plebiscitary democracy, such a leader has the irresistible spell of power on his or her side. Indeed, it depends largely on the overwhelming novelty of the mass media that the theory of charisma does not apply so much to the past, as Weber himself thought, but to the present and even more to the future.

References

Bensman, J., & Givant, M. (1975). Charisma and modernity: The use and abuse of a concept. *Social Research, 42*, 570–614.

Caciagli, M. (1982). Le risorse e i ritardi del Partito socialista obrero español. *Il Mulino, 31*, 669–707.

Cavalli, L. (1981). *Il capo carismatico*. Bologna: Il Mulino.

Cavalli, L. (1982). *Carisma e tirannide nel secolo XX. Il caso Hitler*. Bologna: Il Mulino.

Cavalli, L. (1983). Nuovi leaders per un'Europa nuova. *Città & Regione, 9*(3), 5–20.

Cavalli, L. (1984). *A trend towards plebiscitary democracy in the West. The socialist case in Italy*. Firenze: Centro Studi di Sociologia Politica, Facoltà di Scienze Politiche 'C.Alfieri.'

Ceaser, J.W. (1979). *Presidential selection. Theory and development*. Princeton, NJ: Princeton University Press.

Cohn, N. (1961). *The pursuit of the millennium* (2nd ed.). London: Mercury Books.

Dogan, M. (1965). Le personnel politique et la personnalité charismatique. *Revue Française de Sociologie, 6*, 305–324.

Durkheim, E. (1912). *Les formes élémentaires de la vie religieuse* [The elementary forms of the religious life]. Paris: F. Alcan.

Durkheim, E. (1924). *Sociologie et philosophie* [Sociology and philosophy]. Paris: F. Alcan.

Durkheim, E. (1925). L'éducation morale [Moral education]. Paris: F. Alcan.
Freud, S. (1940). Massenpsychologie und Ich-Analyse [Group psychology and the analysis of the ego]. In S. Freud, Gesammelte Werke (Vol. 13, pp. 71–161). Frankfurt am Main: S. Fischer. (Original work published 1921)
Friedrich, C.J. (1961). Political leadership and the problem of the charismatic power. Journal of Politics, 23, 3–24.
Germani, G. (1980). Democrazia e autoritarismo nella società moderna. Storia Contemporanea, 11, 177–217.
Glassman, R. (1975). Legitimacy and manufactured charisma. Social Research, 42, 615–636.
Hellpach, W. (1906). Die geistigen Epidemien. In M. Buber (Ed.), Die Gesellschaft. Sammlung sozialpsychologischer Monographien (Vol. 11). Frankfurt am Main: Rütten & Loening.
Kavanagh, D. (1974). Crisis, charisma and British political leadership: Winston Churchill as the outsider. London: Sage.
Langer, W. C. (1972). The mind of Adolf Hitler. New York: Basic Books.
Lepsius, M.R. (1978). From fragmented party democracy to government by emergency decree and national socialist takeover: Germany. In J.J. Linz & A. Stepan (Eds.), The breakdown of democratic regimes: Europe (pp. 34–179). Baltimore: Johns Hopkins University Press.
Loewenstein, K. (1965). Max Webers staatspolitische Auffassungen in der Sicht unserer Zeit [Max Weber's political ideas in the perspective of our time]. Frankfurt am Main: Athenäum.
Lyrintzis, C. (1983). Il Pasok: Leadership carismatica e 'personale' politico emergente. Città & Regione, 9(3), 143–158.
Mannheim, K. (1940). Man and society in an age of reconstruction (E. Shils, Trans.). New York: Harcourt, Brace. (Original work published 1935)
Marcus, J.T. (1961). Transcendence and charisma. Western Political Quarterly, 14, 236–241.
Michels, R. (1925). Zur Soziologie des Parteiwesens in der modernen Demokratie. Untersuchungen über die oligarchischen Tendenzen des Gruppenlebens [Political parties: A sociological study of the oligarchical tendencies of modern democracy]. Stuttgart: A. Kröner. (Original work published 1911)
Michels, R. (1927). Corso di Sociologia Politica. Milano: Istituto Editoriale Scientifico.
Michels, R. (1983). Studi sulla democrazia e sull'autorità. Firenze: La Nusva Italia.
Moscovici, S. (1981). L'âge des foules. Paris: Fayard.
Nyomarkay, J. (1967). Charisma and factionalism in the Nazi Party. Minneapolis, MN: University of Minnesota Press.
Panebianco, A. (1983). Tendenze carismatiche nelle società contemporanee. Il Mulino, 32, 507–537.
Parsons, T. (1937). The structure of social action. New York: McGraw-Hill.
Parsons, T. (1951). The social system. Glencoe, IL: Free Press.
Poliakov, L. (1974). The aryan myth. A history of racist and nationalist ideas in Europe. (E. Howard, Trans.). London: Chatto-Heinemann for Sussex University Press.
Schiffer, I. (1973). Charisma. A psychoanalytic look at mass society. New York: Free Press.
Schonfeld, W.R. (1980a). La stabilité des dirigeants des partis politiques: Le personnel des directions nationales du Parti socialiste et du mouvement gaulliste. Revue française de science politique, 30, 477–505.
Schonfeld, W.R. (1980b). La stabilité des dirigeants des partis politiques: La théorie de l'oligarchie de Robert Michels. Revue française de science politique, 30, 30, 846–867.
Tuchhändler, K. (1977). De Gaulle und das Charisma. Munich: Tuduv.
Tucker, R.C. (1968). The theory of charismatic leadership. Daedalus, 97, 731–756.

Tucker, R.C. (1974). *Stalin as a revolutionary. A study in history and personality.* New York: Norton.

Tucker, R.C. (1981). *Politics as leadership.* Columbia, MO: University of Missouri Press.

Weber, M. (1966). Das antike Judentum [Ancient Judaism]. In M. Weber, *Gesammelte Aufsätze zur Religionssoziologie* (Vol. 3). Tübingen: J.C.B. Mohr. (Original work published 1917, 1919).

Weber, M. (1971). Politik als Beruf [Politics as a vocation]. In M. Weber, *Gesammelte politische Schriften* (3rd ed., pp. 493–548). Tübingen: J.C.B. Mohr. (original work published 1919).

Weber, M. (1980). *Wirtschaft und Gesellschaft* [Economy and society]. Tübingen: J.C.B. Mohr. (Original work published 1922).

Chapter 6

Power and Leadership in Lewinian Field Theory: Recalling an Interrupted Task

Carl F. Graumann

Kurt Lewin and the Change in Social Psychology

Consulting the social psychological literature on leadership inevitably leads one back to the so-called pioneer studies of Kurt Lewin and his students published between the late 1930s and 1960s. However, as inevitable as they seem to be, references to these studies are of an intriguing ambivalence. On the one hand, they state and sometimes emphasize the historical significance of Lewin's and the Lewinians' conceptual and empirical contributions to power and leadership in groups, mainly in connection with the application of field theory to group problems, with the beginning of cognitive social psychology and with experimentation with groups in laboratory settings. On the other hand, the reader gets the feeling that this emphasized significance is merely historical, since the field-theoretical approach, with its topological and dynamic constructs, does not seem to have been continued, nor have the findings from the classic studies on group atmospheres or styles of leadership been reliably replicated. (For recent explicit evaluations of Lewin's role in contemporary social psychology, see Evans, 1980; Festinger, 1980; Schellenberg, 1978). Furthermore, if we consider that neither Lewin nor his students presented an explicit theory or model of leadership, some justification is needed in the 1980s for discussing the Lewinian contributions to our understanding of leadership or even to resume his mode of thought.

In this chapter, I shall argue (1) that the Lewinian school of thought is still most relevant for our present thinking about power and leadership, and that (2) historically speaking, this approach, interrupted by Lewin's untimely death and uncompleted by his students (most of whom were not his disciples), has all the dynamic characters of a "tension system" inducing the resumption of the interrupted scientific activity. For that purpose, I shall not restrict my arguments to Lewin's own statements, but shall include all those ideas of his students that may properly be called Lewinian, that is, those that can be shown to be consistent explications and/or interpretations of Lewin's original conceptions. When Dorwin Cartwright presented his systematized essay "Lewinian Theory as a Contemporary Systematic Framework" in 1959—a title that after a quarter century can hardly be upheld—he was still able to proclaim that "Lewin's influence has permeated psychological thinking for more than a quarter-century and ... his own thought was developed in a widely shared intellectual climate" (Cartwright, 1959b, p. 9). Thus, beyond our special interest in changing conceptions of leadership, we shall have to ask the more general question of historical change in the intellectual climate of social psychology if we want to account for Kurt Lewin's impact on contemporary social psychology.

Because in the present context such an account cannot be fully given (cf. the various prefaces to the seven volumes of Lewin's collected works, the German *Kurt Lewin Werkausgabe* [Lewin 1981 ff.]), I shall concentrate on those aspects of Lewin's field theory that are necessary prerequisites and elements of the conception of leadership. This, then, is the second qualification. Leadership will have to be discussed in the context of power, and the latter in the context of group dynamics. In conclusion, the historical change of group dynamics and Lewin's significance for modern social psychology will be discussed.

Power and Leadership in the Field-Theoretical Perspective

Introduction to Field Theory

There have been many discussions about the proper meaning of field theory. The term itself is, at least in its *genus proximum*, misleading rather than helpful. Field theory is not a theory in the sense in which we normally use that term, as we do when speaking of Gestalt theory, learning theory, exchange theory, or a theory of cognitive dissonance. It is rather a metatheory, essentially implied in a methodology. Lewin, who never gave a proper definition of field theory, suggested this implication himself when he stated: "*Field theory is probably best characterized as a method*: namely, a method *of analyzing causal relations and of building scientific constructs*" (Lewin, 1951, p. 45). That is why Cartwright (1959b) is correct in his interpretation that field theory "is a set of beliefs about the proper way to build empirical theories; it is ... a metatheory" (p. 9).

On the other hand, there are more substantive statements about the nature of field theory. They all converge on what is most explicitly contained in a short (and so far unpublished) manuscript entitled "Field Theory and Geometry" (partly printed in Lewin, 1982, pp. 25–26): that the basic assumption of field theory is that any behavior (actions, affects, or thinking) depends on a variety of coexisting and interacting factors which make up the psychological "field." This field is not an abstract frame of reference but contains psychological facts such as the needs of the acting person, the goals and wishes of the individual, the manner in which the individual sees his or her past and future, the groups to which the individual belongs, the individual's friends and his or her own position among them, and so on.

Leaving aside Lewin's concern for the analysis of constructs and for formalization, I shall concentrate on two basic statements of field theory, namely, that "(a) behavior has to be derived from a totality of coexisting facts, (b) these coexisting facts have the character of a 'dynamic field' insofar as the state of any part of this field depends on every other part of the field" (Lewin, 1951, p. 25). The first statement refers to the "life space," which includes the person and the psychological environment, whereas both the first and the second statement have been formalized and simplified into the well-known and controversial formula according to which all behavior is a function of the person (P) and the environment (E), where both P and E are conceived of not as independent but as "interdependent variables" (Lewin, 1951, p. 25). The concept of interdependence is a central one in field theory. In many respects, field theory is the formation and use of constructs "which characterize objects and events in terms of interdependence rather than of phenotypical similarity or dissimilarity" (Lewin, 1951, p. 149).

The transition from the Aristotelian to the Galileian mode of thought (Lewin, 1935a) is a shift of focus from individual entities to their inter-relations. As postulated by Cassirer (1923), thing-concepts were replaced by relational (or functional) concepts, and interest in the constancy of elements by an interest in the constancy of relations (cf. Lewin, 1949). This Galileian interest in interrelations led Lewin not only to a topological representation of the structured life space with its paths, regions, boundaries, and barriers; it also helped him to describe the dynamic features of the life space. The basic construct for such descriptions is "force," which characterizes for any given point of application in the field the direction and strength of the tendency to change or to resist changes. Usually, there is a combination of several forces acting at a given point and time, yielding a resultant force (Lewin, 1951, p. 256). Forces have been distinguished as driving forces, which are tendencies to change or locomotions from one region to another region of the field, and as restraining forces, which correspond to barriers to such locomotions. Furthermore, Lewin distinguished between own forces (corresponding to a person's own needs), induced forces (corresponding to the actions of another person), and impersonal forces (corresponding to impersonal aspects of the situation). Because, as a rule, many forces of several types exist at the same time, but at different regions of the life space, the latter is construed as a force field. (For further characteristics of the total situation construed as a force field, cf. Lewin, 1951, pp. 256–272.)

The Concept of Power

It is within this formal framework of an organized (differentiated) and dynamic field that the concept of power is developed. It is a matter of definition or axiom that parts within a whole are interdependent, but in order to be distinguishably different parts, they also have to be independent to some degree. For simple interdependence this means that "part a will not be affected, as long as the alteration of part b is within certain limits. However, if the change of b surpasses this limit, the state of a will be affected" (Lewin, 1951, p. 305). This simple case of dependence is not applicable to highly organized (i.e., hierarchically structured) units where "organizational dependence" obtains. "For organizational dependence the important characteristic of a is its power to induce a change of state in b and this power seems to have no direct relation to the amount of change in a ... " (Lewin, 1951, p. 335). The force field here, where induced forces play the major part, is a "power field":

> This concept, which has shown its usefulness in social psychology, indicates the ability of one person to induce forces acting on another person. One can distinguish the strength and the scope of the power field. It is one important aspect of the relation between leader and led that the power field of the "leader" over the "led" is stronger than that of the "led" over the "leader." (Lewin, 1951, p. 126)

I will only briefly add that as a possible measure of the power of b over a, Lewin (1951, p. 336) suggested the quotient of the maximum force that b can induce on a and the maximum resistance that a can offer—a measure that later (by Cartwright, 1959a, p. 193) was changed from the ratio of maximal values to maximal difference of those forces, induced as well as resisting, that can be activated by b (i.e., neglecting resistance activated by a).

Before we turn to the possible social psychological meaning and significance of this field-theoretical approach, it is essential to see that both concepts, that of power as well as that of the prototypical leader-led relationship, do not in themselves denote social or interpersonal relations. Lewin developed and defined his construct of power in an appendix to an article on "Regression, Retrogression, and Development," entitled "Analysis of the Concepts Whole, Differentiation, and Unity" (Lewin, 1951, pp. 305–338). In the whole context there is reference to social psychology, but most examples are intra- rather than interpersonal. The power of b over a is the power of one region over another, whether this region be a subregion of the person or of the environment, an individual, a group, or an impersonal (e.g., normative) aspect of the situation. Whichever source is able to induce changes in some other region of the field has power over that region. Since the concepts of power and power field are meant to represent the leader-led relation, "which is characteristic for organizational dependence" (Lewin, 1951, 126), we should explicate and discuss the general meaning of the field-theoretical construct of power in order to understand and evaluate its social psychological utility.

1. Power is the ability of a source to induce changes in other regions of the field. Power is neither the direct effect of b on a nor b's influence on a, but rather the capacity to exert influence. This emphasis on power as potentiality is a very important and unambiguous conceptional clarification, which has been overlooked or misunderstood by a lot of social psychologists who identify (social) power with (social) influence or consider social power a special class of influence (e.g., Irle, 1971, p. 13; Lasswell & Kaplan, 1950, p. 76). What these authors miss is one of the psychological and social essentials of power, namely, that it does not have to be executed, but *can* be, whether under prescribed conditions or in an arbitrary manner. The psychology of potentiality implies a cognitive rather than a learning theory of power. The power of the hydrogen bomb lies in the anticipation and apprehension of it rather than in past experience; so it is with the power of the Almighty and of Satan as well as of many institutions of the state and of groups in society.

To the extent that power is a potentiality for inducing forces in other regions of the field, the social and self-attribution of power has become an interesting field of psychological research (see below). However, the conception of power as the potentiality of a field region does not psychologize power. Power is not necessarily a property or need of a person, nor is it dependent on a specified set of behaviors. It is a possible dynamic relationship in a field, highly probable in hierarchically structured fields, the source of which is an agent (Cartwright, 1959a, p. 196) capable of acts. The agent may be personal or institutional, individual or collective. As a potential dynamic relationship between regions of a differentiated field, the Lewinian concept of power is very close to system-theoretical conceptions of power as a generalized mechanism or medium of living systems (cf. Luhmann, 1975; Parsons, 1951, p. 121; 1970, p. 6). There is, in spite of different theoretical orientations, full agreement between the field and systems approaches to power (a) in the notion that power essentially is potentiality and "effective as such" (Luhmann, 1975, p. 24) and (b) that power is a dynamic relationship that emerges in the process of system differentiation as a structural field or system property.

2. If power is a dynamic relationship between two regions or agents in a field, then what are the formal characteristics of the relation? Because this question has already been addressed by Cartwright (1959a, pp. 196–199), I can be brief. The usual conception that a power relation is nonsymmetric is not warranted by Lewin's concept of the power field. He only insists that for the leader-led relation it is characteristic "that the power field of the 'leader' over the 'led' is stronger than that of the 'led' over the 'leader' (Lewin, 1951, p. 126). This statement does not qualify the power relation as symmetric or nonsymmetric. The statement "a has power over b" should, however, be read

as "*a* has more power over *b* than *b* over *a*." For all practical psychological purposes one may call such a relation a nonsymmetric one, but relationships of balanced power are equally probable. As such the power relation is not necessarily symmetric or asymmetric.

The same applies to transitivity. If *a* has power over *b* and *b* over *c*, it is neither conceptually implied nor excluded that *a* has power over *c*. In a hierarchical institution, *a* would have power over *c*, especially if given a *Führerprinzip*. According to Lewin (1951, p. 126) it is even possible to measure the degree of any hierarchical organization of wholes "by the number of strata each of which rules a ruled stratum." In nonhierarchical systems, such as informal interpersonal relationships, *a* would not have power over *c*, but may influence *c* by holding power over *b*, if *c* depends on *b* (Cartwright, 1959a, p. 198). The relational character of power has resulted in a relativistic conception of leadership, in which leadership in group dynamics was defined as "the potential social influence of one part of the group over another" (French & Snyder, 1959, p. 118). Because usually every group member has some potential influence over other members, "leadership is widely distributed throughout the group. Those who are popularly called 'followers' are members with less leadership" (French & Snyder, 1959, p. 118). That, of course, leaves the traditional question unanswered: Who will be more or less leading or following, and for what reasons?

3. Less for Lewin than for Cartwright (1959a, p. 199), the answer is found in a closer analysis of the actual and potential acts of the agent. The basic definition of power as potentiality suggests that intentionality is not a logical prerequisite for setting up forces in another person's life space. Imitation of a model's unintentional behavior may be less frequent than imitation of intentional acts. Nevertheless, what Lippitt, Polansky, Redl, and Rosen (1960) have called "behavioral contagion" is as effective as direct influence, or behavior intended to influence other people's behavior. More important than intentionality, at least in these field studies with children, is the attribution of power. Within the groups studied there was a high consensus on "who is able to get the others to do what he wants them to do" (Lippitt et al., 1960, p. 747). Imitation of or deferential behavior toward some group members was found to covary with the attribution of power to those members, who for themselves showed the tendency to utilize the power attributed to them. Related studies have confirmed the latter finding that the more attributed power an agent perceives, the more likely he or she is to attempt influence (and to get away with it).

The attribution of power would then be one of the bases or resources of power, although a secondary one, if power is attributed to an agent by others who perceive or assume that the agent has resources, that is, properties "which can be made available to others as instrumental to the satisfaction of their needs or the attainment of their goals" (Wolfe, 1959, p. 100). Here the motivational basis of the Lewinian conception of power becomes evident. Although Lewin's concept of dynamics generally refers to any conditions of change (locomotion), for the life space needs as intrapersonal tension systems correlated with valences in the psychological environment are the major conditions for change. Power as contingent upon assumed resources then presupposes needs and efforts to have access to the means of need satisfaction and goal attainment. The consideration that "any conceivable property which can be utilized by other persons may be a source of power" (Wolfe, 1959, p. 108) enables the psychologist to deal with the motivational aspects of power situations, but it may also help to prevent the psychologization of power and power resources.[1]

In the Lewinian conception power is related to potential acts rather than to the real exercise of influence. As a consequence the study of social power is not the observation of behavior (i.e., of a's acts of social influence on b) but the investigation of b's cognitions, basically of b's assessment (hope or fear) of all acts a could perform at a given time plus the ensuing attribution of power to a (including a's self-attribution). Only then are the real attempts at influence and resistance to influence of interest. If this is a typical design of cognitive social psychology, then we should not forget that it was Kurt Lewin to whom we largely owe this research pattern. We can restrict ourselves here to the question of the relationship between influential behavior and potential acts. For our everyday conception and for some social theories of power and authority, there seems to be a consensus that those systems are most powerful that do not need the regular manifestation of power by executive acts. Instead, they are based on belief. For Max Weber (1964), who distinguished between power (*Macht*) and authority (*Herrschaft*),[2] "the basis of every system of authority, and correspondingly of every kind of willingness to obey, is a *belief*, a belief by virtue of which persons exercising authority are lent prestige" (Weber, 1964, p. 382). Also for mere power relations, however, we may conclude that the probability that one actor will have his or her way, even against resistance, is known or at least apprehended by his or her potentially resisting opponent.

On the other hand, every manifestation of power carries with it the risk of failure. Attempts at influence may fail in two ways: (1) the intensity of the force activated is too weak to bring about the intended change, so that other forces in the field may neutralize the effort; or (2) the intensity of the force is so strong that it meets with resistance to change. Whether this is due to a quasi-stationary equilibrium of the field (Lewin, 1951, pp. 199–237), to the

---

1. The atheoretical but helpful typology of "power bases" (French & Raven, 1959), which clarifies some formal kinds of resources, is still widely used, but will not be discussed here.

2. In Weber's writings *power* is the probability that one actor in a social relationship will be in a position to carry out his or her own will despite resistance, and *authority* the probability that a command will be obeyed (Weber, 1964, p. 152). Recently *Herrschaft* has been translated by *domination* (cf. the chapters by Cavalli and Lepsius on charismatic domination).

potential character of threat in manifestations of power, or to other principles accounting for the fact that strong rather than gentle forces evoke counterforces (cf. Skinner, 1965, on control and countercontrol in social groups), it is improbable that "when O has strong acts in his repertory he will tend to perform them" (Cartwright, 1959a, p. 203). This, however, may be a case for differential psychology; social intelligence and social skills are not evenly distributed in the population. However that may be, the problem of which acts to select for the manifestation of power remains a cognitive and motivational one.

4. A seeming triviality that illustrates a serious limitation of the Lewinian approach to power has to do with the reality of the social. When Cartwright (1959a) summarized the empirical findings of research on the use of power, he came to the conclusion "that whenever the use of power involves the giving up of resources or the possible reduction in one's power then might arise restraints against the use of power," and he added that a "complete analysis of this problem would involve matters of motivation, ideology, and strategy in the use of power" (Cartwright, 1959a, p. 203).

In interpersonal relations it is easy to think of cases in which a (an individual or a group), trying to overpower b, gives up after realizing that going on to "win" means the loss of all power resources. It may be different, however, if matters of motivation are involved. In cases of heightened affectivity (such as hatred or jealousy) or mental disturbance, a might knowingly or blindly go on to the bitter end, as many rulers, generals, and governments have done and as Pyrrhus, King of Epirus, did in his ill-famed victories over the Romans, until he realized, "One more victory and we are lost."

Very often, however, it is the ideology or value system that either makes a consider whether further loss of resources still makes sense, whether costs in the long run will be higher than the reward (rational or economic values), or make a carry on, against all common sense, in loyalty to traditional principles (irrational, conservative, or revolutionary values). It is more than an educated guess that such matters of ideology are still more important for the manifestation of power in groups, and even more so in institutions and states. Institutional representatives such as politicians and administrators may well have realized long ago that unlimited economic growth (in terms of industrialization, urbanization, and mechanization) and the ever-increasing speed of the arms race will exhaust the natural and economic resources of social or national power; however, there are ideological and political commitments that act as strong counterforces against the many attempts at changing the dominant policies.

Although Lewin (1951, p. 41) insisted that ideology and values are constructs that have the same psychological status as power fields (which means that they, too, are possibilities of inducing forces), he usually kept the usage of these constructs restricted to individuals or small groups. Even though he (1951, passim) insisted that field theory, with its emphasis on the total situation and on interdependence, is a method equally suited for psychology and sociology, the field in which it was used was almost exclusively the individual and the social environment of the small group. It is true that Lewin criticized the attitude of psychologists "to regard only individuals as real" (1951, p. 191), but, with one exception to be discussed below, the only other social reality he considered worth studying (or had the time to study before his early death) was that of group atmosphere or leadership. Thus, social psychology remained the study of interpersonal relations, primarily as represented in cognitive processes and structures. Social structures, in a social science sense, remained foreign to psychology (cf. Lewin's concept of the quasi-social, meaning the "social facts as they affect the particular individual concerned," in Lewin, 1935b, p. 75). As such, the social as well as the physical remain outside psychology, as mere boundary conditions of a life space defined as "the person and his psychological environment" (Lewin, 1951, p. 240). The only exception to this methodological rule we find in Lewin's "psychological ecology" (Lewin, 1951, pp. 170–187). Here the field approach goes beyond the total situation when Lewin demands that scientific predictions "should be based on an analysis of the 'field as a whole,' including both its psychological *and nonpsychological* aspects" (1951, p. 174; emphasis added). Unfortunately, this field approach, which includes culture and group life as field forces, has remained foreign to the further development of Lewinian social psychology and its cognitive encapsulation, as Brunswik (1943, p. 266) noted in his criticism of Lewin's approach. The field approach, which could have enriched social psychology ecologically, has remained an uncompleted task. It is definitely not too late to resume it.

Leadership as Group Property

Although Lewin's name may be closely associated with the notions of autocratic and democratic leadership (and here, of course, with Lippitt and White), there is no theory of leadership in Lewin's work. There is a method of research, a method of training leaders, and there are findings.

1. It is one of the usual adornments in the historiography of psychology to make Lewin the pioneer of experimenting with groups. Although this is historically incorrect, Lewin has deserved a special mention in this respect. He could argue, from his conceptual and methodological system of field theory, that groups as structured and dynamic wholes, defined by the interdependence of their parts, have no special methodological status different from that of individuals. Thus, the rationale for doing experiments with groups is in principle no different from that for the experimental study of individuals. The properties and behavior of the unit group may, in principle, be observed, categorized, and rated just as well as the traditional unit of the individual subject. Correspondingly, the methods used by Lewin

and his collaborators are observations, stenographic and movie records, ratings, and a kind of self-report by the leader.

In this way working with groups experimentally was normalized, and for some time it seemed to be normal for social psychologists to do experiments with groups. Gradually, however, group size was diminished, and although interaction and interdependence remained major research interests (cf. Thibaut & Kelley, 1959 versus Kelley & Thibaut, 1978), the experimental social psychology of groups shrunk to a psychology of dyads or of the "minimal social situation." This development was symptomatic of the basic individualism of social psychology which had not been truly overcome by the Lewinians (cf. Steiner, 1974; Graumann, 1979). The more cognitive social psychology has become in recent years, the more its central research focus narrows down to intraindividual structures and processes (Graumann, 1986).

2. I shall not discuss the methods of leadership training. On the one hand, it is possible to say that with training groups and leadership training Lewin had set something in motion that up to this day, under the name of *group dynamics*, has grown "beyond words" and extended outside the scientific community (cf. Back, 1973). On the other hand, it would be unfair to make Lewin responsible for the significant changes inflicted upon his originally experimental three-step program for changing leadership habits by sensitizing the social perception of leaders (Bavelas, 1942; Bavelas & Lewin, 1942; Lewin, 1951, p. 159), but this is already part of the findings from the leadership studies.

3. The general results of the almost classic studies of leadership by Lewin, Lippitt, and White (Lewin, 1938; Lewin & Lippitt, 1938; Lewin, Lippitt, & White, 1939; Lippitt, 1939, 1940; Lippitt, Polansky, Redl, & Rosen, 1952/1960) are too well known to be reiterated here. This is not to say, however, that they have been universally accepted, at least not at face value. It is more than a coincidence that the different studies on leadership have been titled and referred to almost interchangeably as studies on "leadership," "leadership styles," "social climates," or "group atmospheres." These terms are not necessarily synonyms, nor are they disjunctive categories. They all refer to a holistic character of groups, which in the beginning (Lewin & Lippitt, 1938) was called *group ideology* to be approached by a total behavior methodology. Ideology indeed it was. Domination and integration in the social behavior of children, partly in experimental play situations, had been studied before (Anderson, 1937a, 1937b; Hanfmann, 1935), and in 1939 Anderson had even looked into dominative and integrative contacts between teachers and children. From this time we may count an uninterrupted and increasing series of investigations, contributing to what today is educational psychology, which is mainly the study of educational styles. However, it took Lewin, a man with an outspoken political philosophy and an emigrant from Nazi Germany, to try to miniaturize the social and ideological issues of the time so that they could be experimented

with, and to use the explicitly ideological or political labels of *democracy* and *autocracy*. The methodological and conceptual tool was meant to be field theory; the goal was insight into the dynamics and laws governing different types of leadership. For leadership was the issue. What was manipulated, however, was the behavior of a leader (in terms of decisions, instructions, praise and criticism, helping, admonishing, etc.). What the investigation was to yield was the description of states and degrees of tension, frequency of interactions, ascendance and submission among group members, expression of hostility, scapegoating, amount of cooperation, constructiveness, feelings of "we"-ness versus "I"-ness, stability of group structure, feeling for group property and goals, and so on.

As is easily seen, these studies did not aim at single behaviors that could be identified as leading or following, nor did they introduce personalities with specific traits, who were "disposed" to be leaders. Theoretically, to speak of leadership was to speak of the group as a whole and of the way forces inducing changes are distributed in the field. If the power field of the group is centered and has a well-differentiated unity, the structure of the group tends to be autocratic; if many regions are able to induce changes in an equally differentiated whole, there is not less power but a different distribution of inducing forces. Power, we realize, is not leadership. The region (individual or group) able to induce changes in other regions is also capable of leading, but it is only the ensuing acts (of social influence) that make those who have power actually lead others.

Thus, there is no real leadership without power. Power, however, need not result in leadership. Hence, what the Lewinians wanted to demonstrate is that leadership is neither a quality of an individual person nor a position or office, nor is it merely in the eyes of the beholders, or otherwise definable from the followers' perspective. In a field-theoretical (i.e., truly Galilean) sense, leadership is a quality of a dynamic whole, a group property which, like cohesiveness, cannot be inferred from individuals taken alone. Neither would we learn much about leadership from the prototypical experimental dyad. Because we need a group to study social power, our understanding of social power enables us to grasp what leadership is, and secondarily what it means to be a leading and/or powerful person or group.

Yet as much as we recognize the Galileian spirit in the Lewinian conception of power, in terms of interdependence in a power field, Lewinian empirical leadership studies are open to a critique of inconsistency if we consider the experimental treatment, that is, the way autocratic or democratic leadership was brought about. The experimenter or the experimenter's confederates were trained to act in an either autocratic or democratic or laissez-faire manner or style. That the leader's behavior and nothing but the behavior was taken as the independent variable is underlined by the fact that, in some experiments, it was one and the same person who had to act differently in three (originally two) experimental settings (Lewin et al., 1939). On the other hand, the dependent variable was what White and Lippitt

(1960) rightly called "member reactions," or the followers' behavior toward their leader and toward each other.

If we take these two classes of variables alone, the design is conventional and does not reflect a field-theoretical philosophy: Instead of demonstrating the interdependent character of leadership, the behavior of group members was shown to be a function of a leader's pattern of behavior. If you train or retrain a given leader to act in a specific way, this training, if successful, will affect the behavior of others. There was, as a matter of fact, this pragmatic philosophy behind some of the Lewinian leadership studies: to promote training in democratic leadership or, even more to the point, the "rapid retraining of mediocre leaders into efficient democratic leaders" (Bavelas & Lewin, 1942; cf. Bavelas, 1942). We are here at the roots of the post-Lewinian T-group movement (cf. Back, 1973).

The underlying philosophy, however, much more in harmony with Lewin's scientific credo, was to do experiments with groups (e.g., on leadership, aggressiveness, productivity) within the context of field theory. These studies had to be experimental, because "only in this way the factors influencing group life will not be left to chance" (Lewin & Lippitt, 1938, p. 292). At the same time, however, these experiments were not meant to be searches for one-factor influences; the group as such was defined by interdependence, the core construct of field theory (Lewin, 1939). Yet, given the rather conventional setup of the experiments, how could interdependence ever turn up as a variable or as data? The alternative could have been one of the earlier forms of multivariate analysis, but statistics was for Lewin too much of an Aristotelian instrument to be acceptable for field-theoretical purposes.

Thus, the only place where we may find interdependence is in the description of the treatment effects, if and only if the observers had been trained to observe the properties of the group as such instead of observing the properties of individuals. It is indeed in these interpretive rather than descriptive records of the leadership studies, mainly in the "continuous interpretive running account" (as in Lewin et al., 1939), that the spirit of field theory becomes flesh. Equally manifest, however, is the problem that the holistic-dynamic constructs of field theory cannot be related to the proper data in an unambiguous way. Hence, the hybrid nature of these investigations: As experiments they are, in principle, Aristotelian, with an independent variable (leader's behavior) influencing dependent variables (members' behaviors). The results, however, are discussed and interpreted in the Galileian discourse of Lewin's dynamic psychology. The question of compatibility or even conflict between these two parts of the leadership studies depends on our assessment of whether these investigations were proper experiments or exploratory studies.

Historically, it may be true that Kurt Lewin not only described the transition from Aristotelian to Galileian modes of thought (hence the title of the German original of 1931) and the conflict between them (as the English title suggests), but practiced both in his own research. The leadership studies, then, are instances of both transition and conflict—leaving us a considerable amount of tension to be resolved. Lewin, who had described the dynamics of marginal man (Lewin, 1939), was a scientist in transition in still another respect. As a social psychologist he saw the necessity to deal with the group as a whole, which by the principle of interdependence is perhaps not more but something else than the sum of its constituent members. But was not (and is not) the group as a whole a traditional problem and category of sociology (Lewin, 1939)? Because it was, every now and then Lewin felt himself to be trespassing (fortunately, he did not care). Furthermore, it was in the observation of nonexperimental groups, traditionally a domain of sociology and anthropology, that Lewin had hoped to corroborate his experimental findings (Lewin & Lippitt, 1938, p. 300; Lewin et al., 1939, p. 297). His interest in group ideology and his field-theoretical emphasis on interdependence in the total situation implied the need to consider the broader social and cultural context—a need that, after the dismissal of mass psychology and *Völkerpsychologie*, could only be satisfied in the social sciences outside psychology. To overcome this problem and the separation of psychology from the other social sciences, Lewin offered his field theory as a comprehensive and unifying approach (Lewin & Korsch, 1978). After Lewin's death, Dorwin Cartwright repeated this offer when he gave his collection of Lewin's theoretical articles the title *Field Theory in Social Science* (Lewin, 1951).

Individualism and the Galileian Principle: An Unresolved Conflict

Today it would be a mistake to maintain that the social sciences have accepted field theory as a unifying frame of reference. It would also be overoptimistic to expect that they will do so in the near future. Nevertheless, what we still carry with us is Lewin's basic field-theoretical postulate. This postulate asks the psychologist, or any social scientist, to approach a particular object of study from the larger context or, more precisely, from the particular total situation, or even from the field as a whole, including both its psychological and nonpsychological aspects (Lewin, 1951, p. 174). Lewin was aware that with his conceptual analysis of and experimental attacks on groups as wholes he was in opposition to traditional procedures. He used the experiment (and the case of leadership) to prove that such dynamic wholes and their properties were real. For traditional psychologists only individuals were real, and for some only their behavior. The prototype, however, the experimental subject, was (and still is) an isolated individual, methodologically cut off from his or her social context.

This 'Aristotelian' restrictedness of experimental social psychology Lewin tried to overcome by means of his field approach. Deeply convinced that interdependence is the 'Galileian' principle of all dynamic wholes, and that the person-environment relationship is inseparable, he tried to leave the individual in his or her situation, even experimentally. He knew it was going to be difficult and he himself was not convincingly successful, but as he wrote in 1947, the year of his death, "To vary a social phenomenon experimentally the experimenter has to take hold of all essential factors even if he is not yet able to analyze them satisfactorily. A major omission... makes the experiment fail" (Lewin, 1951, p. 193). Lewin challenged experimenters in social research "to take into consideration such factors as the personality of individual members, the group structure, ideology and cultural values, and economic factors," and he looked forward with the confidence that experimentation with groups "will... lead to a natural integration of the social sciences" (Lewin, 1951, p. 193).

Today we know that this hope has not come true, that the spring of group dynamics as experimental small-group research was a very brief period, and that, in the present intellectual climate (which we should take to be as real as Lewin's "social climate"), the theoretical and methodological individualism that Lewin had opposed has not only been fully restored, but "cognitively" strengthened. The intellectual climate in which Lewin could develop his idea of social psychology has changed, and so has social psychology. Lewin was not only in harmony with the intellectual climate of his time; he actively contributed to it. His last contribution, in 1947, was entitled "Frontiers in Group Dynamics" (Lewin, 1951, chapter 9). The confidence expressed there (and quoted above) is the confidence of a frontiersman. He felt he could do something to promote social science, social work, and human relations. He was in accord with the many who, after the bloodiest war in history, strove for "one world," for truly united nations, for international cooperation, and against discrimination and aggression. His work with groups and leadership styles was not only motivated by pure and basic research interests, but also instrumental for understanding and implementing democracy. The tremendous activity of his last few years did not leave Lewin enough time to realize systematically what he himself had postulated. Therefore quite a few inconsistencies in his conceptions as well as between theory and research remained. As we have tried to indicate, he never did in his research on autocratic and democratic leadership what he asked to be done, namely, account for the field as a whole—for the cultural, political, and economic boundary conditions of such group dynamics experiments. He died in the middle of the journey, leaving this intriguing task unfinished.

But what about its resumption? It is true that the postwar enthusiasm and optimism to achieve a more human society, briefly but passionately revived in the years following 1968, have given way to an attitude of so-called realism, to critical rationalism and skepticism. The individual has withdrawn from the public scene, encouraged not only by conservative politicians. A new individualistic humanism, operative in a seemingly ever-increasing variety of therapies, advises and helps individuals to actualize themselves toward enhancement, personal growth, and the expansion of potentiality. Elsewhere I have tried to evaluate critically the new humanists' "emphatic focus on the individual personality" (Graumann, 1981, p. 13). Here it will do to refer again to Kurt Back's testimony to the gradual and irresistible fusion of originally Lewinian (East Coast, Bethel, National Training Laboratory for Group Development (NTL) T-group dynamics with the less academically rooted West Coast (Esalen) encounter group dynamics (Back, 1973). If it is true that this fusion gave birth to the contemporary group dynamics movement, it is still illegitimate to trace its modern individualist cult of self-expression and self-realization back to Lewin. Social psychologists, hardly ever acting as social scientists, have concentrated on cognitive processes and structures hypothesized to function inside an individual's mind. Today's frontiersmen preferably focus on such schemata and mechanisms as can be simulated or represented in sophisticated software. Maybe Lewin himself accelerated what came to be called the cognitive revolution (or at least the cognitive turn) when he encapsulated the person in his or her environment. Maybe Steiner (1974, p. 99) is right when he criticizes "the Lewinian tendency to emphasize the life space of the individual member, rather than overt, ongoing behaviors," the emphasis on "who *thought* something" instead of who did something as a contribution to the increasing cognitive individualization of social psychology. For Lewin one should, however, add that this was against his original Galilean principle.

Yet "Lewin," (i.e., Lewin as we read him) is still there, still powerful as long as he is able to induce changes in the field of psychology, for example, to remind us that the scope of social psychology is broader than we nowadays see it, that the field approach, although difficult to implement, is ultimately inevitable for a truly social psychology, and that we still have to solve the problem he left us, namely, the reconciliation of psychological and nonpsychological forces within one theoretically unitary field; this is the unfinished task of a socially and ecologically enriched social psychology.

References

Anderson, H.H. (1937a). An experimental study of dominative and integrative behavior in children of pre-school age. *Journal of Social Psychology, 8*, 335–345.

Anderson, H.H. (1937b). Domination and integration in the social behavior of young children in an experimental play situation. *Genetic Psychology Monographs, 19*, 341–408.

Anderson, H.H. (1939). Domination and social integration in the behavior of kindergarten children and teachers. *Genetic Psychology Monographs, 21*, 287–385.

Back, K.W. (1973). *Beyond words—The story of sensitivity training and the encounter movement*. Baltimore: Penguin.

Bavelas, A. (1942). Morale and training of leaders. In G. Watson (Ed.), *Civilian morale* (pp. 143–165). New York: Reynal & Hitchcock.

Bavelas, A., & Lewin, K. (1942). Training in democratic leadership. *Journal of Abnormal and Social Psychology, 37*, 115–119.

Brunswik, E. (1943). Organismic achievement and environmental probability. *Psychological Review, 50*, 255–272.

Cartwright, D. (Ed.). (1959a). *Studies in social power.* Ann Arbor, MI: University of Michigan Press.

Cartwright, D. (1959b). Lewinian theory as a contemporary systematic framework. In S. Koch (Ed.), *Psychology: A study of a science* (Vol. 2, pp. 7–91). New York: McGraw-Hill.

Cassirer, E. (1923). *Substance and function, and Einstein's theory of relativity.* Chicago: Open Court.

Evans, R.I. (1980). *The making of social psychology.* New York: Gardner Press.

Festinger, L. (Ed.) (1980). *Retrospections on social psychology.* New York: Oxford University Press.

French, J.R.P., & Raven, B. (1959). The bases of social power. In D. Cartwright (Ed.), *Studies in social power* (pp. 150–167). Ann Arbor, MI: University of Michigan Press.

French, J.R.P., & Snyder, R. (1959). Leadership and interpersonal power. In D. Cartwright (Ed.), *Studies in social power* (pp. 118–149). Ann Arbor, MI: University of Michigan Press.

Graumann, C.F. (1979). Die Scheu des Psychologen vor der Interaktion. *Zeitschrift für Sozialpsychologie, 10*, 284–304.

Graumann, C.F. (1981). Psychology: Humanistic or human? In J.R. Royce & L.P. Mos (Eds.), *Humanistic psychology—Concepts and criticisms* (pp. 3–18). New York: Plenum.

Graumann, C.F. (1986). The individualization of the social and the desocialization of the individual. In C.F. Graumann & S. Moscovici (Eds.), *Changing conceptions of crowd mind and behavior* (pp. 97–116). New York: Springer-Verlag.

Hanfmann, E.P. (1935). Social structure of a group of kindergarten children. *American Journal of Orthopsychiatry, 5*, 407–410.

Irle, M. (1971). *Macht und Entscheidung in Organisationen.* Frankfurt am Main: Akademische Verlagsgesellschaft.

Kelley, H.H., & Thibaut, J.W. (1978). *Interpersonal relations: A theory of interdependence.* New York: Wiley.

Lasswell, H.D., & Kaplan, A. (1950). *Power and society.* New Haven: Yale University Press.

Lewin, K. (1935a). The conflict between Aristotelian and Galileian modes of thought in contemporary psychology (German original 1931). In K. Lewin, *A dynamic theory of personality* (pp. 1–42). New York: McGraw-Hill.

Lewin, K. (1935b). Environmental forces in child behavior and development. In K. Lewin, *A dynamic theory of personality* (pp. 66–113). New York: McGraw-Hill.

Lewin, K. (1938). Experiments on autocratic and democratic atmosphere. *The Social Frontier, 4*(37), 316–319.

Lewin, K. (1939). Field theory and experiment in social psychology: Concepts and methods. *American Journal of Sociology, 44*, 868–897.

Lewin, K. (1949). Cassirer's philosophy of science and social science. In P.A. Schlipp (Ed.), *The philosophy of Ernst Cassirer* (pp. 271–288). New York: Tudor.

Lewin, K. (1951). *Field theory in social science* (D. Cartwright, Ed.). New York: Harper.

Lewin, K. (1981ff.). *Kurt Lewin Werkausgabe* (Vols. 1–7; C.F. Graumann, Ed.). Bern: Huber, and Stuttgart: Klett-Cotta.

Lewin, K. (1982). Aspects of field theory (unpublished). German translation in *Feldtheorie* (C.F. Graumann, Ed.). *Kurt Lewin Werkausgabe*, Vol. 4, pp. 25–26). Bern: Huber, and Stuttgart: Klett-Cotta. (The complete manuscript "Field Theory and Geometry" will be translated and published in Vol. 3 of the *Werkausgabe*).

Lewin, K., & Korsch, K. (1978). Mathematical constructs in psychology and sociology. *The Journal of Unified Science, 8,* 397–408.

Lewin, K., & Lippitt, R. (1938). An experimental approach to the study of autocracy and democracy: A preliminary note. *Sociometry, 1,* 292–300.

Lewin, K., Lippitt, R., & White, R.K. (1939). Patterns of aggressive behavior in experimentally created 'social climates.' *Journal of Social Psychology, 10,* 271–299.

Lippitt, R. (1939). Field theory and experiment in social psychology. Autocratic and democratic group atmospheres. *American Journal of Social Psychology, 45,* 26–49.

Lippitt, R. (1940). An experimental study of the effect of democratic and authoritarian group atmospheres. *University of Iowa Studies on Child Welfare, 16,* 45–195.

Lippitt, R., Polansky, N., Redl, F., & Rosen, S. (1960). The dynamics of power: A field study of social influence in groups of children. In D. Cartwright & A. Zander (Eds.), *Group dynamics* (2nd ed.). (pp. 745–765). Evanston: Row & Peterson. (Original work published 1952).

Luhmann, N. (1975). *Macht.* Stuttgart: Enke.

Parsons, T. (1951). *The social system.* New York: Free Press.

Parsons, T. (1970). *Social structure and personality.* New York: Free Press.

Schellenberg, J.A. (1978). *Masters of social psychology.* New York: Oxford University Press.

Skinner, B.F. (1965). *Science and human behavior.* New York: Free Press.

Steiner, I. (1974). Whatever happened to the group in social psychology? *Journal of Experimental Social Psychology, 10,* 94–108.

Thibaut, J.W., & Kelley, H.H. (1959). *The social psychology of groups.* New York: Wiley.

Weber, M. (1964). *The theory of social and economic organization.* (T. Parsons, Ed.). New York: Free Press.

White, R., & Lippitt, R. (1960). *Autocracy and democracy.* New York: Harper.

Wolfe, D.M. (1959). Power and authority in the family. In D. Cartwright (Ed.), *Studies in social power* (pp. 99–107). Ann Arbor, MI: University of Michigan Press. (1959a), 99–107.

Chapter 7

The Contribution of Cognitive Resources and Behavior to Leadership Performance

Fred E. Fiedler

Theories of leadership have not fared too well in their attempts to explain the role of intellectual abilities in team or organizational performance. In fact, most theories of leadership have ignored intellectual ability altogether (Campbell, 1977). And yet, intelligence must play an important part in determining the performance of leaders and their groups or organizations. This is clear when we consider the essentially intellectual nature of such critical leadership functions as planning, decision making, and coordinating the work of others. Not surprisingly, most organizations prefer to hire bright rather than stupid managers. Why then, do we find such low correlations between leader intelligence and organizational performance? I shall trace the development of a new leadership theory that attempts to deal with this intriguing question.

Antecedents

Empirical leadership research had its beginnings at the turn of the century when Lewis Terman (1904) published a study on the relationship between children's intelligence and their leadership status. Terman's research was followed by a stream of papers that attempted to find correlations between leader intelligence and leadership performance. Stogdill (1948) reviewed more than 100 of these studies and reported a preponderance of low positive correlations between intelligence and leadership performance, typically accounting for less than 4 or 5% of the variance. Remarkably similar findings were subsequently reported in other reviews (Ghiselli, 1966; Mann, 1959). As a result of these disappointingly low correlations, most researchers and theorists turned to greener pastures in the leadership area.

It is difficult, however, to ignore this problem. On the one hand, the most frequently cited theories virtually ignore intelligence and such other cognitive variables as job knowledge, experience, or technical competence as elements in their systems. This includes, for example, McGregor's Theory X and Theory Y (1967); House's path–goal theory (1971); Vroom and Yetton's normative decision model (1973); Maslow's management theory (1965); and this author's contingency model (Fiedler, 1964, 1967). On the other hand, measures of intellectual abilities continue to be extensively used in selection procedures, especially by headhunters and assessment centers (e.g., Bray, Campbell, & Grant, 1974; Byham, 1970) in their search for executive talent.

Instead, the major thrust in the leadership area since World War II has come from the vast amount of research conducted on leader behaviors. Among the best-known earlier studies were those by Lewin, Lippitt, and White (1939), Bales (1950), and the Ohio State University group under the direction of Shartle (1956). This line of research assumed that it would be possible to identify effective leader behaviors and to teach these leader behaviors in order to improve organizational performance.

The Ohio State University group identified the two well-known leader behavior dimensions of consideration and structuring. However, neither these measures of leader behavior nor similar measures identified by other researchers consistently correlated with, or predicted, effective task performance (Bass, 1981; Korman, 1966).

Many leading theorists in the 1950s and 1960s (e.g., Likert, 1967; Maslow, 1965; McGregor, 1967) also espoused the advantages of nondirective behavior and participative management. Empirical studies did not show, however, that democratic or nondirective leadership necessarily resulted in more effective task groups (French, Israel, & As, 1960; Fox, 1954; Morse & Reimer, 1956) nor were structuring leaders more effective than leaders who were nondirective (Korman, 1966).

In retrospect, we must ask why such leader behaviors as directiveness, structuring, or participative management should necessarily improve performance. Surely, the question is not whether the leader is directive or nondirective but rather what the leader directs the group members to do, and whose abilities are used when the leader fails to direct the group.

This question is generally neglected by such leadership programs as the managerial grid (Blake & Mouton, 1964) and life cycle theory (Hersey & Blanchard, 1969). The training tells the leader when to be directive and when to be nondirective or considerate. But this surely cannot be enough. A leader's choice of a participative or autocratic strategy provides no guarantee that either the group's participation or the leader's unilateral direction will result in effective performance. Leaders who are stupid but directive are not necessarily effective, and asking incompetents for their advice is unlikely to produce sage counsel.

We need to be concerned with the intellectual content of the leader's plans and decisions as well as the leader's directions for implementing them. In addition, we must consider that even the most intelligent leader will have an effective team only under certain conditions, e.g., if the leader's attention is focused on the assigned task, and if the group members are motivated to follow. Hence, we need to identify the specific conditions that enable the leader to influence group performance. This is the main problem to which this chapter addresses itself.

Contributions of Leader Intelligence to Task Performance

My own research and that of my associates frequently uncovered unexpected negative relations between leader intelligence and performance. These were difficult to explain, yet too consistent to be conveniently shoved under a rug. For example, Fiedler, Meuwese, and Oonk (1961) reported a series of studies in which leader intelligence and task knowledge correlated positively with performance when the leader was accepted by the group, but negatively when the leader was not accepted or experienced stress (Fiedler & Meuwese, 1963; Fiedler, Meuwese & Oonk, 1961; Meuwese & Fiedler, 1965).

One early attempt to explain these findings resulted in a "multiple screen model" (Fiedler & Leister, 1977) which proposed that the products of the leader's intelligence (e.g., plans and decisions) must pass through various screens or barriers in order to affect group action. The model postulated that the leader's intelligence cannot contribute to the task unless the leader is motivated, the group is willing to accept the leader's direction, and the leader has a relatively stressfree relationship with the boss. The data supported these hypotheses. In particular, the empirical findings pointed to the importance of stress between the leader and the immediate boss in preventing the leader from making effective use of his intelligence.

The effect of stress on the leader's intellectual contribution to task performance was further investigated in a more recent series of studies (Fiedler, Jobs & Borden, 1984; Fiedler, Potter, Zais & Knowlton, 1979; Frost, 1983; Potter & Fiedler, 1981). These showed that the leader's intelligence correlated positively with rated performance when the leader reported low stress with his boss, but negatively when stress with his boss was high. (Stress with boss and performance were unrelated.) Performance in this case was measured objectively, that is, by grade point average in the U.S. Coast Guard Academy (Barnes, Potter, & Fiedler, 1983). Furthermore, a dissertation by Blades (Blades & Fiedler, 1976) showed that the leader must be directive in order to communicate his or her plans, decisions, and action strategies.

These studies have led to a new theory of leadership that attempts to identify the role of cognitive abilities in determining the organizational effectiveness.

Cognitive Resource Theory

Discussion in this chapter is limited to situations in which the leader supervises interacting task groups. We shall not consider groups engaged in decision making, policy discussions, or creative tasks. The model advances the following propositions:

A. The leader's cognitive resources (e.g., intellectual abilities, technical competence, or job-relevant knowledge) determine the quality of the leader's plans, decisions, and strategies. The leader must therefore be directive in order to communicate these plans, decisions, and strategies and see to their implementation. Hence:

Hypothesis 1. Relevant leader abilities correlate with group performance when the leader manifests directive behavior.

B. Implicit in the first hypothesis is the assumption that such cognitive resources of the leader as intellectual abilities or job knowledge will contribute only to the extent to which the task requires these particular cognitive resources. That is, athletic teams require athletic but not necessarily musical ability. Hence:

Hypothesis 2. The leader's cognitive resources correlate with performance in those tasks that require these particular cognitive resources.

C. As pointed out earlier, we cannot expect the leader's abilities or task-relevant knowledge to influence group performance unless the group listens to the leader and supports his or her plans, decisions, and strategies. Hence:

Hypothesis 3. The correlations between task performance and the leader's cognitive resource variables will be higher when group support for the leader is high than when it is low.

D. The leader's behavior is determined by the interaction of personality and situational factors. Research on the contingency model has shown that the leader's tendency to be directive in his or her interactions with group members is determined to a substantial degree by the leader's task motivation or relationship motivation (least preferred co-worker, LPC), by intelligence, and by situational control (e.g., Fiedler, 1972; Larson & Rowland, 1973; Meuwese, 1964; Sample & Wilson, 1965). Because this particular relationship is highly complex and has already been dealt with in the literature at some length, we shall not consider it in detail in this paper.

Propositions A, B, and C are incorporated in a partial model presented in Figure 7-1. The elements of the model are (a) the leader's directive behavior, (b) the leader's cognitive resources, (c) the group's support and consequent compliance, (d) the requirements of the task, and (e) task performance criteria.

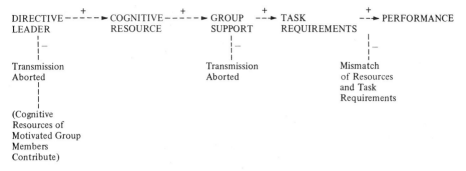

Figure 7-1. A partial model depicting the conditions under which the leader's intellectual abilities or other relevant cognitive resources affect group performance. Positive signs indicate that condition exists (i.e., leader is directive, group does support leader, cognitive resource does meet task requirement), negative sign indicates that these conditions are not met. (This figure does not show the conditions determining the leader's directive behavior.)

As can be seen, directive behavior is required and group support is desirable if the leader's cognitive resources (e.g., intelligence, job knowledge) are to contribute to group action. Group action will contribute to task performance only to the extent that the task requires the particular abilities the leader has available (Figure 7-1). In the next section, data are presented that support the model.

Initial Empirical Support for the Cognitive Resource Theory

A complete test of the model is, of course, well beyond the scope of this chapter. However, results from three studies are presented here to illustrate support for the cognitive resource theory.

Mess Halls

The first set of analyses is based on a study of 48 U.S. Army mess halls by Blades and Fiedler (1976). These mess halls were directed by a mess steward, who supervised 3 to 6 cooks as well as enlisted men assigned on a day-by-day basis to perform various menial tasks. The mess stewards' behavior was described by their cooks. We obtained intelligence scores for the mess stewards as well as time spent in various Quartermaster Corps training courses, on the assumption that task ability and job knowledge would be related to amount of training in mess management and food service.

Mess stewards completed a 10-item group atmosphere (GA) scale on which they described the group as friendly or unfriendly, cooperative or uncooperative, helpful or unhelpful, and so on. The GA score indicated the leader's perception of the members' support and group harmony (McNamara, 1968). Performance was evaluated by brigade food officers and the commanders of the company the mess hall served.

The first analysis addresses the hypothesis that the cognitive resources will correlate more highly with performance of directive than of nondirective leaders. Also presented is evidence suggestive of support for Hypothesis 2, that is, that task performance will be predicted more highly the more highly the cognitive resource is relevant to the task: Training in mess management presumably is more relevant to running a mess hall than is general intelligence.

The crews were divided according to whether the mess stewards were rated by their cooks as high, moderate, or low in directive behavior, and performance was then correlated with leader intelligence and amount of training (Table 7-1).

As can be seen, the data support the hypothesis in showing that the more directive leaders' intelligence and training affect performance to a greater extent than do the intelligence and training of less directive leaders. We also find a slightly but not significantly higher correlation between performance and amount of training than between general intelligence and performance (Table 7-1).

It is of particular interest that the correlations between performance and the cognitive variables are significantly negative under low leader directiveness. The reasons for these negative correlations are not yet completely clear. One tentative explanation is that a leader creates animosity among group members when he or she is able but fails to direct the group sufficiently. Group members may resent the trained and knowledgeable leader who permits them to flounder.

A further analysis tested Hypothesis 3, that the leader's cognitive resources will contribute more highly in supportive than in nonsupportive

Table 7-1. Correlations Between Intellectual Ability and Technical Knowledge of Mess Stewards and Performance of Army Mess Halls for Directive and Nondirective Leaders

	Leader Directiveness		
	High ($n = 10$)	Moderate ($n = 24$)	Low ($n = 13$)
Leader intelligence	.34	.11	−.56[a]
Leader technical training	.45	.22	−.56[a]

[a]$p < .05$.

groups—in effect, when the group was willing to listen to the leader's directions. Table 7-2 shows the result obtained when mess hall crews were further divided into those with relatively directive and nondirective leaders, and relatively high and low group support (GA). This process of partitioning an already small sample obviously makes interpretation of the data difficult, but it is nevertheless of theoretical interest (Table 7-2).

Table 7-2 shows that the correlation between leader performance and job knowledge was significant only when the directive leader rated the group as supportive. However, when the leader was nondirective, the leader's cognitive resources did not contribute to performance and may in fact have detracted from performance.

Army Squad Leaders

The second study was based on 138 U.S. Army infantry squad leaders (Bons & Fiedler, 1976). These men supervise the work of a basic infantry unit consisting of 10 men. The present data were obtained after the squads had been together for 6 to 8 months. The Army General Classification Test (AGCT) constituted the measure of intellectual ability. Leader behaviors were described by squad members, using items from the Leader Behavior Description XII Questionnaire (LBDQ XII; Stogdill, 1974). The Directiveness factor was based on items usually found in Stogdill's Structuring and Production Emphasis factors.

Two criterion ratings were obtained from the squad leaders' superiors, namely, the platoon leader (a second lieutenant) and the platoon sergeant. These were task performance (mission accomplishment) and personnel performance (morale, discipline, rapport with squad). We would expect that intellectual ability is more closely related to task performance than to the maintenance of morale, discipline, and rapport. As can be seen, this was the case (Table 7-3).

Table 7-2. Correlations Between Intellectual Ability and Technical Knowledge of Mess Stewards on Performance of Supportive and Less Supportive Mess Hall Groups[a]

Leader Directiveness	Intelligence and Performance		Training and Performance	
	High MS[b]	Low MS	High MS	Low MS
High	.58[c]	−.48	.61[c]	−.16
Low	−.10	.02	−.44	.10

[a]Ns for all groups = 11.
[b]MS, member support.
[c]$p < .05$.

Table 7-3. Correlations Between Intelligence and Task and Personnel Performance
for Squad Leaders With High, Moderate, and Low Directive Behavior

	Directive Behavior		
Performance Type	High ($n = 36$)	Moderate ($n = 38$)	Low ($n = 35$)
Task performance	.49[a]	.29[b]	.01
Personnel performance	.33	−.23	−.08

[a]$p < .01.$
[b]$p < .10.$

Table 7-4 presents the correlations between leader intelligence and task
and personnel performance when we also take into consideration the
leader's perception of the group's support. Again, the leader's intelligence
correlated significantly with task performance only when the group was
supportive (high GA); it did not correlate with the personnel performance
criterion.

As we had discovered earlier in research related to the multiple-screen
model, stress with the boss was one important factor in determining whether
the leader's intellectual abilities would contribute to leader performance. It
is well known, of course, that high stress and anxiety lower intellectual
performance (e.g., Sarason, 1972; Spielberger, 1972,) especially when this
stress is caused by authority figures. Most people have had the misfortune
of knowing a dreaded teacher or boss who could reduce them to a state of
babbling imbecility.

We need to consider that interpersonal stress with the boss is an
emotionally charged and anxiety-producing problem that does not yield to

Table 7-4. Correlations Between Squad Leader Intelligence and Performance Under
Directive and Nondirective Leaders With High and Low Group Support

	Leader Directiveness			
	High		Low	
Performance Type	High GS[a] ($n = 27$)	Low GS ($n = 24$)	High GS ($n = 26$)	Low GS ($n = 30$)
Task performance	.49*	.38	.13	−.03
Personnel performance	.01	−.28	.19	.00

[a]GS, group support.
[b]$p < .01.$

rational solutions. There is no logical argument by which a subordinate can convince a boss that he or she is loyal and trustworthy; it is equally difficult to change a boss's unreasonable demands. The anxiety aroused by this type of stress tends to distract from the task and thus prevents the individual from focusing his or her intellectual abilities on the job (Barnes, Potter, & Fiedler, 1983).

This point was made by a series of studies that compared the correlations between leader intelligence and leadership performance for those reporting low stress and those reporting high stress with the boss (Borden, 1980; Fiedler, Potter, Zais, & Knowlton, 1979; Frost, 1983; Potter & Fiedler, 1981). The main finding of these studies was that the correlations between the leader's ability and performance were significantly higher when the relationship between leader and the boss was relatively free of stress than they were when the leader reported stress with basis of leader directiveness and boss stress. Table 7-5 shows the correlations between leader intelligence and performance when we subdivide the squad leader sample on the basis of leader directiveness and stress with boss ratings by the leader.

As hypothesized, the leader's intellectual abilities correlated quite highly and significantly with performance when the leader was not only directive buy also had a stress-free relationship with the boss. Again, as expected, personnel performance was not related to intellectual ability of the leader.

Public Health Teams

A study of 41 small public health teams (Fiedler, O'Brien, & Ilgen, 1969) shows that the hypotheses are supported not only in military settings but also in civilian groups with informal leaders. The study was conducted in Honduras and Guatemala. These teams, composed of high-school-age volunteers, organized and conducted vaccination and inoculation pro-

Table 7-5. Correlations Between Squad Leader Intelligence and Performance Under Directive and Nondirective Leaders With High and Low Stress With Boss

| | Leader Directiveness | | | |
| | High | | Low | |
Performance Type	Low SB[a] ($n = 29$)	High SB ($n = 25$)	Low SB ($n = 29$)	High SB ($n = 24$)
Task performance	.58[b]	.10	.15	.14
Personnel performance	−.04	−.13	.28	.18

[a]SB, stress with boss.
[b]$p < .01$.

Table 7-6. Correlations Between Leader Intelligence Scores and Task and Interpersonal Performance in Public Health Teams

	Directive Behavior		
	High ($n = 12$)	Moderate ($n = 14$)	Low ($n = 13$)
Community development	.61[a]	.16	−.23
Intragroup relations	−.28	−.05	−.19

[a]$p < .05$.

grams and performed community development work. These groups lived and worked for 3 weeks under relatively primitive conditions in small rural villages. The work environment varied in stressfulness, depending upon the degree to which village officials and villagers welcomed or resented these volunteers. Team performance was rated by the project director and his staff. Ratings are shown here for performance in community development work, which was intellectually most demanding, as well as for intrapersonal performance, which presumably is not highly related to intellectual ability.

We divided the teams into those in which the informal leaders were rated by teammates as relatively high, moderate, or low in directive behavior. We then correlated leader intelligence with performance (Table 7-6). A further analysis was based on villages that were further divided into those rated by the project director as providing a relatively easy or relatively difficult working environment (Table 7-7).

As can be seen, the correlation between intelligence and task performance

Table 7-7. Correlations Between Leader and Member Intelligence and Performance Under Directive and Nondirective Leaders in Relatively Stressful and Stress-Free Villages

	Leader Directiveness			
	High		Low	
	High GS[a] ($n = 6$)	Low GS ($n = 11$)	High GS ($n = 11$)	Low GS ($n = 6$)
Community development	.51	−.33	−.40	.13
Intragroup relations	.30	−.23	−.24	−.29

[a]GS, group support.

measures was higher for directive than for nondirective leaders, and higher for tasks requiring intellectual ability than for the ability to maintain good interpersonal relations. Correlations between intelligence and task performance again were relatively high for directive leaders in a low-stress environment.

Discussion

This chapter briefly outlined one aspect of a new leadership theory. Cognitive resource theory proposes that intelligence, task ability, and job-relevant knowledge cannot affect the performance of the organization or the group unless the leader (a) directs the group, (b) does so in an intelligent and knowledgeable manner, and (c) the criterion task requires the abilities the leader has available. In retrospect, these conclusions are painfully obvious. This is perhaps a sign of a believable theory.

The cognitive resource theory exhumes intelligence from its premature grave, and shows that intellectual abilities play an important part in leadership performance under certain conditions. These require that the leader not only direct the group, but that the leadership situation permits the products of the leader's intellectual efforts to be implemented by the group. Our data cast considerable doubt on the uncritical acceptance of participative leadership.

It is important to point out that these results may not apply for temporarily assembled groups which perform such tasks as solving puzzles, inventing stories, or making decisions. In tasks of that nature, the leader does not have to be directive in order to perform or modify the group product. Thus, if a story is to be invented, or a group position is to be written, it is the leader who does the writing, and can, therefore, substantially influence the group's product. This is not possible in the more typical task group in which the leader supervises the group effort but takes no active part in performing the task.

The empirical data presented in this paper may well be insufficient to convince a skeptical reader, nor are they intended for that purpose. Rather, the data are shown to indicate that the theory is plausible and warrants serious consideration.

This chapter did not discuss the problem of predicting directive leader behavior. Other studies show, however, that the contingency model provides the basis for making this prediction (Fiedler, 1970). The present formulation in effect extends the contingency model by suggesting the reason why the interaction between LPC and situational control predicts leadership performance. It is hoped that the cognitive resource theory can provide a model for further research that integrates intellectual, behavioral, task, and personality variables into one coherent theory of leadership.

Acknowledgments. The author wishes to express his appreciation to Sarah M. Jobs for her constructive criticism of this manuscript. The research in this paper was supported in part by a grant from the Naval Personnel Research and Development Center, San Diego, California, under Battelle Contract DAAG29-81d-0100, Order 0683. A more extensive treatment of cognitive resource theory is provided in a forthcoming book by Fiedler and Garcia, to be published by John Wiley and Sons, Inc., New York.

References

Bales, R. F. (1950). *Interaction process analysis.* Reading, MA: Addison-Wesley.

Barnes, V. E., Potter, E. H., & Fiedler, F. E. (1983). The effect of interpersonal stress on the prediction of academic performance. *Journal of Applied Psychology, 68,* 686–697.

Bass, B. M. (1981). *Stogdill's handbook of leadership: A survey of theory and research.* New York: The Free Press.

Blades, J. W., & Fiedler, F. E. (1976). The influence of intelligence, task ability, and motivation on group performance. Seattle: Organizational Research, University of Washington.

Blake, R. R., & Mouton, J. S. (1964). *The management grid.* Houston: Gulf.

Bons, P. M., & Fiedler, F. E. (1976). Changes in organizational leadership and the behavior of relationship and task-motivated leaders. *Administrative Science Quarterly. 21,* 433–472.

Borden, D. F. (1980). Leader–boss stress, personality, job satisfaction, and performance: Another look at the inter-relationship of some old constructs in the modern large bureaucracy. Unpublished doctoral dissertation, University of Washington, Seattle.

Bray, D. W., Campbell, R. J., & Grant, D. L. (1974). *Formative years in business: A long-term AT&T study of managerial lives,* New York: Wiley-Interscience.

Byham, W. C. (1970). Assessment centers for spotting future managers. *Harvard Business Review, 48,* 150–160.

Campbell, J. (1977). The cutting edge of leadership: An overview. In J. G. Hunt, & L. L. Larson (Eds.), *Leadership: The cutting edge.* Carbondale: Southern Illinois University Press.

Fiedler, F. E. (1964). A contingency model of leadership effectiveness. In L. Berkowitz (Ed.), *Advances in Experimental Social Psychology.* New York: Academic Press.

Fiedler, F. E. (1967). *A theory of leadership effectiveness.* New York: McGraw-Hill.

Fiedler, F. E. (1970). Leadership experience and leader performance—Another hypothesis shot to hell. *Organizational Behavior and Human Performance, 5,* 1–14.

Fiedler, F. E. (1972). The effects of leadership training and experience: a contingency model interpretation. *Administrative Science Quarterly, 17,* 453–470.

Fiedler, F. E., Jobs, S. M., & Borden, D. F. (1984). *Downward transmission of stress and its effects on the performance of motivated and unmotivated leaders.* (Tech. Rep. No. 84-2). Seattle: University of Washington.

Fiedler, F. E., & Leister, A. F. (1977). Leader intelligence and task performance: A test of a multiple-screen model. *Organizational Behavior and Human Performance, 20,* 1–14.

Fiedler, F. E., Meuwese, W., and Oonk, S. (1961). An exploratory study of group creativity in laboratory task. *Acta Psychologica, 18,* 100–119.

Fiedler, F. E., & Meuwese, W. A. T. (1963). The leader's contribution to task performance in cohesive and uncohesive groups. *Journal of Abnormal and Social Psychology, 67,* 83–87.

Fiedler, F. E., O'Brien, G. E., & Ilgen, D. R. (1969). The effect of leadership style upon the performance and adjustment of volunteer teams operating in a stressful foreign environment. *Human Relations, 22,* 503–514.

Fiedler, F. E., Potter, E. H. III, Zais, M. M., & Knowlton, W. Jr. (1979). Organizational stress and the use and misuse of managerial intelligence and experience. *Journal of Applied Psychology, 64*(6), 635–647.

Fox, W. M. (1954). An experimental study of group reaction to two types of conference leadership. Unpublished doctoral dissertation, Ohio State University, Columbus.

French, J. R. P. Jr., Israel, J., & As, D. (1960). An experiment on participation in social power. Ann Arbor, MI: Institute for Social Research.

Frost, D. (1983). Role perceptions and behavior of the immediate superior: Moderating effects on the prediction of leadership effectiveness. *Organizational Behavior and Human Performance, 31,* 123–142.

Ghiselli, E. E. (1966). *The validity of occupational aptitude tests.* New York: Wiley.

Hersey, P., & Blanchard, K. H. (1969). Life cycle theory of leadership. *Training and Development Journal, 23,* 26–34.

House, R. J. (1971). A path goal theory of leader effectiveness. *Administrative Science Quarterly, 16,* 321–338.

Korman, A. K. (1966). "Consideration," "Initiation of Structure" and organizational criteria. *Personnel Psychology, 18,* 349–360.

Larson, L. L., & Rowland, K. (1973). Leadership style, stress, and behavior in task performance. *Organizational Behavior and Human Performance, 9,* 407–421.

Lewin, K., Lippitt, R., & White, R. K. (1939). Patterns of aggressive behavior in experimentally produced social climates. *Journal of Social Psychology, 10,* 271–301.

Likert, R. (1967). *The human organization: Its management and value.* New York: McGraw-Hill.

Mann, R. D. (1959). A review of the relationships between personality and performance in small groups. *Psychological Bulletin, 56,* 241–270.

Maslow, A. H. (1965). *Eupsychian management: A journal.* Homewood, IL: Dorsey Press.

McGregor, D. (1967). *The human side of the enterprise.* New York: McGraw-Hill.

McNamara, V. D. (1968). *Leadership, staff, and school effectiveness.* Unpublished doctoral dissertation, University of Alberta, Edmonton.

Meuwese, W. A. (1964). The effect of the leader's ability and interpersonal attitudes on group creativity under varying conditions of stress. Unpublished doctoral dissertation, University of Amsterdam.

Meuwese, W., & Fiedler, F. E. (1965). *Leadership and group creativity under varying conditions of stress.* Urbana, IL: Group Effectiveness Research Laboratory, University of Illinois.

Morse, N. C., & Reimer, E. (1956). The experimental change of a major organizational variable. *Journal of Abnormal and Social Psychology, 52,* 120–129.

Potter, E. H., & Fiedler, F. E. (1981). The utilization of staff member intelligence and experience under high and low stress. *Academy of Management Journal, 24*(2), 361–376.

Sample, J. A., & Wilson, T. R. (1965). Leader behavior, group productivity, and rating of least, preferred coworker. *Journal of Personality and Social Psychology, 1,* 266–270.

Sarason, I. G. (1972). Experimental approaches to test anxiety: Attention and the uses of information. In C. D. Spielberger (Ed.), *Anxiety: Current trends in theory and research* (Vol. 2). New York: Academic Press.

Shartle, C. L. (1956). *Executive performance and leadership.* Englewood Cliffs, NJ: Prentice-Hall.

Spielberger, C. D. (1972). Anxiety as an emotional state. In C. D. Spielberger, (Ed.), *Anxiety: Current trends in theory and research* (Vol. 1). New York: Academic Press.

Stogdill, R. M. (1948). Personal factors associated with leadership: A survey of the literature. *Journal of Psychology, 25*, 35–71.

Stogdill, R. M. (1974). *Handbook of leadership*. New York: Free Press.

Terman, L. M. (1904). A preliminary study of the psychology and pedagogy of leadership. *Pediatric Seminars, 11*, 413–451.

Vroom, V. H., & Yetton, P. W. (1973). *Leadership and decision-making*. Pittsburgh: University of Pittsburgh Press.

Chapter 8

Leadership as a Function of Group Action

Mario von Cranach

Without Action, There Is No Leadership

There are many different ways to scientific understanding. For me, it is a precondition of comprehension to grasp the investigated objects' functions in their context. It is my impression that, despite some remarkable developments, leadership theory and research remain incoherent and miss some important problems; therefore, their practical usefulness must also be limited. To improve this unsatisfying state, I propose that we enlarge our scope and look at leadership phenomena from a systemic perspective. If this can be achieved as I hope, the more partial theories and findings will fall into their place, and we may even integrate them with additional hitherto neglected viewpoints to form a more general theory. The perspective I propose is the concept of group action: I conceive of groups (or other social systems, like organizations or even masses) as acting systems which actively strive, by means of directed behavior, toward internal and external goals. I further assume that the structural properties of groups evolve at least partly in the service of group action functions. This is particularly the case with leadership, which includes some most important functions of group action, namely, steering, energetizing, and control, and often contributes essentially to the groups identity and coherence as a precondition of enduring adapted activity.

Because the concept of group action is so crucial for my approach, I shall first outline its essentials. The main part of this chapter will be devoted to the most important functional and structural aspects of leadership: its relations to the structure of the task and of the group, its functions in directing the group's action (cognitive and emotional information processing) and in its energetization (motivational and emotional processes). In these considerations, I shall mainly refer to leadership as a general category and only in some cases in which personalization is salient shall I speak of the "leader". I cannot treat the differences between leaders as persons, leading committees, and so forth, although these are interesting problems. Limitation of space forbid me from discussing the immense literature on leadership problems but I feel that this can be tolerated, because my basic assumptions are, to my knowledge, more or less new. Space also prevents me from elaborating the relations of this theory to other conceptions of leadership.

This is a very short summary of complicated propositions. To achieve a better understanding, I strongly refer the reader to the extensive paper on which these considerations are based (von Cranach, Ochsenbein, & Valach, in press).

Basic Features of Group Action

Human groups are self-active systems composed of human individuals; their behavior has the properties of self-active systems in general, and some of the specific features of human goal-directed action in addition. Let us first therefore look at these.

The Directed Behavior of Self-Active Systems

Self-active systems form a particular class of living systems (see, e.g. Miller, 1978), which, in order to make their living, act on their environment: They actively strive toward certain ends by means of behavior that is directed toward the achievement of future states. Thus, a self-active system is not just instigated by external stimuli and forces, but instantaneously activated by internal energy and steered by internal information; directed behavior means that this internal information depicts the behavior and/or its results. Until the moment of operation, it is normally contained in an information store or memory. At the moment of activation, the information elicits the (physical) energy and steers the behavior.

Both energy and information are created from the system's constant interchange with its environment and stored and elaborated within the system. To the extent that the stored information is stored on the system's individual level, its ontogenetic history leads to the formation of specific individual traits: self-active systems tend to develop individuality (or "personality").

The information-processing system of higher self-active systems tends to be differentiated according to *function* and *hierarchy*. Different subsystems subserve different tasks, as, for example, information input and retention or steering of execution, and we can distinguish more central and normally superordinated subsystems from more peripheral and normally subordinated ones, although hierarchical orders tend to be relative and characterized by mutual interaction. Making use of the information about future ends and the means to get there, this form of organization makes possible directed behavior and control processes. The latter can refer to the system's own state. This self-monitoring tends to be linked to the system's central structures and adds to the formation of its individuality.

Now, given that directed behavior forms the characteristic activity of self-active systems, what are its features? First, to avoid misunderstandings let us note that it includes reactive behavior, in the sense that any behavior includes reactions to environmental conditions, without which it would be unadapted. Outward directed adaptation to environmental requirements is, however, only one side of the coin; the system must also instantaneously and constantly cope with the requirements of its own complicated inner structure (inward-directed adaptation). It is in the service of these two basic functions that all the various component processes of directed behavior must be understood. We can subdivide them into classes: directing and energetizing.

Directing

Here we have to deal with those processes that steer the system's behavior in a certain direction. They subserve the resolution of a few universal tasks which I can only briefly enumerate:

Perception of the environment, or the constantly ongoing perception and evaluation of environmental circumstances which contain clues for the steering of the behavior;

Self-monitoring, or the constant monitoring of the system's own state, at least in respects that are of behavioral consequence;

Selection of aim, or development of representations of the future state at the end of the behavior—a feed-forward process;

Choice of a program, which depicts the behavioral steps from the present state to the aim;

Transformation of the program into behavior, in order to produce the effects;

Control of execution, to ensure that the behavior is correctly executed—mostly by feedback processes;

Stopping the behavior when the aim is reached—again by feedback processes;

Evaluation and consummation of the outcome;

Final evaluation and storing of the essential features of the whole sequence, in order to learn and improve.

Energetizing

I consider energy as a physical or physiological concept to explain the movement or matter of the behavior of living systems. It is indispensable for the explanation of directed behavior, but it is not a psychological concept. Psychology deals with aspects of the arousal, inhibition, termination, and steering of energetic processes, mainly through information processing to make a distinction, I prefer to speak of energetization. This term refers to psychological problems that are treated in some theories of motivation (e.g., Atkinson & Birch, 1970; Lorenz, 1978) and of the will (e.g. Ach, 1910; James, 1890; Lewin, 1926), the latter of which is just reappearing in psychology (von Cranach, Maechler, & Steiner, 1985; Kuhl, 1983). In spite of their long history, however, the theoretical conceptions of energetization and especially of the relationship between steering and energetization are as yet insufficiently developed, and so I must restrict myself to some very basic statements. I assume that energetization serves the following functions:

To initiate and to terminate directed behavior;
To overcome specific difficulties in the execution of directed behavior;
To change the direction of behavior when it is forceful or fast;
To resolve conflicts between competing aims of programs.

I assume that energetizing is particularly elicited through environmental perception and self-monitoring.

Under normal conditions, energetizing occurs unnoticed with steering; it is mainly in the presence of difficulties that it becomes visible as a problem in its own right. This happens principally when directed behavior is to be started or maintained under difficult conditions.

Specific Features of Human Goal-Directed Action

The concept of human goal-directed action refers to an actor's consciously goal-directed, planned, and intended behavior, which is socially directed and controlled (von Cranach, Kalbermatten, Indermühle, & Gugler, 1982; von Cranach & Harré, 1982; von Cranach, Maechler, & Steiner, 1985). It is directed behavior with all its typical features, but it possesses some additional characteristics that can be derived from the properties of human cognition, especially conscious representation, and from the specific forms of human social organization. Some of its features that are important for our discussion are the following:

Setting of Milieu
The specific ecological section of reality to which the act is related (Barker, 1968). I further distinguish between the act's physical environment and the socially defined situation (Fuhrer, 1983).

Task
The task is the social demand that requires an act or a sequence of acts from the actor. Insofar as it contains more detailed information about goals, plans, and other features, I shall speak of a task structure.

Social Representation
Social representations (Farr & Moscovici, 1984). refer to a reference group's system of social knowledge, including norms, rules, values, and scripts, which have been adopted by the individual actor and steer and regulate his

or her action (cf. von Cranach et al., 1985; Thommen, Amman, & von Cranach, 1982).

Three-Dimensional Organization
The well established concept of three-dimensional organization refers to the organization of the actor's cognitions and hence his or her actions in sequence, hierarchy, and complexity (Fuhrer, 1983; Hacker, 1978; Volpert, 1982; von Cranach et al. in press). Sequence refers to temporal order, hierarchy to patterns of super and subordination, and complexity to simultaneously ongoing actions. This organization also forms the basis of feed-forward and feedback processes.

Conscious Representations and the Integration of Lower Self-Monitoring Systems into Conscious Cognition
Here I refer to the various information processing systems that represent (or depict) selected information about the actor's own state (e.g., proprioceptive sensations, pain, emotions, and conscious cognitions). Each self-monitoring system delivers messages of a particular quality, which are related to the system's code and its specific functions. It is a particular feature of human information processing that all of these messages are integrated into conscious cognition and thus at least partly participate in the latter's properties, as for example, reference to objects, independence of space and time, and the ability to construct metasystems (von Cranach, 1983; von Cranach & Ochsenbeing, in press).

Volitional Processes
As we have argued, energetizing processes operate on the basis of information processing. Thus they can be subject to conscious cognition: The will is a process of conscious cognitive energetizing. Its most distinctive forms appear at the beginning of acts (resolution or resolve) and when facing difficulties that demand great expenditure of energy (strain). Volitional processes also direct cognitive processes, such as perception and thinking (attention, concentration) and emotion (self-control).

Linguistic Encoding
Linguistic encoding of cognitions brings about the unique features of human interaction, linguistic representation, and communication, which are essential for group action: Action-related cognitions and feelings can be communicated.

The Structure of the Group Action Process

So far I have listed many of the features of directed behavior and of human goal-directed action that I consider important. To understand their function in group action, we must see them in the context of the group process, as we have done in our theory. Here are its essential steps:

1. The group action process starts from a situation in which a group, with a

given group structure, is confronted with a task. I refer primarily to cases in which group and task exist already. I believe, however, that the theory can be adapted to cases in which one or both of these have to be developed in a process of coevolution: Our theory can be extended to a theory of group development.

2. As a consequence, the task structure is projected onto the group structure, so that each part of the task is related to one (or several) specific positions in the group. This is, of course, the aspect of work division.

3. If there is no (or an insufficient) group structure in the beginning, it will develop during the action.

4. As with any directed behavior, group action is based on information processing. It operates on two levels: On the individual level, individual cognition and emotion operate in their usual form of three-dimensional organization (primary information processing). On the group level, information is processed through action-related communication (secondary information processing). To be effective for group action, this communication must proceed in accordance with the group action structure. By the distinction of these levels we acknowledge that cognitions, emotions, and the like are exclusively individual processes. They form the source and the material of group information processing, namely, communication. In group communication, individual ideas are discussed, elaborated, changed, and enhanced, and through group communication they are finally fed back into individual cognitions and emotions.

5. Consequently, group action execution is also a two-level process. On the individual level, execution is individual action (as analyzed in action theory). On the group level, group action is executed through cooperation between the group members according to the group action structure. Disturbed information processing can result in execution conflict.

Thus, the structure of information processing brings about a similar structure of execution. The theories and findings about the organization of individual action must be fully applied to the individual level of group action execution. On the group level, however, with cooperation and conflict, we meet with new and additional problems. In the next section we shall discuss the features of the group action process under the specific aspect of leadership. Therefore our emphasis will be different than in the more general framework.

Leadership in Group Action

Leadership Functions, Task Structure, and Group Structure

An Outline of Leadership Functions
I have preliminarily determined leadership to be the allocation of important

group action functions to certain positions in the group structure. Let us now consider the problems that hide behind this formulation.

First, I believe, we have to deal with the question: Just what are these important group action functions? As I have already mentioned, the directed behavior of self-active systems serves, in a very general sense, the functions of externally and internally directed adaptation. Analyzing group actions, we find that some are directed at the achievements of the group in the external world, as for example, production or the relationship to other groups. Others aim at the solution of the group's internal problems, such as the more or less constant regulation of structural patterns, intragroup communication, and the relationships between individual members. Let us further note that these two types of functions are correlated in a kind of dialectical manner; important changes in external relations instigate internal change, and vice versa (consider how the developments in a couple's relationship change their relations to their families and friends). As for leadership, it was noted long ago that the external and internal tasks give rise to two different leadership functions; this is the famous distinction between task-oriented and socioemotional leadership functions (Bales, 1958).

Second, the equally basic distinction between directing and energetizing processes in directed behavior is highly relevant for leadership functions. The group's acts must be appropriately steered, and they must be released, encouraged, and sustained. This requirement, widely accepted for individual action, is even more salient for group action, and the logic of the sequential-hierarchical model as well as common sense suggest that energetizing is a domain of leadership. These four viewpoints form the basis for our discussions in the following sections. Note, however, that so far our discussion has not hinted at any reason why these functions should be allocated to only one or a few positions in the group structure, instead of being distributed over the whole group. If we can observe this specialization so often, hitherto-unmentioned factors must be responsible.

Task Structure and Leadership

As already stated, in group action the task structure is projected onto the group structure. Let us have a closer look at the implications of this relationship. What is a task? In industrial psychology, which deals extensively with goal-directed activity, a task is understood as a socially prescribed goal-plan unit (Krogoll & Resch, 1984), which comprises logical and procedural aspects of the act as well as normative components. Within this general frame, group tasks possess characteristics that are important for our problem:

1. Most tasks are imposed on groups in the context of higher-order social systems. The working unit in a factory, the military platoon, the parliament's consulting committee, as well as the jury all act in the execution of tasks they have received from the organization of which they form a part. Sometimes the task consists, at least partly, in the

elaboration of a frame task, as in the case of research groups or seminar groups of a university. Sometimes, as in the work of consulting or surgical teams, the frame has to be filled in with more specific task elements specified by a client.

2. Typically, groups in their social context are specialized for certain kinds of tasks. Surgical teams perform various kinds of operations, but they do not pilot airplanes. Orchestras play different pieces of music, but they do not repair canals. Specialization is quite variable in degree, but as a principle it is ubiquitous in modern society. This highly refined division of work finds its continuation in the differentiation within the group, because the group's tasks also tend to possess a complex structure.

3. Under the aspect of division of work, task structures show a horizontal and a vertical dimension. The first results from the aspect of complexity, the second from that of hierarchical organization, both mentioned above. Within the same task, there are different subtasks to be performed, but there are also super- and subordinated information processing and execution. Thus, the subtasks of replacing trees by the city parks office of Dresden are located on a vertical as well as on a horizontal structure: selecting kinds of trees as information processing differs in quality from planting as execution; planting is superordinated to digging the hole (see Figure 8-1). To a degree, however, these two dimensions tend to be confounded: superordinated tasks tend to differ from subordinated ones over in content and quality.

4. Thus the task is a hierarchical design, and it shares two frequent properties of hierarchies: inclusiveness (a given higher-level unit tends to include several lower-order units) and concentration of competence (a given hierarchical unit is competent for several or all processes on a given level). The latter organizational pattern allows for simplicity of coordination and helps to avoid confusion. (For example, one sergeant is responsible for several soldiers in most respects of service.)

5. Thus, to an extent, hierarchical combined with qualitative work division is contained in the task. It is for this reason that leadership is (at least partly) projected onto the group, together with the task; the task demands structural solutions which may include forms of leadership. Practically this may appear in the implicit or explicit expectations of the group's social environment and be frozen in social representations, rules, and regulations. (For example, it may be prescribed by law that a ship approaching a harbor be led by a pilot.) Note, however, that the task is only one of the factors that contribute to the emergence of leadership; others will be discussed below.

Leadership in the Context of Group Structure

Apparently, leadership results at least partly from an interaction between task and group: The task demands leadership functions from the group, and the group creates leadership in response (which may in turn lead to the

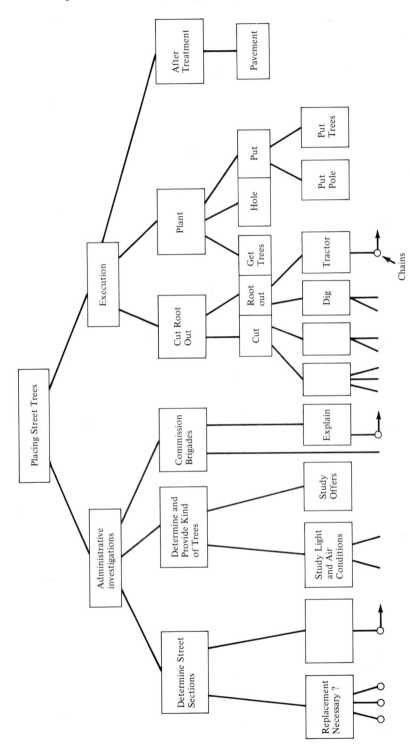

Figure 8-1. The logical structure of the task: replacing street trees. (Actor: the city park office of Dresden.) (Example provided by W. Hacker, 1985, unpublished.)

creation of new tasks). Now we have to consider the manifold phenomena of group structure.

Social psychology offers us a number of viewpoints, which have sometimes been called dimensions to hide the lack of understanding of their relations: role, hierarchy, status, power, communication, and affect structure. The question of how leadership in group action is related to these structural features can help us to understand their coherence.

Role and hierarchy. Let us begin by looking at what we have already learned in our discussion: Because the task structure demands and the group's social environment expects it, certain hierarchical and content aspects tend to coincide. In the resulting pattern leadership refers to high-ranking activities of a specific content and quality. These activities are also expected by the group members; they are part of a role differentiation, as the role theory of leadership has proposed (e.g., Bales & Slater, 1955; Gibb, 1969; Whyte, 1943). In this respect, leadership refers to complementary roles in a system of mutual relations: a system that, as we have seen, combines vertical and hierarchical aspects. In leadership roles, important task aspects and high hierarchical position tend to be combined. The leader performs acts that are different from those of his or her followers and that occupy a high place in the action structure, such as setting goals, developing plans, and making decisions.

Power and influence. Furthermore, it is a part of the leader's role to make his or her followers perform the lower-order task components that follow from the leader's own performance—in other words, to execute the leader's plans. These role demands require power: the possibility to influence the group members so that they cooperate in the performance of the task, and, if necessary, to enforce certain acts upon them and from them. This leadership power stems from all of the various bases that French and Raven (1959) have described. I believe that in group action, however, some of these sources, such as legitimation, expertise, and information, are mediated through the task, because it spells out in detail what the leader and reciprocally the group can do, should do, and have to do. I therefore see the task as a mediator of power. Thus, the trainer of a soccer team can, to a degree, legitimately control the players' diet, drinking, and smoking, because these things influence their fitness and are therefore related to the trainer's acknowledged task of increasing their efficiency; he cannot, however, control what they read. In these considerations, we should not of course forget the legitimation from superordinate social systems, which is often complementary to legitimation from the task.

Status and prestige. Power, of course, grants the holder of leadership functions a large share in the gains and products of group action, which in turn, together with its elevated position in regard to task and hierarchy, contributes to the prestige of leadership roles and their high position in status hierarchies; this position, of course, depends greatly on the success of group action.

Thus there remain communication and affect (or emotion) from the classical repertory of group structure dimensions. However, because I see these as information processes which form essential components of the group action, I shall discuss them more thoroughly in the following sections.

Leadership Functions in Information Processing

Action on the Group's Environment

Action-related information processing constitutes one of the most important leadership functions. In this section we concentrate on those functions that result from the group's striving for external adaptation: interaction with and action on its environment.

1. The group's action-related information processing proceeds on an individual and on a group level. On both levels, leadership plays an important role and performs some of its most essential functions; thus we have to investigate it on both levels, in respect to individual cognition and to communication. On both levels, leadership has to process high-ranking action-related (steering, controlling, evaluating) information: those that concern the higher topics in the hierarchical structure of the task. Therefore leadership is concerned with the comprehensive representation of the situation, task, group, and action rather than that of subordinated aspects; it is concerned with the development of supergoals rather than of subgoals, with general plans rather than with the details of execution, and with far-reaching rather than short-range decisions. (The detailed knowledge of these processes which action theories provide can be applied here.) It is only in the specific case that we can determine what is high- and what is low-ranking information. There is one exception to the general rule, however: to the extent that the leader is also a teacher, he or she must care for the details. For example, if the skipper of a yacht is also a sailing instructor, he or she will have to care for the knots. For the performance of these tasks, the leader must also have access to important information from outside and inside the group.

2. Cognition and communication serve closely connected and partially vicarious functions. First, no cognition becomes effective in its leadership function unless it is also communicated to the group. Second, leadership does not need to be the source of the action-related information, as long as it controls it. Thus, the arguments of a group discussion may be closely analogous to the cognitions in individual decision making and lead to similar results; in this case, leadership consists in the adoption and final reinforcement of a solution. Practically, the leader will often be the one who summarizes, formulates, and thus also legitimizes the outcome of group work.

3. Like any other actions, those of leadership consist of information processing and execution. As a general principle, however, the higher we go in the task structure, the more difficult we find the distinction to make. Very often both sides of the action fall together, as in the case of the skipper who determines the yacht's course by drawing lines on the map, and what is execution on the leadership level may be considered information processing on the group level (like the command, which the skipper finally utters to the helmsman).

4. Elsewhere (von Cranach, Ochsenbein, & Valach, in press) we have pointed to some of the analogies between individual cognition and group communication. Our argument was based on the assumption that group communication shows degrees of explicitness just as individual cognition possesses degrees of conscious representation, and that fully communicated messages are analogous to consciously represented cognitions. We have also argued that we need an attention mechanism to explain the transition from the nonconscious to the conscious, and that the function of consciousness, its requirement in action allows to predict the direction of attention, von Cranach, 1983; for empirical support of these ideas see Ochsenbein, 1982). Here I want to extend these ideas to leadership, the function of which seems analogous to the individual attention mechanism: if the leader has attended to a problem, the group has attended to it unless the nature of the problem demands that it should be communicated; in the latter case, it is the function of leadership to make it communicated. I assume that, on this basis, some of the leadership processes can be predicted, and likewise it should be possible to specify its dysfunctions. In a way, leadership functions as an attention mechanism: and as an agent of voluntary attention in group: information processing.

5. Group action is always complex action; its information processing does not proceed in a linear way but constitutes a network in which several communications to variable addresses tend to occur simultaneously. Although the traditional studies of communication networks (e.g., Shaw, 1964) reflect reality only insufficiently, I subscribe to their conclusion that leadership is associated with privileged positions in the network. In fact, a great amount of leadership activity is related to creating and maintaining a network suitable to leadership functions, and I believe that a combination with group action theory could lead communication network theory out of its present stagnation).

6. In two respects, the leader serves the group as its major link to its social environment. The leader is the one who represents the group, and therefore is often obliged to act for the group in its outside communication. This representation is often explicitly or implicitly anchored in normative systems, as for example the role of the father in the traditional European family. In close connection with this obligation, the leader is also principally responsible for the group's observing, in its acts, the

prescriptive social representations of its higher social systems. Thus the traditional father is also responsible for the conduct of his family members.

Emotional Group Processes and Group Identity
We have to consider emotion in a dual sense: as an action-related emotional process and as a structure of mutual feelings of the group members. As a third topic, we must discuss the role of emotion in group identity. Leadership is essential in all these matters.

1. What is an emotion? To give a short answer to a difficult question, we consider it as a part of individual information processing: a self-monitoring system, based on physiological processes and providing the individual with information about his or her own global state, including basic evaluations and reaction tendencies, in a given situation (von Cranach & Ochsenbein, in press). The emotional code is relatively simple, too simple for a complex syntax; it consists in the representation of a few selected states in a holistic way. Emotions are often reflected in conscious cognition. As to action, they serve attention-directing and motivating (arousing and inhibiting) functions.

2. Group emotional processes are two-level processes, like group information processing in general: The first level is made up by the individual emotion, the second by communication between group members. Communication about emotional matters is to a high degree nonverbal. But what happens on the group level, and why is it justified to speak of the group emotional process? Let us consider the process itself. When a member communicates an emotion verbally or nonverbally to other members, it is likely to elicit an emotional reaction, which the member then perceives and evaluates and which is likely to reinforce or weaken his or her own reaction. Very similar mutual influences occur when members react independently to external events: The group provides positive or negative feedback to its members.

3. It is not difficult to understand the process that operates in the emotions related to their interaction with and action on their environment. If somebody is, for example, the only one who is afraid in a certain situation, he or she is likely to be comforted; if all the members are afraid, their fear will increase because of "positive feedback", in some cases to the level of hysteria and panic. (The opposite case leads to phenomena like the so-called "risky shift," the tendency to make more risky decisions in group than in solitary situation). However, because the emotion includes reaction tendencies, influences the action-related cognitions, and exerts motivating influences, it will exert a strong impact on the acts to be chosen and on the way they will be executed. In stable situations, the fluctuating feelings of all members in their interaction will act as "negative feedback" and build up something like a homeostatic system, which contributes, along with habits and other factors, to a typical style

of group action: Certain circumstances tend to be observed, certain definitions of situations are adopted, and certain acts tend to be chosen, and in their execution a typical level of motivation will be maintained. (Consider as examples the listless seminar group that never rises to the heights of inspired work, or the jazz quartet whose members by mutual instigation rise to an extraordinary level of performance.)

4. The case of the group's emotion structure is more difficult. Of course, if we consider the group as a multitude of dyadic relationships, as is done in the sociometric method (e.g., Lindzey & Byrne, 1968), each dyad may exhibit relatively stable positive or negative mutual feelings. This conception is all too simple, however. First we have to understand that the quality of any dyadic relationship depends on and changes with its social environment, in this case the group. Thus, a couple's relationship changes with the advent of children, and a family's friends are no longer the same after a divorce. Second, mutual liking and disliking is a variable process, the dynamics of which depend on homeostatic regulation in the group. This is a very complicated affair, and Heider's (1958) balance theory represents only a part of it, in a simplified way. As a whole it establishes a flowing equilibrium, a homeostatic system again which is often called group climate or atmosphere; it forms an important part of cohesiveness. In such a system any change is likely to be paralyzed through regulation; this is why a group climate is so difficult to change. Group climate is of course closely related to the emotional processes we have considered.

5. Having considered these connections, it is less difficult to understand the leader's part in the group emotional process. Because of his or her role in task fulfillment and action, the leader is focal in a dual sense: as the focus of attention (consider Chance's [1967] concept of attention structure) and as the focus of projection of the group members; the leader therefore plays a key role in the group's emotional dynamics. His or her feelings exert a major influence on the feelings of all the others in their interconnection, as a standard and anchoring point. Moreover, it can be part of the leader's task and role to control, influence, and change the emotions of the group and its members. On the other hand, if the leader is also sensitive to the group he or she may strongly react to the group's emotions and function as an amplifier. Thus, the leader's role is always ambivalent, as the one who is simultaneously most influential and most in danger of being influenced.

6. Groups have an identity that originates from the members' cognitions and emotions as a system of mutual feedback on the group level. It serves as a source of unity and stability and forms an important part, in turn, of the members' social identity (e.g., Tajfel, 1982). Because of the various properties we have hitherto discussed, the leader is likely to form the nucleus of this structure.

Leadership Functions in Group Action Energetization

Motivation and the Will

Energy is necessary for any process in nature, and energetization is indispensible in a psychology of action: Without energy, nothing moves. Therefore, energetization is also essential for group action. Like information processing, it must be considered as a two-level process: The energy of the group consists of the physiological energy of its members, aroused in individual energetization processes which are stimulated and influenced by the group. To achieve clarity, it is again important to keep both levels apart but to understand their interaction. In the psychology of the individual, the two concepts of motivation and of volition (or the will) have been used to explain energetization. Although the accent is very differently put in the various approaches, motivation (in a general sense) refers to the conception of an action tendency which includes both steering and energetizing components. Action-related emotions contribute to this process. In certain stages of human activity the two components tend to be separated, so that we can distinguish between action-related cognition and volition—for example, the goal and the resolution (Rubinstein, 1977).

Why introduce the will, in addition to the concept of motivation? It explains action phenomena that are frequently experienced and observed, but for which motivation alone cannot account, namely (to put it in William James's words), resolution and effort. The first term refers to the arbitrary beginning of an act by means of a partly conscious volitional process, something like a start command; the second refers to the conscious clinging to an intention when its execution meets with difficulties. Both of these are based on cognitive processes of positive feedback, which include the (partly conscious) selection of the incoming and cognitively and emotionally processed information, so that the tendency to act is progressively strengthened. James (1890) and Ach (1910, 1935) have already partly described these processes; Kuhl (1983) has recently published a model that integrates motivational and volitional constructs.

Energetization at the Group Level

Let us assume that task and goal are given and that the individual knows his or her role in the total performance. What then is the group's contribution to energetization? Here we ask for those group properties and processes that influence individual energetization, which in turn steers the dynamics of individual physiological energy.

1. As we know from many examples, the group can have a positive, but also a negative effect on the individual; it will arouse and enhance, or inhibit and decrease individual energetization. In a more extensive analysis, we should investigate whether positive and negative group energetization follow different rules.

2. Groups have enduring characteristics which may exert an energetizing effect. These properties refer to certain task and action requirements. They are rooted in the group's history and reflected in the evaluation the group receives from its social environment and its members, and they can be related to the group's structural features (for example, the soccer team's conviction that "We always had a strong defense") or recurring group processes ("With this strategy, we can deal with equals, but we cannot beat strong adversaries"). They form an important aspect of group identity. Group energetizing properties can strongly influence individual energetizing processes. Consider, as examples, the instigating *esprit du corps* of military units, the paralyzing impact of the soccer team in decline, or the case of the volleyball team whose members are convinced that "We always fail in the decisive set" and consequently do so. How does the influence of such group properties operate in detail? To become effective, any psychological property must be translated into a process. Let us therefore turn to group energetizing processes.

3. Obviously, group processes can only affect individual energetization if they influence the individual's cognitions or emotions. There are many different ways of achieving this. There is direct social influence through command, admonition, and example. The group may set norms for output and performance, it may serve as a standard for performance, or it may serve as a standard for comparison processes and provide cues for competitive behavior. In all of these instances, emotional arousal plays a major role. Due to the mutual influence between group members, positive or negative feedback processes occur which resemble those we have discussed in the context of emotions. Thus the soccer team member who sees that his comrades are not really fighting may become discouraged himself, or he may in a kind of stubbornness born of despair fight even more fiercely. Which of the two will happen is a question for more detailed theorizing and empirical research, but whatever the individual does is likely to influence the other group members' behaviors.

4. Finally, we also have to consider multiple energetization processes, which result from the fact that many processes take place simultaneously in the group context, as is also reflected in the network character of intragroup communication. Depending on his or her position in the group structure, the member receives many different messages which draw him or her in the same or in a different direction. The group member can choose between different examples and, to a degree, select his or her reference persons. The dynamics that result from these circumstances should make a fascinating topic for empirical investigations.

The Leader's Key Role

As in directing, the leader plays a most important role in group action energetizing. Let us see how this influence operates, and what the sources are from which the leader draws.

1. An unproblematic routine action does not need particular energetization. As William James (1890) described it under the heading of the "ideomotor action," the goal, plan, or other steering information is sufficient to make the action take place. In regard to routine group action, we can make very similar observations: The leader's instruction, command, or even a mere indication suffices to release the group's activity. Thus, the yacht skipper's command to turn, under normal conditions of sailing, does not need to be accompanied by additional encouragement. Even in those cases where preparation and execution of the command are separated, this division serves more the timing of the act than additional energetization. Steering (the choice of the proper act) and energetizing (the sequence of information processing that ends with the group members' physiological activity) are contained in the same communication.

2. The impact of leadership on the level of motivation in long-term activities is much more obvious. Several properties of leadership combine to produce this effect. At the basis there is the central position of leadership in the task and group structures. Further, the leader or leading group may be distinguished by valued personality characteristics. It does not really matter to what degree these have a valid foundation or are only attributed or made up by propaganda. As a result of all of these factors, the group's specific pattern of leadership forms a part of the group identity. As a result, the leader becomes a target of projection and is put into the constant focus of attention. (The relationship to the emotional processes already discussed is obvious.) These are the reasons why the leader exerts such an impact on the group processes of motivation and regulation: The leader serves as a standard (*Sollwert*) in the cybernetic system. His or her high spirits will raise and depressions lower the motivation of the group. Leaders tend to be well aware of this function and try to demonstrate confidence and firm determination. Consider how President Reagan quite successfully raised the spirits of a majority of the American people. Writers have often described these attitudes in their stories (e.g., Forrester's *Horatio Hornblower* or the captain in Buchheim's *The boat*).

3. Finally, the leader forms the center of the group's volitional functions. Just as in individual action, these are required when specific difficulties in the course of action arise, as often happens when an act should be started or when hindrances arise which demand for particular efforts. It is in these moments that the leader's direct incitements, encouragements, or even threats are of particular importance. Further, as another volitional function, the leader has to protect the acts that have been chosen against conflicting action tendencies: The ideas of giving up or of

changing goal and plan have to be defeated. Of course, these functions are closely related to action directing and steering. Clinging to the chosen action cognition is again the essence of the volitional function. Here again the analogy between individual conscious cognition and intragroup cognition is useful, because volitional messages, to be effective, must be clearly communicated.

A Remark on Charisma

Charisma, defined by Weber (1922) as the attributed endowment of a person with extraordinary, even magical power is so often reported in records of the impact of historical leaders that we can hardly doubt its existence. In social psychology, however, it has not received much attention. From the preceding discussion about emotional and energetizing leader–group relationships, we can hypothesize that charisma is not an attribute of the leader himself, but a relational property that results from interactional processes: It is born out of the interaction between the group members and between them and the leader. How could this interaction create charisma? As we have seen, intragroup interaction is nearly invariably combined with cybernetic processes, which reinforce and regulate individual cognitions, emotions, and motives. Let us now imagine that attributional projections are strengthened by an intragroup communication which results in positive feedback. From this idea we can understand why charismatic impressions on the followers' side can reach an incredible force and give the leader tremendous power over their ideas, feelings, and motives, a power that in turn changes the leader's feelings, cognitions, and self-image. We can also understand why charisma can so suddenly dissolve into nothingness. It is a process very similar to the rise and fall of the "star" in the modern entertainment industry. To a degree, leaders are stars, and to this degree they can be artificially created. Charisma, of course, helps the leader to serve his or her functions, but as with all processes of positive feedback, it contains great risks for the system's survival, as is documented by many historical examples.

The Future of Leadership

It is my conviction that group action theory, including these ideas about leadership functions, bears interesting implications for social psychology in general. Beyond its scientific meaning, however, it has many practical consequences. Let us end by considering one of them.

In the last few years we have witnessed a variety of real-life experiments in group action and leadership in various fields, and the principle of leadership in general has been put into question. In our private lives, we have all learned to claim more autonomy. New styles of group life have been developed in various settings, and new forms of teamwork and team decision have been tested. Egalitarian movements, deeply convinced that democratic decisions should be made at the grass roots, have propagated the idea that leadership is altogether unnecessary and even harmful. Can we dispense with leadership in a society that aims at freedom and equality? From the previous considerations, we can try to give an answer.

1. Our analysis has shown that, as a principle, leadership is an indispensable function of group action; it provides the group much of its direction and energy. Moreover, leadership forms an important part of the group's identity. A group without leadership behaves like an individual without a cerebral cortex, at least as far as outward- and inward-directed action is concerned. Without well-adapted action, a group cannot survive.

2. Our analysis, however, has not investigated the many different ways of realizing leadership functions, and hence our conclusions do not suggest any particular solution. We cannot, for example, comment on the various possibilities of distribution of leadership functions or of turntaking, which are in line with today's democratic values. In a given case, the preferred solution will largely depend on the given structures of task and group, but in the long run task and group structures may be changed in the course of social progress.

3. The solution of the leadership problem therefore certainly cannot be found in a minimization of leadership functions, which would deteriorate action. Quite the contrary, our complicated and vulnerable democratic societies will have to strengthen their leadership functions. It seems obvious to seek the answer in the distribution of leadership functions and in leadership control. These are, besides the necessary empirical foundations of our theory, promising directions for future research.

References

Ach, N. (1910). *Über den Willensakt und das Temperament*. Leipzig: Quelle und Meyer.

Ach, N. (1935). Analyse des Willens. In E. Abderhalden (Ed.), *Handbuch der biologischen Arbeitsmethoden*. (pp. 1–483). (Band VI). Berlin: Urban und Schwarzenberg.

Atkinson, J. W., & Birch, D. (1970). *The dynamics of action*. New York: Wiley.

Bales, R. F. (1958). Task roles and social roles in problem-solving groups. In E. E. Maccoby, T. M. Newcomb, & E. L. Hartley (Eds.), *Readings in social psychology*, (pp. 437–464). New York: Holt, Rinehart & Winston.

Bales, R. F., & Slater, P. E. (1955). Role differentiation in small decision-making groups. In T. Parsons & R. F. Bales (Eds.), *Family, socialization and interaction process*. New York: Free Press.

Barker, R. G. (1968). *Ecological psychology: Concepts and methods for studying the environment of human behavior*. Stanford, CA: Stanford University Press.

Chance, M. R. A. (1967). Attention structure as the basis of primate rank orders. *Man. 2*(4), 503–518.

Cranach, M. von, Kalbermatten, U., Indermühle, K., & Gugler, B., (1982). *Goal-directed action*. London: Academic Press.

Cranach, M. von, & Harré, R. (1982). *The analysis of action: Recent theoretical and empirical advances*. Cambridge, England: Cambridge University Press.

Cranach, M. von. (1983). Über die bewusste Repräsentation handlungsbezogener Kognitionen. In L. Montada, K. Reusser, & G. Steiner (Eds.), *Kognition und Handeln*. (pp. 64–77). Stuttgart: Klett–Cotta.

Cranach, M. von, Maechler, E., & Steiner, U. (1985). The organisation of goal directed action: A research report. In M. Brenner, J. Ginsberg, & M. von Cranach (Eds.), *Discovery strategies in the psychology of action*. (pp. 19–61) London: Academic Press.

Cranach, M. von, & Ochsenbein, G. (in press). "Selbstüberwachungssysteme" und ihre Funktion in der menschlichen Informationsverarbeitung. Schweizerische Zeitschrift für Psychologie.

Cranach, M. von, Ochsenbein, G., & Valach, L. (in press). *The group as a self-active system. A research report*. European Journal of Social Psychology.

Farr, R. M., & Moscovici, S. (Eds.). (1984). *Social representations*. Cambridge, England: Cambridge University Press, and Paris: Editions de la Maison des Sciences de l'Homme.

French, J. R. P., & Raven, B. (1959). The bases of power. In D. Cartwright (Ed.), *Studies in social power*, (pp. 150–167). Ann Arbor, MI: University of Michigan.

Fuhrer, U. (1983). *Mehrfachhandeln in dynamischen Umfeldern*. Göttingen: Hogrefe Verlag.

Gibb, C. A. (1969). Leadership. In G. Lindzey & E. Aronson (Eds.), *The handbook of social psychology* (Vol. IV, pp. 205–282). Reading, MA. Addison-Wesley.

Hacker, W. (1978). *Allgemeine Arbeits- und Ingenieurpsychologie*. Bonn: Deutscher Verlag der Wissenschaften, and Bern: Hans Huber Verlag.

Heider, F. (1958). *The psychology of interpersonal relations*. New York: Wiley.

James, W. (1890). *Principles of psychology*. New York: Holt.

Krogoll, T., & Resch, M. (1984). *Aufgabenbezogene Arbeitsanalyse*. (Berichte und Reprints aus dem Institut für Humanwissenschaft in Arbeit und Ausbildung der TU Berlin, No. 2). Berlin: Technical University.

Kuhl, J. (1983). *Motivation, Konflikt und Handlungskontrolle*. Berlin: Springer-Verlag.

Lewin, K. (1926). Untersuchungen zur Handlungs- und Affektpsychologie II: Vorsatz, Wille und Bedürfnis. *Psychologische Forschung, 7,* 330–385.

Lindzey, G. & Byrne, D., (1968). Measurement of social choice and interpersonal attractiveness. In G. Lindzey & E. Aronson (Eds.), *Handbook of social psychology* (Vol. II, pp. 452–525). Reading, MA: Addison-Wesley.

Lorenz, K. (1978). *Vergleichende Verhaltensforschung. Grundlagen der Ethologie*. Vienna: Springer.

Miller, J. G. (1978). *Living systems*. New York: McGraw-Hill.

Ochsenbein, G., (1982). *Aufmerksamkeitsprozesse in zielgerichteten Handlungen*. Unpublished thesis, Psychologisches Institut, University of Bern.

Rubinstein, S. L. (1977). *Grundlagen der allgemeinen Psychologie* (7th ed.) Berlin: VEB, Volk und Wissen.

Shaw, M. (1964). Communication networks. In L. Berkowitz (Ed.), *Advances in experimental social psychology*. (Vol. I, pp. 111–149). New York: Academic Press.

Tajfel, H. (1982). *Social identity and intergroup relations*. Cambridge, England: Cambridge University Press.

Thommen, B., Ammann, R., & Cranach, M. von. (1982). *Handlungsorganisation durch soziale Repräsentationen*. Forschungsbericht aus dem Psychologischen Institut der Universität Bern.

Volpert, W. (1982). The model of hierarchical-sequential organization of action. In W. Hacker, W. Volpert, & M. von Cranach (Eds.), *Cognitive and motivational aspects of action*. (pp. 38–58). Amsterdam: North Holland.

Weber, M. (1922). Die drei reinen Typen der legitimen Herrschaft. *Preussische Jahrbücher, 187,* 1–12.

Whyte, W. F. (1943). *Street corner society*. Chicago: University of Press.

Chapter 9

Contests, Conquests, Coronations: On Media Events and Their Heroes

Elihu Katz and Daniel Dayan

In their classic paper, Lazarsfeld and Merton (1948) identified "status conferral" as one of the major functions of mass communications. The media enhance and legitimize the status of those to whom they call attention. This formulation, however, understates the reciprocal character of the process. In fact, there are two senses in which persons of status reciprocate: First, they affirm and enhance the status of the media that have access to them; secondly, and more fundamentally, the pronouncements and actions of persons of status are essential to the very practice of journalism. Implicit in the theory of Western journalism is the axiom that the talk and deeds of individuals—particularly those in office—are the basic force in social stability and change.

This is the point at which journalism and social science part company. Whereas the social sciences and academic history tend to discount the importance of individual action in favor of anonymous social, political, and economic forces, journalism shuns these forces, proposing instead that great men and women still live among us and that it is they who make history. This concern with greatness is not explained simply by the visual bias of the modern media. Rather, the media's celebration of personality stems more deeply from a belief in voluntarism—of will—that attributes social change to the deliberate actions of individuals. Journalism, in other words, is strongly antideterministic.

Boorstin (1962) would insist that the heroes of modern journalism are only pseudoheroes, products of the collusion between public relations officers and journalists. The true heroes of modernity, argues Boorstin, are occupied with problems of such complexity that the popular media cannot even cope with them; moreover, he would insist, modern heroes work not alone but in teams.

Whether or not Boorstin is correct, this chapter will argue that true heroes can still be found, at least on certain occasions, in the press and on the screen. Of course, whether or not he is right, Boorstin's yearning for real heroes and real events does not conflict with the proposition that journalists and heroes, true or false, need each other.

Heroes and the Daily News

The heroes of the everyday, true or false, do not have much of a chance anyway. News is deviation from the normal, and typically it is about conflict: between man and man, between man and society, and—as in cases of disaster—between man and nature or God. In reporting on routine conflicts, the daily news does not generally allow great individuals to flourish unchallenged for very long. Most of the news is about routine contests in which the two contending parties are presented as equals, and as each side does battle with the other, both sides have hits and misses and suffer tarnished images. Nevertheless, heroic figures do sometimes emerge in the daily news, to illustrate the process of the dependence of heroes and journalists on each other and on their joint client, the public.

Henry Kissinger's shuttle diplomacy is a good example. Descending from the sky and surrounded by the journalists who had won the coveted places on his plane, Kissinger would announce that the crisis he had come to solve was all but impossible of human solution. Moreover, he would say, he had only three days to give, as equally worthy crises elsewhere were pleading for his attention. Thus, he portrayed himself, and was portrayed by those assigned to cover him, much as Weber (in Schwartz, 1983) would have hoped: self-appointed, self-confident, an outsider who is called to a mission, rejecting "rational" administrative conduct in favor of the particularistic dispensation of power and justice, leaving implementation and routine to disciples and successors, achieving and maintaining authority by putting extraordinary talents to use in the performance of miraculous feats, deriving prestige by the seizure and effective use of power, and thus demonstrating "strength in life."

In listing these attributes of the charismatic leader, Schwartz (1983) proposed that Weber showed no awareness of a competing form of democratic leadership, that of George Washington. Such a man is reluctantly drafted into leadership, riddled with self-doubt; he administers power and justice according to universalistic standards, exhibiting no extraordinary talent or political feat, but dedicating himself to institution building, and deriving prestige almost from the avoidance and relinquishment of power, thereby demonstrating "virtue." Curiously, Schwartz showed us that Washington was looked upon "as the most extraordinary moral hero of his time . . . [because] in late eighteenth century America . . . the refusal to accept power and haste in giving it up, were the ingredients that went into political spectacles."

Putting aside this competing conception of self-effacing leadership for consideration elsewhere, let us return to the charismatic Kissinger and his shuttle. Our interest in this case focuses not only on the man and his deeds but on the journalistic form in which they were reported. For it can be shown that the form itself—the story type invoked by journalists to report on heroic mediators commuting between embattled parties—is an essential part of the message. In other words, the particular manner in which the hero and his or her personality and actions are packaged is essential to an understanding of their effect. Thus, the afternoon newspaper and the evening television news offer us the melodrama of a hero setting out on a journey in which he will face an almost insurmountable obstacle, accompanied by story tellers who will inform readers and viewers, from day to day and even from hour to hour, what the hero is doing and saying and, above all, whether he is winning. Note that the journalists have all but excluded themselves from access to outside sources, depending very heavily on the reports of the hero. Manipulated into this situation by the *deus ex machina* himself, they have been invited aboard as members of the wedding and will tell their story in typically breathless and awe-stricken fashion. When the story form is fixed, it may sometimes turn into a measure of the adequacy of reality, as when reporters question aloud whether George Shultz has not been miscast in the role of hero.

The form of the story itself has consequences. In the present case, journalists and officials from all sides have conspired to create a suspense story that (1) spotlights a seemingly dire situation, requiring extraordinary measures; (2) creates a mood of desperation, implying that there is no recourse beyond this last one; (3) thus putting great pressure on the parties to yield, as the whole world looks on; and (4) setting a great machinery into motion on each side in order to prove that the fault is elsewhere, should, God forbid, the negotiations fail.

Media Events

This example of how establishments and journalists use each other also serves to show how the genres of the daily news subtly change from routine stories of conflict to the more melodramatic story of conquest, as when David faces Goliath or Gandhi faces the British Empire. In the television era, there is a genre of journalism that does this even more dramatically, one that invites great men and women onto the stage of the world and frames them to show how they transform things before our eyes. We refer to the live broadcasting of historic occasions such as the moon landings, the journeys of the Pope, the visit of Sadat to Jerusalem, the funeral of President Kennedy, the Olympic games, and the televised Watergate hearings of the United States Congress. Each of these events is also a ceremony celebrating the unity of a nation or of several nations.

These events have in common that they are interruptions of our lives and of the schedules of broadcasting. They are transmitted as they are happening, in real time. Unlike other live broadcasts, however, they are preplanned, announced and advertised days or weeks, sometimes years, in advance, Viewers—and, indeed, broadcasters—had only a few days notice of the exact time of the broadcast of Sadat's arrival, but Radio-Telefis Eireann advertised the Pope's visit to Ireland a few weeks in advance and the 1984 Los Angeles Olympics were heralded for more than four years. Typically, these events are hailed as "historic," both in advance and while they are being broadcast.

Media events, by our definition, are organized outside of the media. Thus, in the United States, the League of Women Voters and the two major political parties organized the last three presidential debates (1976, 1980, and 1984); the Royal Family and the Church of England planned and produced the Royal Wedding; the Olympics are mounted by the International Olympic Committee. Of course, the events may be planned with television "in mind," or there may be collusion between broadcasters and organizers, or state-operated broadcasting systems (in Poland, not in England or Israel) may be indistinguishable from the organizers, but the exceptions only serve to prove the rule. The organizers, on the whole, are public bodies such as governments, legislatures (parliamentary commissions), political parties (national conventions), international organizations (the Olympic Committee), and the like. Organizers of such events are unlikely to be from outside the establishment or the consensus. Therefore Woodstock was presented to the public via film, not as a live television broadcast; the live broadcast of Ayatollah Khomeini's return was halted almost before it began.

Although the broadcasters are not the organizers, media events are typically presented by the former with reverence. Broadcasters and even seasoned journalists suspend their normally critical stance and preside over the broadcast with respect. Garry Wills (1980) characterized media coverage of the Pope in America as "falling in love with love," and referring to the almost priestly role played by journalists on such occasions, he calls it ironically "the Greatest Story Ever Told." Of course, the very flow of ceremonial events is courtly and invites awe. There is the playing of the national anthem, the funereal beat of the drum corps, the diplomatic ceremony of being escorted from the plane, the rules of decorum in church and at Senate hearings. The point is that television rarely intrudes; it stands at attention for the anthems and for the passing of the bier, interrupting only to identify the music being played or the name of the chief of protocol. It upholds the definition given the event by its organizers, explains the meaning of the symbols of the occasion, and only rarely intervenes with analysis and almost never with criticism.

Events of this kind celebrate not conflict—the subject of most news programs—but reconciliation. They call for a cessation of hostilities, at least for a moment, as when the Royal Wedding "asked" for a stop in the street fighting in Brixton and the terror in Northern Ireland, or when Sadat came to Jerusalem or the Pope to Poland, asking for a more permanent truce. Even Nixon's resignation ushered in for America a period of national reintegration (Alexander, 1982).

These ceremonials electrify very large audiences—an entire nation or large parts of the world. They are gripping, enthralling. They are characterized by a norm of viewing in which people tell each other that it is mandatory to watch, that they must put all else aside. These broadcasts integrate societies in a collective heartbeat, overriding divisiveness and contentiousness. They cause viewers to celebrate the event by gathering before their television sets in groups, rather than alone. Often, they participate actively in this expression of *communitas* (Turner, 1977) causing people to ask themselves why society can't be this good all the time. Here, too, the packaging and worldwide delivery of the event by television contributes to its effect, as will be demonstrated below.

A Typology of Media Events

Let us distinguish among three types of such televised events: We call them *contests, conquests*, and *coronations*. Contests are live broadcasts of ceremonial competitions between matched individuals or teams, tilting with each other in an arena according to predetermined rules, often with a referee and a live audience. We have in mind such sporting events as the World Cup and political events such as the presidential debates in the United States and elsewhere. "Who will win?" is the essence of the drama of such events. Most contests are cyclical events, although occasionally an unscheduled contest such as the senate Watergate hearings presents itself for our attention.

Conquests are live broadcasts of "great steps for mankind" whereby a hero, facing insuperable odds, enters the enemy camp unarmed, as did the Pope in Poland, or Sadat in Jerusalem, or the astronauts on the moon. The dramatic question is "Will he win?" and the dramatic action is the crossing of a forbiddent frontier (Katz, Dayan, & Motyl, 1983).

Coronations are the rites of passage of great individuals: their inaugurations, their marriages, their departures. Broadcasts of these events invite the television audience to participate in the process of ritual transformation of the hero from one status to the next, as the mysteries of traditional ceremony harness and channel the forces of nature, assuring the continuity of society (Shils & Young, 1956; Dayan & Katz, 1983).

These great events of mass communication do not occur frequently; they cannot do so, of course, without losing some of their effectiveness. They emerge, rather, at moments of crisis when a change is to be made either in the rules of the game, as Sadat changed Middle Eastern politics, or in the players, as in the mourning after Kennedy. Even regularly scheduled contests, such as sports events and political ceremonies are given more or less attention as a function of the salience of the larger conflicts of which they speak. Even when Israel competes in the European song contest, it is a symbolic event of considerable importance.

Events and Their Heroes

Each type of event proposes a different set of heroes, or great men (Table 9-1). Contests, ironically, are the least charismatic. Like the less ceremonial conflicts of the daily news, they symbolize the equality of opposing forces and, above all, the predominance of the rules. They are thus rather rationalistic events, in which the loser is seen to have certain of the winner's qualities. Although the victor is presented as a potential candidate for coronation and conquest, contests offer the chance of a "next time" to the defeated side and no more than a temporary reign to the victor. Still, the winners of contests often receive great acclaim, all the more so when the underdog wins: Recall Kennedy's victory in the 1960 debate with Nixon.

Coronations, on the other hand, put a great man on view, sometimes as the product of ascription, more often as the product of achievement. Here, however, the great man acts out a ritual role in which initiative is minimized, dwarfed by the august setting of cathedral or cemetery and by the strictness of protocol. Ironically, these are great men stuffed with the symbols of voluntarism, but unable to act it out: the dead Kennedy or Mountbatten is a mere symbol of the man himself.

The arena of true greatness is the live broadcasting of conquest. These are "missions impossible" where the odds against the hero are so great and the risks so real that humanity holds its breath to witness the challenge and its outcome. Consider Sadat in Jerusalem, for example, or the Pope in Poland. Each of these stories begins with the hero's climb from humble origins to great stature, culminating in a deliberate and carefully calculated decision to try to change the world. In both cases, we find the enemy actually daring the hero to try. In both cases, the hero talks over the heads of his rivals to enlist the attention of the rival's ostensible following—the Israeli and Polish peoples—inviting them to invest the hero with the charisma that will allow him to charm them. Of course, the rivals—the Israeli and Polish governments—stand to benefit too if the hero succeeds. Risking failure and perhaps his life, the hero offers himself as a sacrifice in the very act of making the journey. In response, he is offered a show of welcome whose pomp and ceremony are difficult to exaggerate. The hero wants more, however, and gives more to get it. On the potlatch principle, there is a consequent escalation of demands and of gestures of largesse.

Table 9-1. Dimensions of Contests, Conquests, and Coronations

Dimension	Type of Event		
	Contests	Conquests	Coronations
Periodicity	Fixed (cyclical)	Not fixed (one-time event)	Not fixed (recurrent)
Rules	Agreed-upon rules	No rules (antistructure?)	Ritual rules
Participants	Man vs. man, etc.	Hero vs. nature, society	Culture, society vs. nature
Odds	Even	Against hero	Against society
Drama	Who will win?	Will hero win?	Will ritual succeed? Can we keep reality out? Who's next?
Relation to conflict resolution	Frames, miniaturizes, symbolizes conflict; makes other side human too	Invites suprapartisan identification	Reflexive: reminds audience of basic values of society; provides intermission
Role of audience	Partisan rooting; audience as judge	Invests hero with charisma; audience in awe	Renews contract with center; audience loyal
Role of television presenter	Neutral or partisan	Reverent	Reverent
Locus	Arena	Frontier (*limen*)	Aisle
Somatic contact	Hug	Kiss	Tears
Message	Rules are supreme; victory, defeat reversible. Best man will prevail	Great men: great leap for mankind	Continuity is assured; great men as symbols
Role of performers	Demonstrate character, mobility	Demonstrate charisma	Ritual performance
Time Orientation	Present	Future	Past

The Role of Television

By agreeing to package these ceremonies as media events, television augments their gestures, their symbols, and their drama. In the live broadcasting of contests, the television presentation underscores the deep rivalry between the sides and the symbolic meaning of the encounter. Sports events have this character (Comiskey, Bryant, & Zillman, 1977). In coronations, television rehearses the audience in the ceremony they are about to witness; it carefully spells out the meaning of its symbols, thus framing the event by separating it from daily life, embroidering it, upholding its official definition, and offering a story line and commentary to shape its interpretation. Thus, television made a Cinderella of Lady Diana and held high the symbols of marriage, family, mobility, nobility, and, above all, Britishness and *communitas*. Television offered viewers various opportunities to "participate" in the event—by suggesting, for example, that viewers prepare the Royal Wedding breakfast menu at home. By means of effects such as split screen and montage, television created an experience that was altogether different from that of the crowds or even of the invited guests. Indeed, the television show co-opted the crowds and the guests and, adding them to the minidocumentaries, commentaries, and special effects, virtually moved reality of the streets, out off the churches and palaces, and into the living room (Dayan & Katz, 1983).

As for conquests, it is easy to see that the arrival of the hero, his deplaning, and his kissing the ground or reviewing the honor guard are endlessly more compelling when the whole world is watching. The very arrival of Sadat at the Tel Aviv airport represented, long before the words came, the recognition by an Arab leader for which Israel had waited so long. Israel and the world understood the gesture immediately and changed their attitudes toward Egypt, even as they ignored the hard line that the smiling hero took in his speech to Knesset. Similarly, the openness of the Pope in Poland was read in his gestures, not in his words, thus reversing the priority of the verbal over the visual that characterizes normal television news (Katz, Adoni, & Parness, 1977). Television offers such persons a messianic role on the stage of the world, inviting them to outdo themselves and each other in the making of history.

Media Events and Conflict Management

The integrative character of media events should not blind us to their relationship to the conflicts of the daily news. After all, these are ceremonial occasions in which conflict is put into the larger perspective of the basic values of the society, so that conflict can be expressed, respoken, and overcome. Thus, the live broadcasting of contests—the Olympic Games, for example—is, in effect, a symbolic transformation of political conflict.

Televised contests (see Table 9-1) frame conflicts and miniaturize them, sometimes taking them outside the realm of politics into sports or song.

Conquests are a process whereby conflicts, as in the Middle East before Sadat, evaporate in the aura of a hero who evokes universal admiration and focuses it on a new symbolic order; thus peaceful gestures, and not only hostile ones, entered the realm of Middle Eastern possibilities. The hero's daring seems to invite admiration and identification even from those who are disadvantaged by his triumph. One suspects (we are not certain) that the Russians, who lost the race to the moon, were no less dazzled by the astronauts, just as the Arab states, deeply embarrassed by Sadat, may have admired his dramaturgy, if not his message.

Coronations are a call for intermission in daily conflict in order to recall shared values. Thus, the marriage of Charles and Diana spoke of the glorious British heritage that transcended a failing economy, the riots in London neighborhoods, and the fighting in Northern Ireland. The wedding was a truly liminal (Turner, 1977) interlude in which conflict could not play a role. Had Britain's conflicts not been suspended voluntarily, as they were, they would have been altogether overlooked by television. Is the rallying to tradition and *communitas* less real than the fighting? We think not. Holidays are as real as ordinary workdays.

Thus, media events do not simply avoid conflict or substitute for it, as might be thought. They are not merely escapist. Rather, they often look straight into the eye of conflict and make an effort to contain it. In this respect, each of the three genres of media events addresses conflict in its own way. Contests miniaturize and frame conflict; coronations redirect attention to shared values; conquests direct attention to a great human achievement around which both supporters and opponents can rally. Media events can accomplish these things by activating great publics to "thrust greatness" upon an occasion and its heros.

Acknowledgments. The "Media Events" project is funded by the John and Mary F. Markle Foundation. Thanks are due to Ambassador S. Dinitz for inspiring our analysis of shuttle diplomacy.

References

Alexander, J. (1982, January). *Media ritual in social crisis: The Senate Watergate hearings.* Paper presented at the Symposium on Communication Media and Social Integration, Annenberg School of Communication, University of Southern California, Los Angeles.

Boorstin, D. (1962). *The Image.* New York: Atheneum.

Comiskey, P., Bryant, J., & Zillman, D. (1977). Commentary as a substitute for action. *Journal of Communication, 27,* 150–152.

Dayan, D., & Katz, E. (1983). Rituels publics á usage privée: Metamorphose televisée d'un mariage royal. *Annales: Economies, Sociétés, Civilisations, 38,* 3–20.

Katz, E., Adoni, H., Parness, P. (1977). Remembering the news. *Journalism Quarterly, 54*, 231-239.

Katz, E., Dayan, D., & Motyl, P. (1983). Television diplomacy: Sadat in Jerusalem. In G. Gerbner & M. Siefert (Eds.), *World communications* (pp. 127-136). New York: Longmans.

Lazarsfeld, P. F., & Merton, R. K. (1948). Mass communication, popular taste, and organized social action. In L. Bryson (Ed.), *Communication of ideas* (pp. 95-118). New York: Harper.

Schwartz, B. (1983). The Whig conception of heroic leadership. *American Sociological Review, 48*, 18-33.

Shils, E., & Young, M. (1956). The meaning of the coronation. *Sociological Review, 1*, 63-82.

Turner, V. (1977). Process, system and symbol. *Daedalus, 106*, 61-80.

Wills, G. (1980). The greatest story ever told. *Columbia Journalism Review, 18*, 25-33.

Chapter 10

The Creation of Political Leaders in the Context of American Politics in the 1970s and 1980s

Nadav Kennan and Martha Hadley

The major underlying assumption in the conceptualization and execution of the political process described in this chapter is that a political candidate, whether an incumbent or a challenger, is, at one level, a consumer product (like cottage cheese, salted snacks, or toothpaste) that can be marketed in the same way as such products. Consequently, the political research process discussed here consists of marketing research and marketing strategy processes that were adapted to and have become a part of many political campaign arenas.

This chapter is an analytical description of an action-oriented political process that has been used by our firm, Kennan Research & Consulting, Inc., over the past several years. The specific involvement of the authors with political campaigns has been in terms of researching, "thinking," and conceptualizing campaign strategies. The nature of the political campaigns in which our firm has participated has called for a rather deep involvement in every aspect of the political campaign process. Some of the elements of the research and political process described have been used in different political campaigns by other consultants in the U.S. over the past 10 to 15 years. It is our intention to present a description of our attempts to unify and integrate both new and more established elements into a comprehensive, conceptually motivated and action-oriented process that has been constructed and used successfully by our firm in various political campaigns over the past eight years.

Although the description of the process enables us to conceptualize and to shape a point of view, no special attempts are made to create, establish, or refer to political theories.

The operational flow of this process, which is schematically described in Figure 10-1 and referred to throughout, has been crystallized during and as a result of mayoral, gubernatorial, senatorial, and presidential campaigns.

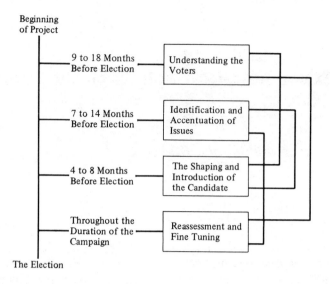

Figure 10-1. The creation of a political leader operational flow.

Although the conceptual flow of campaign activities has been the same regardless of the type of campaign, some specific, rather insignificant modifications and deviations were made in response to the specific nature, size, and complexity of each of the campaigns we have been involved with.

To clarify the components of this process, the following sections provide a description of the players in this process, the voters and their perceptions, the identification and accentuation of social issues, the shaping and introduction of the candidates, and reassessment and fine tuning in the course of the campaign. We conclude with a discussion of some of our own thoughts on this process and its implications.

The Players

Although ostensibly the candidate, whether an incumbent or a challenger, should be viewed as the leading actor or player in a campaign, realistically he or she assumes, at least at times, the role of a puppet whose strings are being pulled by and whose libretto is being composed and even being sung by the members of the candidate's political campaign group. The members of this group, who interact intensively with each other, can be divided into two separate segments, the *creators* and the *implementers* (Figure 10-2).

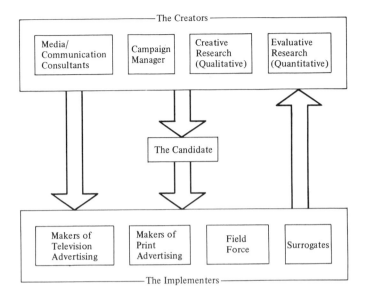

Figure 10-2. The creation of the political leader, creators, and executors of the campaign.

Creators

The creators segment is composed of four groups of players.

The Media/Communication Consultants

These people, who are characteristically political scientists by education with broad experience in political campaigns, assume a key position in the creation and execution of campaign strategy and tactics. They also advise the candidate and the campaign group on issues such as selection of the proper advertising media; the nature, execution, and timing of television commercials; use of print and other forms of communication and advertising; public relations, especially with regard to the media (television commentators, journalists, etc.); and fund-raising activities.

With the exception of the campaign manager, the media/communication consultants are the most active and involved people throughout the campaign. In fact, such people frequently carry more weight, particularly in terms of coordination and setting of direction, than either the campaign manager or even the candidate. Media/communication experts are independent consultants who are hired by the candidate for the duration of the campaign.

The Campaign Manager

The campaign manager is usually a person who grew up within the political party or the political machine context. He or she is usually directly employed by the candidate (and/or the party) and is basically an administrative coordinator. The campaign manager, together with the media/communication consultants, assumes the responsibility for the smooth operation of the campaign group, controls the campaign budgets, and "holds the hand" of the candidate. Although ostensibly this person plays a major role in the creator segment of the campaign group, in reality he or she is more of a coordinator and executor than a creator and direction setter. Throughout the campaign, the campaign manager becomes a permanent "shadow" of the candidate.

The Creative Researcher

The function of creative research is a rather new phenomenon which was recently pioneered in the political campaign arena in the United States by consulting firms like our own. The person who fulfills this function is usually a psychologist who is experienced in conceptualization and implementation of marketing and advertising strategies and tactics. The creative researcher is essentially the "brain" of the campaign group. He or she gathers and analyzes information from voters and, together with the media/communication consultants, conceptualizes and offers the directions for the creation and execution of the campaign strategies as well as the formulation and crystallization of the candidate's political platform. More specifically, the creative researcher is directly responsible for the conceptualization, design, and execution of the qualitative research studies, the analysis of the data, and the presentation of the results as well as being instrumental in the design and construction of the evaluative and quantitative research tools.

Although fully involved with every activity of the campaign group and the candidate (on some occasions also assuming the role of the candidate's therapist), the creative researcher makes every attempt to remain in the background of the campaign—those who take the position of outsider are often able to see things more clearly. Throughout the campaign, this person interacts intensively with the media/communication consultants, the campaign manager, the evaluative (quantitative) researchers, the creative people such as the makers of the television commercials and other advertising materials, and obviously, the candidate.

The Evaluative Researcher

The evaluative researcher is better known in the American political world as the pollster. Up until a few years ago, and actually to some degree even now, some pollsters (especially the more famous ones) fulfilled many, if not all, of the functions presently undertaken by the creative researcher. However, because of some obvious shortcomings of quantitative political polls, which result from the fact that such polls offer only very limited diagnostic information, the trend in the United States is to use polls and pollsters for evaluative rather than creative, direction-setting purposes. The pollster is usually an experienced quantitative researcher, especially in the areas of sample selection, construction of polling questionnaires, and interpreting computer tables. He or she interacts with the campaign manager, the media/communication consultants, the creative researcher, and, to a limited degree, the candidate. However, there are some four or five highly reputable and famous pollsters in the United States whose involvement with the campaign group and the candidate is very intensive.

The Implementers

Producers of Television Advertising

These people usually work for or are associated with advertising agencies. Their area of responsibility is in shooting, editing, and packaging the television commercials created for the campaign. Although they report directly to the media/communication consultants and the campaign manager, the conceptualization of the political commercials they create is usually done by the media/communication consultants and the creative researcher on the basis of the analysis of exploratory, qualitative, creative research. The commercials produced are never aired before being qualitatively tested and evaluated by the creative researcher.

Producers of Print Advertising

These people are very similar in their area of expertise to the makers of television advertising, but their specialty is in the creation of print advertising: pamphlets, leaflets, outdoor posters, bumper stickers, and so forth. They report directly to the campaign manager and maintain only limited contact with other members of the campaign group.

The Field Force

These people, who report directly to the campaign manager, are usually either newcomers to the political world or lower-level politicians. They fulfill the function of direct, personal interaction with the voters by distributing leaflets, pamphlets, and other campaign-related communication material as well as by "shaking hands" and attempting to personally convince voters to vote for the candidate. The decisive majority of these people work on a volunteer basis and usually operate within the neighborhoods in which they live. These people maintain only limited contact with the members of the campaign group other than the campaign manager.

The Surrogates

These people usually come from the political or business community, where they occupy positions of opinion leaders. They work on a purely volunteer basis and are usually friends or close associates of the candidate. After the election, if it is successful, they are included in one way or another in the new administration. The surrogates operate by following instructions given to them by the campaign manager, the media/communication consultants, and the creative researcher. They organize voter meetings, give speeches, pull strings behind the scene, and at times are asked to give testimonials in favor of the candidate through either television or the print media. Their involvement in the campaign is also extremely valuable in terms of fund raising.

This description of the campaign group presents only the key participants. Obviously, many other people are actively involved with the campaign, but, with minor exceptions, all of these clearly fall into one or more of the eight functions described.

The Voters and Their Perceptions

Understanding the voters, in terms of their independent constituencies and cumulative perceptions within the prevailing political and social context, is perhaps the most crucial and significant objective of the campaign process. This understanding enables the precise mapping of the desires, aspirations, agonies, and problems (both evident and latent) of the voters at a particular point in time. Such a descriptive map serves as the most substantial basis for the conceptualization of the campaign strategy, the political platform of the candidate, and the shaping and packaging of the candidate in the most relevant and desirable fashion as defined by the voters' expectations.

Understanding the Voters' Contexts and Voter Segments

The purpose of understanding the voter's contexts as viewed by different voter segments is very simple. In any election, the way voters perceive and side with candidates, issues, or referendums is determined by the way they view the national, state and local sociopolitical situations as they relate to their lives. Consequently, in presenting a political issue, candidate, or referendum, one must have a thorough understanding of how voters perceive their situation and how they are being affected by the prevailing social and political issues and situations.

Research activities, which are conducted in order to gain a clear and precise understanding of the voters' perceptions of the political and social context, are conceptualized and executed in such a way as to enable the clear ascertainment of (a) the issues and concerns (national, state, city, neighborhood, and personal) that voters are aware of and involved with; (b) the way these issues are perceived and interpreted by voters at a particular time; and (c) the way or ways that such issues are being, will be, or can be crystallized in voters' minds into an election-related point of view.

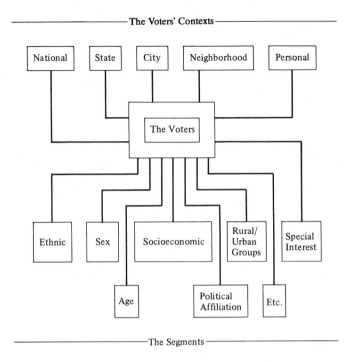

Figure 10-3. Understanding the voters' contexts and voter segments.

Obviously, although many, if not most, of these issues are of common concern to all voters, it is crucial to gauge precisely the degree and nature of this concern by the different voter segments that compose the universe of constituencies for the specific election. Such segments include, among others, ethnic groups, men versus women, socioeconomic groups, rural versus urban residents, special interest groups, and political groups.

In addition to the alternate perspectives on issues obtained from the different constituencies, the perception of more local and larger social and political situations or contexts as contributors to issues is important. It is interesting and at times even fascinating to realize the degree to which the prevailing perceptions of the national situation have an impact on the personal, individual psychology of the voter, with implications even for mayoral elections. Thus, regardless of the type of election (for mayor, senator, governor, etc.), careful exploration and understanding of each of the social and political contexts should be attempted.

An interesting example can be taken from the 1983 mayoral election in Chicago, in which the rather depressed national economic situation resulted in a strong sense of insecurity, a lack of hope, and a sense of personal despair and helplessness among most of the voters, particularly among the unemployed or those who were affected by the recession. (Figures 10-4, 10-5, and 10-6, excerpted from research findings on the election, provide a

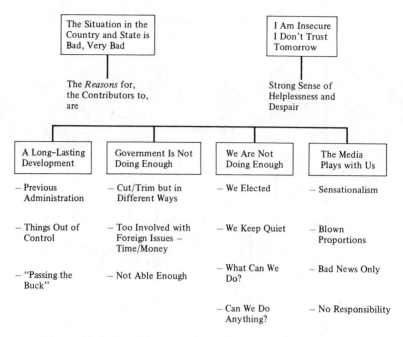

Figure 10-4. People's perceptions of the national situation.

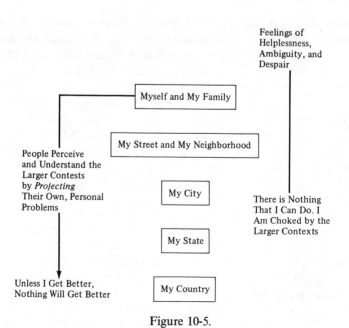

Figure 10-5.

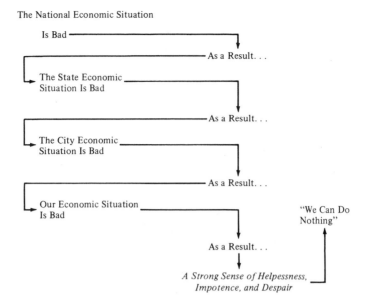

The National Economic Situation

Is Bad ——————————————

As a Result...

The State Economic
Situation Is Bad

As a Result...

The City Economic
Situation Is Bad

As a Result...

Our Economic Situation
Is Bad

"We Can Do
Nothing"

As a Result...

*A Strong Sense of Helpessness,
Impotence, and Despair*

Figure 10-6.

diagrammatic overview of the situation at that time in Chicago.) This sense of helplessness, despair, and lack of hope for a "better tomorrow" expressed by voters resulted in the construction of a reality structure which once understood and crystallized served as an important basis for the identification of the essential attributes and qualities that the people of Chicago desired to see in the mayor of their city, as diagrammed in Figure 10-7.

To reach such an understanding of the voters, part of which can be gained only by penetrating beyond the superficial level of their response, the research activities undertaken are mainly qualitative in nature. These qualitative studies are based on two separate yet highly integrated methodologies described below.

Personal In-Depth Interviews With Opinion Leaders
Opinion leaders, such as union leaders, prominent businesspersons, journalists and reporters, representatives of civic organizations, neighborhood officials, and so on, are interviewed by highly trained psychologists who under no circumstances divulge the real reason and the sponsor of the research study being conducted. Each of these in-depth interviews (IDI), which usually take about one to two hours to complete, is conducted in a form that is ostensibly a free-flowing discussion, but in fact is moderated by the interviewer, who has been given a series of topics to be covered and who carefully probes the responses to each topic until he or she feels that a thorough understanding has been gained of the feelings and perceptions of

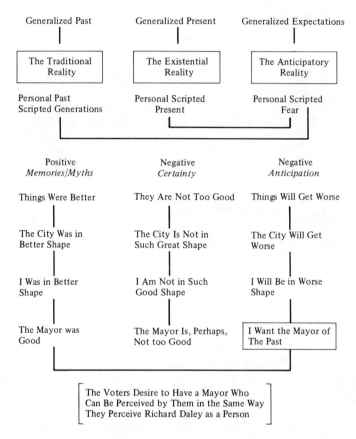

Figure 10-7. The reality structure and the people of Chicago.

the respondents on the given issues. At times the conversation takes on its own direction and form, revealing the significance of issues that could not have been anticipated in the preliminary planning of the interview.

Focus Group Interviews With Voters
Each focus group interview (FGI) is attended by 10 to 12 respondents who are selected to represent the different segments of the voter population (ethnic groups, socioeconomic segments, special-interest groups, political groups, etc.). Each FGI, which takes about two hours to complete and is conducted by a trained psychologist, takes place in a special one-way-mirrored research facility and is tape-recorded (and at times videotaped).

The moderator introduces himself or herself, states the general purpose of the discussion (not revealing the sponsorship), and then proceeds to raise questions and issues and to facilitate their discussion. Generally, the process is guided by a topical outline that is developed ahead of time. However, part of the art of running such groups is enabling the participants to develop what appear to be salient lines of discussion, regardless of whether or not they have been planned. Such a group works best when, in a very short period of time, it develops its own momentum and the interactions between respondents become intense and, at least partially, take on their own direction.

The moderator's role, besides giving everyone a chance to talk and making sure the discussion does not drift to unrelated topics, is to probe issues as they arise and to conceptualize what is being said well enough so that he or she can then throw out the next relevant question.

The guideline for such a group discussion, as with the IDIs, follows a concentric logic. For example, one might begin with a question as broad as, "What is going on in the United States today?" The goal is to encourage respondents to explore various issues and circumstances at the national level as voters see them and as they relate to their own lives, and then move on to the next inner circle or layer, which might be the situation in the given state or city, while always referring back and creating links to the more general issues just discussed. The last part of the interview is focused on current political candidates and their evaluation in the context of neighborhood, city, and state issues as they have been discussed up to this point.

Special attention is given to ascertaining the feelings of the respondents toward the issues and the terminology used by them to express their opinions and feelings. Their ideas on what action-oriented solutions or "next steps" would look like are also explored.

Upon completion of the interviews, the data are analyzed by the moderators, as well as by other analysts who listen to the tapes. A report of findings is issued. Such a report is constructed in a way that (a) clearly communicates the findings and their implications to the candidate and the political campaign group; (b) points out the issues that appear to be the most important and offers initial, hypothetical solutions; (c) presents and recommends the main "building blocks" for the creation and construction of the campaign strategy and tactics; and (d) offers initial directions for the creation of the most desirable, effective presentation of the candidate.

Identification and Accentuation of Social Issues

To begin to lay out the basic parameters and the conceptual and executional directions of the campaign strategy and its tactics, the results of the qualitative research, conducted to gain a clear understanding of the issues and problems of the voters, are presented to and thoroughly discussed with the creators in the campaign group. This presentation and discussion are conducted in the form of a brainstorming session.

Several main topics from the list of issues that voters are concerned with are selected in such a way as to represent those issues which: (a) are most crucial to the voters; (b) have the potential for either action and real improvements or for believable promises regarding future solutions that can be made within the time period preceding the election date; (c) the candidate is being or can be made to be associated with and perceived by the voters as being able to do something about; and (d) are of concern to the largest number of voters, regardless of their ethnic background, political affiliations, socioeconomic status, age, or other characteristics.

After the selection and identification of the key target issues, the creative researcher, the media/communication consultants, and the campaign manager clearly identify, define, and crystallize each of the selected issues primarily in terms of the underlying, deeper implications of each. This process is of extreme importance because, in most cases, the apparent components of a given issue are no more than a rather thin external shell, whereas the deeper, underlying implications are the real and substantial core of the problem. The following example helps clarify this point.

One of the major issues of concern to the Chicago voters in the 1983 mayoral election was public housing, and at the time of the election this issue was symbolized by a low-income housing project called Cabrini Green. This housing project, built about six years prior to the election, had been managed, like all other public housing projects in Chicago, by the Chicago Housing Authority, a municipal organization reporting to the mayor. Over the years, however, people who lived in this housing project (all of whom were either black or Hispanic) experienced numerous problems such as poor security, faulty plumbing, and cockroach infestation in the apartments. About a year before the election, the residents of the project as well as many other Chicagoans became aware that Mr. Swibel, the director of the Chicago Housing Authority, was exercising ineffective management. In spite of the fact that Swibel had been a longtime friend and supporter of Mayor Jane Byrne, she fired him from his position and offered the management of the Chicago Housing Authority to two black people. The residents and almost all the other citizens (including black voters) perceived the newly appointed black officials as not being fully qualified or suited for such a position. These new directors were replaced by the mayor a short time thereafter by three white directors who were better qualified for the job.

While involved in this game of musical chairs, the mayor felt that moving into Cabrini Green would be perceived by the residents of the project and the people of Chicago as a strong indication of her devotion for and concern with the project and the people who lived there. Accordingly, she moved into the project with her family.

Following is a description of the apparent components of the issue, Figure 10-8, taken from a research report submitted by Kennan Research to the campaign group. It points out the underlying, deeper implications of the issue and the way that voters interpreted it with regard to their attitudes toward and images of the mayor.

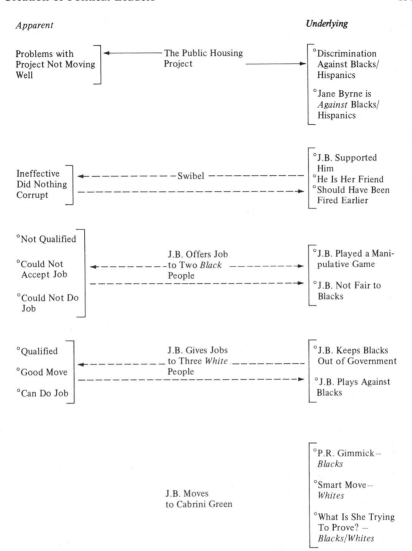

Figure 10-8. The apparent and underlying implicatons.

When this specific issue was redefined and recommunicated to the people of Chicago, it was framed in a way that conveyed the messages that Mayor Byrne: (a) did not discriminate against blacks or Hispanics; (b) was not against blacks and Hispanics, but actually for them; (c) did not support Swibel even though he was her friend and supporter; (d) was not playing a manipulative game in her nominating black directors to the Chicago Housing Authority; (e) was not attempting to keep blacks out of city government; and (f) did not move into Cabrini Green as a public relations activity, but as a statement of commitment.

This recommunication was successfully implemented by the following actions, among others: (a) a series of meetings with black public opinion and community leaders; (b) nomination of two more black people, who were housing-related professionals, to the Housing Authority; (c) "open house" parties for neighbors given by the mayor in her Cabrini Green apartment; (d) several appearances by the mayor in black and Hispanic churches during Sunday services; and (e) two television commercials presenting residents' testimonials regarding the improvements made in the housing project and their firsthand appreciation of the mayor's devotion to and involvement with the project.

During the same initial brainstorming sessions, in addition to the crystallization and framing of issues, decisions are made regarding the types of media and other means, or communication channels to be used in recommunicating issues to the voters. These usually include television commercials, distribution of pamphlets and leaflets, press conferences with journalists, meetings with community leaders and other public opinion leaders, press releases, and so forth. The nature of the recommunication activity is decided upon in light of the perceived severity and importance of each of the issues and the available finances and budgets.

The framing of the issues to be recommunicated to the voters and the exact nature of the means of communication are then discussed with the different executors of the campaign (commercial and print advertisement makers, the field force, and the surrogates), who in turn translate the creators' decision into actual communication activities. Once the final drafts of the various means of communication (television commercials, print advertisements, etc.) are produced, they are tested through a set of FGIs to ensure that these communication tools do in fact communicate what was meant to be communicated and are accepted by the voters as believable and convincing communication pieces. The results of such evaluations enable the final, precise tuning of the communication pieces.

During this stage of the campaign, every effort is made to minimize the exposure of the candidate himself or herself, in order to draw and direct voters' attention to the reframed issues communicated to them.

Shaping and Introducing the Candidate

The purpose of this step in the campaign process, which usually takes place between four and eight months before the election, is to "create" a candidate whose personality characteristics best comply with: (a) voters' perceptions of what the most desirable person for the position ought to be; (b) the reframing of the issues that have been recommunicated and accentuated; and (c) existing images of and attitudes toward the candidate that prevail among the voters (this is especially important when the candidate is an incumbent who has been in the public eye for some time). Obviously, the creation of such a person is not by any means a simple objective to satisfy, especially when the candidate is an incumbent. However, years of experience with such activities have proven again and again that, if carefully and meticulously handled, this objective can be successfully achieved as long as a way or ways are found to utilize the real or perceived personality traits of the candidate in the reframing, in such a way that they are perceived as best fitting the voters' prevailing expectations and needs for the resolution of voters' ambiguities.

As an example, extensive research conducted among the residents of a major New England city showed without a shadow of doubt that their opinions and perceptions of the personality of the mayor of the city, who was running for reelection, were generally negative. He was viewed by the voters as being "an aloof, arrogant sonofabitch who doesn't give a damn for people, utilizes a very effective political machine, and exhibits obvious disregard for what people think of him." The intensity of the voters' perceptions and opinions was such that any effort by the campaign group to change it would have been either ineffective or ridiculous. Consequently, the image of the mayor was reframed to present a mayor "who is highly capable of successfully running the city in a way that the majority of city residents benefit from because he *is* an aloof, arrogant, sonofabitch who is tough, determined, action oriented, not influenced by political pressures, and not a prisoner of political debt." The major theme of this campaign, which was communicated to the voters mainly by insinuation rather than directly, was "You don't have to love me as a person, but rather appreciate the positive results of my actions and activities as the mayor of this city." (It is interesting to note that when Kennan Research first got involved with this campaign, the mayor was running 26 percentage points behind his challenger in the polls, yet on election day he won the election with 56 percent of the votes.)

In shaping the candidate, much attention and very careful planning are devoted to the following: (a) What is to be said by the candidate, to whom, and when? (b) the exact language and terminology used by the candidate in his or her speeches, press releases, and television commercials; (c) the specific issues and subject matter that the candidate is to communicate to the voters; and (d) the actual physical appearance of the candidate, including haircut, style of clothing, and the like. An excellent example that shows how the precise shaping of a candidate 'through meticulous reframing and communication of such reframing to the voters' has great potential for success is the 1980 gubernatorial campaign in West Virginia. At the beginning of Jay Rockefeller's campaign for reelection (he had already served one term), the voters in West Virginia were negatively predisposed toward him on two separate yet highly integrated levels. As an individual, "Jay" was viewed as being neither forceful nor effective as a leader. As a

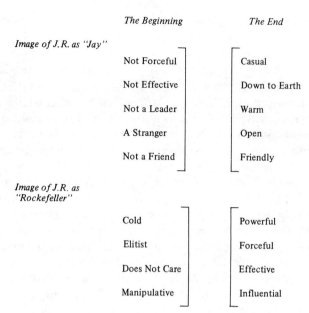

Figure 10-9. Voter evaluation of Jay Rockefeller at the beginning and the end of the campaign.

member of a very well-known family, the Rockefellers, he was viewed as being cold and elitist, not caring for others, and manipulative. (These were images that the people of West Virginia attributed to the Rockefeller family.)

However, a careful study and analysis of voters' opinions showed that each of these negatives could be interpreted as having a positive counterpart. Consequently, Jay Rockefeller was reframed and represented to the voters in a way that emphasized the positive counterparts of the negatives. By the time the election took place, Jay Rockefeller enjoyed a decisive victory and became the only major Democrat to win reelection during the Republican landslide victories at the time of the election of Ronald Reagan. Figure 10-9 summarizes the changes in voters' assessment of the candidate as a result of his successful reframing.

The framing of a candidate who is a challenger is usually a simpler process than the reframing of an incumbent. Whereas an incumbent's image in many cases has to be redefined, changed, and repositioned, the image of the challenging candidate can often be created from scratch.[1]

---

[1]This is especially true with regards to "new" less known challengers. There are, however, exceptions when the challenger has been a known entity and carries substantial political equity.

Obviously, even when creation from scratch is possible, great care and attention should be devoted to ensuring that voters can find logical as well as emotional bases in their attempts to associate the image created with the challenger himself or herself.

An example of this situation is provided by one of the younger sons of a very wealthy and rather well-known Midwestern family, who became the challenger in a senatorial election. The level of awareness of this person among the voters was not only very low but almost nonexistent. People had no idea who the challenger was, what experience and capabilities he had, or what kind of senator he might make. What people did know was his name and the fact that he was very young—34 years of age.

In the creation and presentation of this challenger, two main objectives had to be achieved: (a) to introduce him as a person who, because of his background, past experience, enthusiasm, and devotion, could become a good senator and deliver what is expected of a senator; and (b) to minimize the age-related negatives. The first objective was fulfilled by presenting, in a logical, down-to-earth manner, the candidate's performance qualities and attributes—the logical base. The second objective was fulfilled by playing on the strings of parents' love for their young adult children and bringing the voters to relate emotionally to the challenger in the same way they would relate to their own offspring. The presentation of the challenger was achieved through the candidate's television comments, his personal meetings with voters' groups, visits to retirement homes, interviews with local journalists and television personalities, and similar tactics.

The major shortcoming (which at times can lead to backfiring) of any attempt to create an image for a challenger is the high potential for crossing the thin line of believability. The exact identification and understanding of this thin line is crucial and highly complex because the personality characteristics of voters of different parts of the United States are not the same. The people of New York, who tend to be rather cynical, would offer much stronger believability opposition than the people of Arkansas, who are more receptive and easily won over. The people of Minnesota have very strong roots in and adhere to their conservative, "don't-move-too-fast," Scandinavian heritage, and therefore they are less apt to accept a new challenger than the people of Southern California, who tend to be rootless, having no tradition or heritage to which they subscribe, and thus offer a higher potential for accepting any new challenger who is presented to them in a spontaneous, convincing manner.

Our experience with political campaigns has proven again and again that as long as the reframing of an incumbent or the framing of a challenger is meticulously and carefully conceptualized and executed, and the financial capabilities of the candidate are sound and sufficient, with only few exceptions the presentation of the candidate to the voters yields successful results—the person is elected.

Reassessment and Fine Tuning

The value and the degree of success of each of the actions and steps we have discussed are strongly related to, if not heavily dependent on, the nature and quality of the research activities conducted. Two types of research studies are necessary: direction-setting and evaluative research.

Direction-setting research enables one to understand "where the voters' heads are at" with regard to the issues, the candidates, and the election. As we have indicated, the results of such research are crucial for the conceptualization, establishment, and implementation of campaign strategy and tactics as well as the creation and framing of the candidate.

Evaluative research is based on a set of qualitative and quantitative research studies which serve as longitudinal evaluative tools for the campaign activities. Whereas direction-setting research serves as the basis for the starting point of the campaign, evaluative research enables the reduction of uncertainty and a continuous, dynamic fine tuning of the campaign activities.

Timing and Execution of Direction-Setting Research

As previously discussed, the research studies conducted to meet this objective are chiefly qualitative in nature. Usually, these studies are conducted as the first step of the campaign activities within 9 to 18 months of the election date. These studies are based on both individual IDIs and FGIs.

In-Depth Interviews
These IDIs are conducted with opinion leaders, journalists, and other prominent representatives of the voters' universe. From 15 to 20 such interviews are conducted for mayoral, gubernatorial, senatorial, or congressional elections, and between 50 and 100 for presidential elections. All of these interviews are conducted by highly trained psychologists and are tape-recorded and analyzed by trained research analysts or psychologists. The final results and evaluations are then presented to the campaign group.

Focus Group Interviews
These FGIs are conducted among the voting population. Each FGI involves 10 to 12 participants who are selected to represent the different segments that comprise the voters' universe. The respondents for these FGIs are screened through telephone interviews, and eligible individuals are invited to attend the group discussion. The participants are paid $15 to $40 per person for their participation. All group interviews are conducted in a specially designed facility that provides a one-way-mirrored room to allow discrete viewing of the discussion by the campaign group.

The FGIs are moderated by highly trained psychologists and are taped, analyzed, and presented to the campaign group. From 6 to 10 direction-setting FGIs are conducted for mayoral elections, 10 to 20 for gubernatorial, senatorial, or congressional elections, and 100 to 300 for presidential elections.

Timing and Execution of Evaluative Research

Evaluative research is primarily composed of both qualitative and quantitative longitudinal studies. In addition, ad hoc television evaluative research studies are conducted (communications evaluative research).

Longitudinal Evaluative Research: Qualitative Component
From about a month after the campaign activities begin until three to four weeks before the election, "waves" of FGIs are conducted, with intervals of two to three months between each wave. The purpose of these waves, which are usually conducted among specific voter group segments, is to gauge qualitatively the impact of the different campaign activities and the voters' reactions to them. These FGIs are never viewed as having statistical value, but rather as an indispensable source of diagnostic information, which is of extreme importance for the deep and thorough understanding of data gathered by quantitative evaluative research.

Rather frequently the information gathered through such waves of qualitative evaluations proves to be more incisive than results of large-scale quantitative studies. For example, about eight weeks before the 1983 Chicago mayoral election, the results of several waves of quantitative public opinion polls clearly indicated that the incumbent, Jane Byrne, had a clear and significant lead of about 12 to 15 percentage points over her opponents—Richie Daley and Harold Washington. However, the results of a wave of several FGIs strongly indicated that Byrne might lose the election to Harold Washington (a black candidate) if the noticeable yet seemingly small sparks of an emotional/ethnic spiritual uprising syndrome kept growing and turned into a full-fledged flame.

When these results were presented to the campaign group, a reaction of disbelief prevailed and no counteractions were conceptualized or executed. (In fact, we seriously doubt that there was any chance at that point of Byrne winning over Washington, regardless of any campaign activities that could have been executed). Thus, in spite of the quantitative public opinion polls which predicted a clear victory for Jane Byrne, she lost her election to Harold Washington.

Longitudinal Evaluative Research: Quantitative Public Opinion Polls
From the onset of the campaign up to about four weeks before the election, a wave of quantitative public opinion polls is conducted about once a month. During the last four weeks of the campaign, such polls are conducted about once a week. The questionnaires used in these polls are constructed to ascertain, among other things, the following: respondents' opinions regard-

ing campaign issues, their opinions of the candidate overall and with respect to his or her specific attributes and qualities, and their awareness and rating of the campaign commercials and other candidates' commercials. In addition, the question is asked, "If the election were taking place today, whom would you vote for?"

Generally such questionnaires include very few open-ended questions and are mainly based on structured rating scales. The sample for such studies is drawn in a way that allows random selections of representatives of the universe of voters. The sample size for each of these wave ranges from about 400 respondents in a mayoral, gubernatorial, senatorial, or congressional election to 1,500 respondents in a presidential election. The data collected are tabulated and presented to the campaign group along with computer printouts which include demographic and some attitudinal breaks. All interviews are conducted by telephone.

Communication Evaluative Research
With only a few exceptions, all television commercials prepared for the campaign are evaluated prior to being televised. Such evaluations are conducted through a set of FGIs with respondents who are selected to represent the specific target segments toward which such commercials are directed. The results of these FGIs help to eliminate commercials that miss the point, and they serve as a substantial, action-oriented basis for improving commercials that are well directed but would benefit from additional fine tuning.

Regardless of the type and nature of the study conducted, whether qualitative or quantitative, the results are presented in the form of a final oral and written report within a very short time from the beginning of the interviews. Results of qualitative research are presented within three weeks of the beginning of the interviews, whereas results of quantitative public opinion polls are usually presented within 36 hours after the completion of the interviews.

Reflections on the Process: The Creation of a Political *Leader* or The *Creation* of a Political *Manager*?

The process we have described is one that we have followed numerous times and that has resulted in the successful election of several candidates. Two major questions come to mind. First, "Why is this process successful, or at least, why is it so successful at this particular time and place in American politics?" Second, "Are the people who are being elected through the use of this process political leaders?" The several possible answers we present are not to be viewed as "truths" or even as rigorous points of view; they are simply reflections we have made in the process of working on campaigns and discussing these questions among ourselves.

Why Is This Process So Successful?

The first and rather obvious point is that in the past 20 or so years there has been a major shift of power and of the means of communicating with the voters from the old-line political machines (such as Tammany Hall, the Chicago machine, the Irish Mafia), as we knew them, to the media. By the media we mean both the paid media, from which political candidates or parties purchase time, and free media, which are not paid for by the candidate or party (at least not in dollars), but which provide daily coverage of and commentary on candidates, the political party, and the campaign issues.

Thus, if the media have become enormously powerful in the United States (and they have), in terms of being able to influence and manipulate the public, those who can manipulate the media to their own benefit can become powerful. The process described above is, in a way, a media-manipulating process.

A second point is that during the past 15 to 20 years the people of the United States have become highly trained consumers of goods, information, and concepts; they are greatly influenced by the media with regard to what to buy, when to consume, why to consume, and what opinions to have. These trained consumers rely on the media to explain to them what is happening in the world and what they should do about it. In short, the media interpret reality and provide the trained consumer with seemingly explainable or understandable parameters of beliefs and courses of action, whether it be in regard to what they should eat for breakfast or whom they should vote for in an election. It could even be said that the function the media play today in the lives of the American people is one of shaping or defining reality. This is very much the same function that political ideologies have played in the lives of other peoples at other times. That is to say, in the United States today, media both provide an interpretation of everyday life and of larger events and clearly suggest directions for action. Perceptions of the present and expectations and hopes for the future are greatly influenced by the media, which are the primary means of obtaining information and the primary organizers of this information.

One implication is that the realities being shaped by the media in the United States today are immediate and transient. Because messages are shaped and positioned by different interests at different times with different objectives, they have very little foresight or larger perspective on what has happened before and what will happen in the future.

Another observation is that life in the United States today is extremely complex and on such a large scale that, with the decline of traditional institutions and values (such as solid church organizations), there is a real inability on the part of most people to comprehend or conceptualize what is going on. In fact, the diversity and scale with which the average individual is faced are such that the response is, generally, confusion that results in ambiguity. Thus, *any* conceivable source that reduces this ambiguity, provides even a basic conceptualization of what is going on, offers answers as to why it is going on, or suggests the directions to be followed is a highly attractive source of information that the individual will be most apt to follow.

One of the focal points of the process we have described is its ability to ascertain in some detail the particular ambiguities and confusions that face people at a given time and to resolve them by responding to them in a highly tailored fashion. People find these kinds of clarifications furnished by the media, resulting from the process we have described, highly attractive. They provide concepts and directions that they are immediately compelled to follow simply because they speak so directly to their own confusions and uncertainties.

One of the reasons why the people of this country seem to be in great need of interpretations of current realities and directions for action is that there has been an acknowledged destruction or decline of the meaning of traditional political terminology in the United States. Terms such as *radical, reactionary, liberal, conservative, republican*, and *democrat* no longer have the same clear meanings as in the past. That is, they do not stand for or refer to clear alternative explanations for what is happening, how to relate to it, and what to do about it. Even economic terms such as *supply side, Keynesian, inflation, depression*, and *recession* are not understood or adequate anymore for explaining to the individual (and to the government) why paychecks do not stretch as far as they could three or four years ago. Thus, people are looking for new clarifications of what is happening around them, because the old conceptual system for explaining it and providing various references is proving inadequate.

Perhaps one of the most important transitions that American society has gone and is going through—a transition that has resulted in invalidating the "old" explanations, reference points, and terminologies—is a transition from abundance to relative scarcity. This transition has resulted in the need for redefining one of the most basic tenets of American life: the American dream, based on the belief that those who work hard will be better off than their parents at the midpoint of their own lives. In the face of what most average citizens consider to be an earthshaking awareness that the American dream is no longer feasible for themselves or their children, the need for understanding why this is so, and what the implications are for them for the future, is even greater than simply wanting to understand why the economy is not doing so well.

In short, all of these factors (the growth of the power of the media, the scale and complexity of events today, the changing economic reality, the need for redefinition of the American dream, the inadequacy of traditional political terminology, etc.) have resulted in the evolution of a new contemporary political and social context that includes a great deal of confusion and ambiguity—ambiguity that people yearn to have explained to them and resolved for them.

We are fully aware that these are powerful statements and in many ways overgeneralizations that can be frightening and distorting if taken as absolutes. We mean them as gross generalizations and armchair reflections that are not to be taken without qualification. However, we also believe that stating such points in this extreme way has the advantage of underlining certain rather apparent and crucial trends that do have relevance for why the process we have described is in fact successful in the United States today.

Are the People Elected by This Process Political Leaders?

To answer this question requires some definition of what a political leader is. A precise and accurate definition is not possible, at least within the scope of this paper, and consequently we offer the following as a working definition: A political leader is a person (a) who has a clear ideology, message, set of well-defined beliefs, visions, and future-related directions; (b) who moves forward toward the tomorrows, introduces changes and innovations and opens new or wider horizons, or at least sustains and rejuvenates ideals and beliefs and is able to reinforce these among people; (c) who, because of his or her personality characteristics and beliefs, is able to make people follow him or her; and (d) who is able to introduce and enforce (or at least sustain) the acceptance of the "ten commandments" rather than succumb to and accept the creation by the people of the "golden calf." In light of this definition, the answer to the question, "Does the process we have described create political leaders?" is basically no. We do not create leaders. A political candidate who wins the election as a result of utilizing primarily this process may or may not have his or her own ideologies, beliefs, or messages for the people or new directions to offer. Such a candidate may "play back" to the voters what the voters need to hear, to have, and to follow. Such a person fulfills voters' expectations instead of making the voters subscribe to or follow his or her own ideals. This kind of candidate does not really move forward by introducing changes or significant innovations but rather attempts to maintain or manipulate existing situations according to the voters' expectations. Even when such a candidate introduces changes, they are marginal and motivated by the need to satisfy voters' demands and expectations rather than by a desire to really change or improve those demands. Further, this type of candidate, with only few exceptions, is not able to make the voters follow but rather *accept* and *tolerate* him or her. In sum, such a person would tend to build for the people the golden calf rather than introduce and force them to accept the ten commandments.

In our opinion, the political election process described in this document often enables a person to become a political manager who is very similar in nature to the corporate manager. Some further clarification of this point can be achieved by taking a brief look at the American corporation and its position in the American society and drawing an analogy between the corporate managers and many political leaders of today.

The American corporation is perhaps the most important and visible social structure in the United States. (It would not be surprising if it were recognized, within the relatively near future, as the most important, all-encompassing political structure in the United States.) The contemporary corporate structure offers a clear working model for creating, maintaining, and controlling the essence of the power structure in American society. The conceptual and operational components of the corporation are in the process of being adapted to the American political structure, and the similarities between the political manager and the corporate manager are becoming rather clear. The parallel characteristics outlined in Figure 10-10 provide examples of these similarities.

The Corporate Manager	The Political Manager	The Political Leader
°His/her main responsibility is to promote and maintain the smooth operation of the corporation	°His/her main responsibility to restore, promote and maintain the smooth operation of the government (local or national)	°His/her main responsibility is to improve, promote, advance and create a better government, directions
°Held responsible to short–term "bottom–line"	°Held responsible to short–term performance and budget control	°Held responsible to long–term performance with budget control, per se, not being a major evaluative parameter
°Nominated by the Board of Directors and approved by the shareholders	°Nominated by the party and approved by the voters	°Nominated by the party and approved by the voters
°Not expected or allowed to introduce and execute any significant/ major changes without approval of Board of Directors and shareholders	°Not expected and allowed to introduce and execute any significant/major changes without approval of cabinet/congress senate and the voters	°Expected to introduce and execute major/significant changes and make cabinet/congress/ senate/voters approve such
°Expected to operate within the confines of the corporate policies rather than create such	°Operate within the confines of voters' expectations rather than trying to create such	°Expected to create own context of operation even if it means new creations/changes

Figure 10-10. Some comparisons between corporate managers, political managers, and political leaders.

One wonders if the adaptation of the corporate structure to political life would yield positive or negative results with regard to our social structure, our society, and its individuals. We feel we are in no position, at this point in time, to fully answer this question, because any attempt to judge and evaluate this phenomenon would force us to utilize yesterday's related parameters, and the chances are that these would not be suitable. Further, the newness of this adaptation of the corporate structure to political life does not yet furnish us with a clear and substantial understanding of where it is going to lead and what implications it will have. Finally, the fact that the historical context needed for evaluation and answering this question is still too short, current, and narrow prevents us from assessing it in absolute terms.

However, it appears that American politicians and voters, perhaps without even realizing what is really happening, are accepting or at least adjusting to this transition and seem to be tolerant of and satisfied with it. Years of involvement with political issues and campaigns in the United States made us realize that the American voter, while still professing some mythical desire for real leadership, is more and more expecting and accepting the political manager rather than the innovative, forward-moving leader. It is rather apparent that American voters increasingly view politicians not as a group of individuals who are differentiated from one another, but rather as a commodity composed of undifferentiated and unbranded ingredients.

Chapter 11

Leadership Ms.-Qualified: I. The Gender Bias in Everyday and Scientific Thinking

Lenelis Kruse and Margret Wintermantel

Some Facts and Figures

Only a small proportion of the leadership positions in society are held by women. This applies to women in academic careers at universities, in managerial and executive positions, and in professional fields, as well as in the political realm and in public service. Although women make up about 40% of the work force in countries like West Germany and more than 50% in the United States, they do not hold more than 2% to 4% of the top positions in management. Even in middle-management positions, one finds that no more than about 15% are women. In general, women in professional fields are still concentrated in lower job status categories. Women are consistently paid lower salaries than men, and despite a number of antidiscrimination laws presently in effect, the salary gap is widening rather than decreasing.

Although 40% of the students at West German universities are women, only a small percentage of them will succeed in attaining an assistant professor position. However, as the percentage of women in the middle ranks is gradually growing, the number of women in tenured positions at the top is actually decreasing, although the percentage of women who have acquired the appropriate academic qualifications (*Habilitation*) has markedly increased, by more than 50% from 1980 to 1982 (cf. Bock, Braszeit, & Schmerl, 1983). Whereas the number of male professors grew considerably during that period, the number of women professors went down. Again, it is the female academics who are afflicted most by the growing unemployment rate of Ph.Ds and other highly qualified academics.

Although women constitute almost 53% of the West German population, their share in political responsibility as members of the parliament has not yet reached 10%. Similar or worse proportions hold for most modern democracies: In the United States in 1985 just over 5% of the House of Representatives and 2% of the Senate are women. Even if the average cabinet of a modern government would not present itself without a token woman, women's official role in the political realm is almost negligible. Even increased pressure from legislation for more equal employment opportunities (since 1972 in the United States, and since 1980 in West Germany) has not yet resulted in considerably larger numbers of women in leadership roles.

If newspaper and magazine stories about successful women might succeed in making us believe that more and more women are climbing the career ladder to the top, statistics present a more realistic, although less pleasant picture. Women are still largely underrepresented in recognized leadership positions in the occupational and political realms. The power structure of our society as it manifests itself in its leadership positions is still dominated by men.

What can account for this state of affairs? Several explanations are possible for the differential treatment of women and men. One explanation derives from everyday sex-role or gender stereotyping, which assumes that women lack the attributes, abilities, skills, attitudes, and motivations required for leadership positions. Women are said not to be made for leadership because the characteristics attributed to the female gender role, such as emotionality, sensitivity, expressiveness, and dependency, are perceived as incongruent with leadership prerequisites. Inversely stated, what is demanded in leadership positions are qualities typically associated with men; ambitions, competitiveness, dominance, rationality, and in-dependence.

Another explanation refers to the notion that women are *in fact* inferior to men with respect to actual leadership performance and leadership ef-fectiveness, and it is for this reason that they cannot be leaders, are not found in leadership positions, and will never make it there, a few exceptions notwithstanding. Women's supposed inferiority with respect to leadership effectiveness, however, needs to be explained. Why is it that women make bad leaders, if they do? Explanations are advanced from both person-centered and situation-centered perspectives (Riger & Galligan, 1980). Person-centered explanations stress personality attributes or behavior patterns, such as fear of success (Horner, 1972) and unwillingness to take risks (Hennig & Jardim, 1977) and are, again, prone to gender biases or sex-role stereotypes. Situation-centered explanations stress characteristics of the organizational situation, task characteristics, job environment, group composition, and power structure as critical for women's behavior (e.g. Agassi, 1982; Kanter, 1977; Zellman, 1976). Here again, gender bias may manifest itself in many ways, whether as an aspect of traditional organi-zational structure, as characteristics of peers and subordinates, or as other relevant social-environmental elements.

Whatever explanations, justifications, or excuses are advanced by the lay public or by "experts" for the disproportionate share women have in leadership positions, it is a fact that women do occupy leadership positions and that some of them are recognized as effective, successful leaders. Although their number is still small it is worthwhile to look at their careers, their leadership behavior, and their leadership success and compare them with the respective phenomena on the part of male leaders.

Leadership Research and Theory

If we turn away from facts and figures on women leadership in everyday life and concentrate on the scientific treatment of male and female leadership, this is done with a view to contributing to the review and reconstruction of leadership concepts and theories, as they have developed within psychology and have influenced and determined research questions and approaches. In searching the *Psychological Abstracts* as well as acknowledged reviews of leadership research (e.g., Gibb, 1969; Stogdill, 1974) it becomes conspicuous that until the late 1970s consideration of women as leaders is lacking. Most leadership research before then was carried out by men and dealt almost exclusively with male subjects, whether with student samples or with real-life managers and leaders in corporations and public services. Army officers, senior cadets, chiefs of fire departments, and the like were the preferred subjects of leadership research. When Porter and Geis in 1981 stated that research in the area "deals only with leadership by males, of males, and for males" (p. 39), this is a clear description of traditional leadership research. It has happened only recently that women became of interest for leadership research and that researchers have begun to investigate differences in male and female leadership. It is not only in Bass's revision of *Stogdill's Handbook of Leadership Research* (1981) that the issue of women as leaders plays an important role; quite a number of other recent reviews have dealt extensively with sex differences in leadership (e.g., Brown, 1979; Hoiberg, 1982; Hollander, 1985; Hollander & Yoder, 1980; Nieva & Gutek, 1981; Riger & Galligan, 1980; Terborg, 1977). The fact that until recently leadership research has neither studied women in leading positions, nor considered sex differences an important variable in experimental or field studies of leadership process and success, can be attributed to several causes:

1. Because women have held few positions of recognized leadership it may have been deemed possible to consider them as a negligible quantity.
2. Because scientists are prone to the same stereotypes and biases as laypersons, they may have adhered to the "male-managerial model" (Terborg, 1977) and taken for granted that only men have the aptitudes and skills required for leadership positions. From this perspective, female leaders are to be considered as exceptional or even deviant. Or else, they seem to be endowed with "manlike" qualities, so that findings from male samples can easily be transferred.
3. Another reason that has been advanced to characterize the area and era of sex differences in psychological research in general can easily be applied to leadership research: Many studies using male and female samples have found overlaps and similarities rather than differences

between the two sexes on a multitude of response measures. It then appears only natural to disregard sex differences and to look instead for other variables that could account for variations in behavior. What results is a *psychologie angélique* (Hurtig & Pichevin, 1985), a psychology of "human angels" who are actually thought of as sexless or sex-neutral, but who—in the case of psychology—seem to be predominantly male. Thus, male subjects are taken as representatives of the human species, and inferences from man to mankind become self-evident.

Whatever reason may prove the most important, it is a fact that neither leadership research nor theoretical conceptualizations of the leadership process, of leader-follower interactions, of situational factors favoring different leadership styles, or of other leadership-related variables have explicitly addressed the problem of possible male-female differences (or similarities). That there are differences as well as similarities and that these differences and similarities are often contrary to what the "man in the street" expects or is ready to believe will be shown in the following sections.

As it is not the purpose of this chapter to give a complete account of the literature dealing with sex or gender differences in leadership, we shall restrict ourselves to outlining a few areas of research and pointing to those lines of thinking and theorizing that seem most important to us, in order to demonstrate the gender-related one-eyedness of traditional leadership theory and research.

Women as a Topic of Leadership Research

Sex and Gender as Variables in Psychological Research

As we are interested in the role of women in leadership research and theory, our critical review of pertinent research must not be restricted to those few studies that have investigated women in leadership positions. We have to extend our search into the literature dealing with sex differences in other fields of psychological research. Within psychology, the topic is at least relevant for developmental, differential, and social psychology, but to analyze the problem of male-female leadership in its full scope it would be necessary to cross the boundaries into a number of other fields, with biology, sociology, anthropology, and history as the most important neighboring areas. The present volume has made such an attempt for the analysis of leadership in general. For the special topic of female leadership another round of discussion with the representatives of these various disciplines would be highly desirable and necessary. Yet in recognition of the breadth of the topic and its multidisciplinary nature, we must restrict the present analysis to the perspective of psychology, and of social psychology in particular.

A scholar interested in this field of sex and gender is struck by the wide range of terms used to describe sex-related phenomena, such as *sex roles, sex stereotypes, sex-role norms, sex-role attitudes, sex-role identity, sex typing,* and *gender.* Terminology and conceptualizations are far from clear-cut and have provided a continuing topic of controversy (Deaux, 1984, 1985; Hurtig & Pichevin, 1985; Sherif, 1982; Unger, 1979). We have followed some recent trends in the area and use the term *sex* as a descriptive category for biologically based differences between men and women, and the term *gender* to refer to socially construed psychological characteristics frequently associated with the biological differentiation, either by an outside observer or by individual actors themselves. This term seems to slowly be replacing the term *sex role* and its concomitants with the respective labels of *gender role, gender norm, gender stereotype, gender identity,* and so on:

> Thus studies that select two groups of subjects based on their biological characteristics will be considered appropriate for the use of the word sex. In this context, one is studying sex differences rather than gender differences. In contrast, when judgments are made about nonbiological characteristics or social categories, then gender will be used as a referent. (Deaux, 1985, p. 51)

In considering gender identities and gender stereotypes as sets of culture-specific, consensually shared beliefs with respect to personality characteristics and behavior patterns as typical (gender stereotype) or desirable (gender norms), we could also refer to the notion of "social respresentations" (Moscovici, 1961, 1981) as applied to "the sexes" (Chombart de Lauwe, Chombart de Lauwe, Huguet, Perroy, & Bisseret, 1963; Hurtig & Pichevin, 1985). Such social representations not only are part of the nonmaterial culture of a society but manifest themselves in material products as well.

The Woman as Leader: Stereotypes and Self-Concept

Female Leadership as a Situation of Conflict

As we have shown, women are hardly to be found in leadership positions, and they are rarely appointed to such positions or elected to them. In some areas, however, women have always held positions that should be defined as leadership positions by any reasonable standards, but are not really recognized as such; the head nurse of a state hospital would be a good example. Therefore, being a leader does not merely imply acting like a leader and engaging in leadership functions, but depends on being seen and recognized as a leader by others. Leadership is a social phenomenon (Porter & Geis, 1981), defined by social recognition by followers, colleagues, the constituency, the media, and others. The case of the head nurse may indicate that it is sometimes more important to be perceived and evaluated as competent, powerful, and effective than actually to be those things.

Why is it that women, even if they present actual leadership behaviors or other cues of leadership, are not recognized as leaders? A most simple, even proverbial explanation would read: What may not be, cannot be. In other words, because it is commonly believed that attributes and behaviors typically ascribed to women are just the opposite of what is usually expected from a leader, it is almost logical that women go unrecognized as leaders. Numerous studies show that women as well as men hold the gender stereotype that women are lacking the aptitudes and skills considered to be requisites of leadership. Such gender stereotypes enter the perception and evaluation of men's and women's personality characteristics and performances, which are part of the expectancies concerning appropriate behaviors of men and women and which are the basis for prejudice and discriminatory practices operating against women (most of the time) and against men (once in a while) in their occupational lives and their career aspirations.

Many studies demonstrate the differential perception, categorization, or stereotyping of women and men. Most of them have been predominantly atheoretical, but recent developments in the field of social cognition and, in particular, of stereotyping, provide new theoretical perspectives to understanding the structure and process of gender stereotyping (Ashmore, 1981; Ashmore & Del Boca, 1984; Hamilton, 1981; Wallston & O'Leary, 1981).

A number of studies have shown that stereotypes of how men differ from women match very well our perception and evaluation of how leaders differ from followers. For example, the much quoted work of Rosenkrantz and others (cf. Rosenkrantz, Vogel, Bee, Broverman, & Broverman, 1968; Broverman, Vogel, Broverman, Clarkson, & Rosenkrantz, 1972) showed that men, but not women, are characterized as aggressive, independent, objective, active, dominant, competitive, and decisive, whereas traits attributed to women clustered around gentleness, emotionality, sensitivity, dependency, and submissiveness. It was also found that these stereotypes were not only considered accurate, but "normal and healthy" by mental health professionals. Furthermore, the self-concepts of men and women were found to match these stereotypes, even though the female stereotype is rather unflattering, whereas that of men is couched in more socially desirable terms. These stereotypes, which have a long tradition, have been accepted as a basic description of reality through many generations and by many a science.

Thus, women, who are "born" to be followers, are not prepared for leadership and cannot be successful managers. If they want to be leaders they have to adopt manlike qualities—have to learn to act like a man. This "male-managerial model" (Terborg, 1977) has frequently been confirmed as an autostereotype of women and even women leaders, and as a heterostereotype of the rest of the world. Schein, for example, has demonstrated in several studies (1973, 1975) that male as well as female managers (rating a 92-item leadership characteristic questionnaire) perceive themselves as possessing and demonstrating characteristics, attitudes, behaviors, and temperaments more commonly ascribed to men than to women. Using a so-called Agreement Scale for Leadership Behavior (with items like "see that everyone follows standard procedures," "consider your subordinates' judgment before assigning the work"), Brenner and Bromer (1981) found that self-ratings by female and male managers indicated a significant preference for behaviors that reflect male stereotypic leadership behaviors.

Taking, however, a closer look at those managerial characteristics or behaviors that were not synonymous or in accordance with the male gender stereotype, we find that these characteristics indicate areas in which women presently may be more readily acceptable in management positions. It seems evident that employee-centered or consideration behaviors, such as "understanding," "helpfulness," and "awareness of feelings of others" are requisite leadership characteristics that are more commonly ascribed to women in general than to men in general. Thus, in certain situations, an exhibition of stereotypical female behaviors may be advantageous.

Virginia Schein's conclusion (1976), "Think manager—think male," seems to be a widely accepted standard for women and men alike. It does not yet prove, though, that women show in fact the same leadership behaviors as men. It is their self-perception or self-report of their behavior that resembles those of men.

Because a female leader is more like a man, does this imply that she has become less of a woman? A study by Ahrons (1976), reported by Terborg (1977), seems to indicate that the concept of "career woman" can be subsumed neither under typical feminine occupations (e.g., nurse) nor under typical masculine occupations (e.g. engineer, career man). It rather points to a new prototype. Have we, ten years after Ahrons's study, come any closer to a new proto- or stereotype of the woman in a leading position?

A woman in a leadership position may find herself in a lasting "dual role dilemma" (Darley, 1976), in a conflict between her gender identity as one part of her self-concept and the leader identity as another. As a "good girl," she will have learned what to do as a woman and, some time later in life, how to behave as a leader. As has been emphasized before, schemata and scripts seem to be neither congruent nor overlapping with regard to at least some of the relevant elements or attributes. To be a real woman means for her as well as for the other members of our society to be soft, emotional, and warm. To be a real leader means the opposite, namely, to be hard, rational, and cool. This conflict between contrasting stereotypes, which are both relevant parts of a woman leader's identity, may take the form of a dramatic "double-bind situation," as Deaux (1985) seems to believe, or it may be solved individually by finding a way in between. However, the special problem remains the same for all women leaders. They are confronted again and again with two conflicting clichés characterized by the fundamental polarities between soft and hard, emotional and rational, and so on. Even if a woman leader has solved this conflict at an intrapersonal level she still has to cope with conflicting gender-role versus leader-role expectations held by family members, friends, colleagues, subordinates, and others. The conflict may even be aggravated by media presentations which normally depict women in traditional feminine-typed situations. If women are shown in more exceptional roles it is rather the "princess" than the woman in a leadership position who is portrayed.

If female attributes and leader attributes are seen to be so different, the question is, can a person have both attributes x and non-x simultaneously? The answer depends on the definition of x, especially on its transsituational quality. If a person is always seen and understood as being soft, she cannot at the same time be seen as hard. That persons sometimes are soft and at other times hard is possible, but still difficult to accept, particularly when gender stereotypes co-determine the judgment process. But why should the female leader in her everyday work not be as rational as a man, and why should the male leader in his family life not be as emotional as a woman?

"Switching" between the two ends of the supposed polarity seems to be more problematic for the woman than for the man, as is reflected in the media, in schoolbooks, and elsewhere. The stereotypically desired qualities of men are liked and accepted in all possible situations; the woman, however, is a "real" woman in some situations, namely, those in which she acts in congruence with the gender stereotype, whereas in other situations, when she is functioning as a leader, her behavior is seen as not in accordance with the gender stereotype, although it can be judged as adequate leader behavior.

Two Empirical Illustrations

To Illustrate the conflicts inherent in the situation of women leaders, we report on two of our own studies addressing problems of gender stereotyping in general, and differential stereotyping of women and men leaders in particular.

Media Descriptions of Women and Men Leaders. To find some evidence for the exceptional status of women leaders as compared to men we were interested in finding out whether men and women in leadership positions are described in different ways, and judged by different standards, or whether a single "male-stream" frame of reference, rooted in masculine experience (Siltanen & Stanworth, 1984), is applied. For this purpose we analyzed newspaper portrayals of women and men in recognized leadership positions. This small study was done as part of a larger research project concerning social judgments on the basis of person-descriptive texts (Wintermantel & Christmann, 1983). The first thing one finds in the analysis of both person descriptions and their reproductions is the tendency to construct a coherent picture of the person who is described. This is done in different ways, one of which is the interpretation of actual behaviors in terms of dispositions. Moreover, those behaviors that seem to be typical and distinctive for the person described are likely to be accentuated. In analyzing 10 newspaper descriptions of women leaders and 10 of men we found some striking differences, two of which deserve our special attention.

1. In the descriptions of female leaders there were more typical references to typical leader traits than in the descriptions of male leaders. Does it seem unnecessary to accentuate the leadership traits of a man in a leading position because it is self-evident that he has them? What instead is stressed in our descriptions of men leaders are other attributes, for instance, role as a family father, interests in sports, and personal philosophy of leadership. Thus, the basic schema or cliché of the leading man is presupposed as a kind of background information that needs no explicit mention in the description itself. On the other hand, descriptions of leading women emphasize exactly those traits and performances that are typical for leadership, namely, being dominant, being competitive, taking risks, making solitary decisions, and so on. Again, the stereotypical attributes, here the female stereotype, are not mentioned. They are taken for granted. If in the descriptions of female leaders their leadership qualities are accentuated, it is because those characteristics differentiate her from the gender-role cliché.

2. In the descriptions of female leaders we found more references to the manifestation of dominance in the interaction with subordinates than in the description of male leaders. This again indicates a deviation from the female stereotype that seems to require special mention. Is it that women as leaders are expected to acquire interactive qualities that are atypical for women in general? Our data base is too small to draw any specific conclusions. We could, however, argue that these descriptions of female leaders as compared to male leaders illustrate the existence of a "male-as-norm" principle (Siltanen & Stanworth, 1984), which operates as a frame of reference for the description of female leadership and as a standard for judging its adequacy.

Is the Businesswoman Not a Woman? Our second study concerned the connotative meaning of five concepts that seem to be relevant for the discussion of gender stereotypes and their effects and implications with regard to leadership. The study had two aims. First, it was undertaken to find out whether the gender stereotypes reported in the literature are still with us, and whether they still show the same configuration of attributes that have been found for years. Second, we wanted to analyze the semantic relation between the "pure" concepts of "man" and "woman" and those concepts that are marked with regard to the occupation a person holds in a leading position.

Accordingly, we chose the following four German words: *Mann* (man), *Frau* (woman), *Manager* (manager), and *Geschäftsfrau* (businesswoman), and had 50 male and 50 female students at the University of Heidelberg rate the meaning of these words, using a version of Osgood's semantic differential technique with 25 bipolar seven-point scales. In addition, our subjects rated the abstract concept of *Führung* (leadership). (It should be noted that the

German term for *businesswoman* (Geschäftsfrau) does not share the connotation of career woman as exceptional.)

Our results confirm all the above-mentioned stereotypes. For our sample the meaning of the concept *woman* includes attributes like *soft, warm, tender*, and the like, whereas the concept *man* includes attributes like *hard, cold,*, and so on. But what happens with the terms *businesswoman* and *manager* and the *leadership* concept?

Table 11-1 presents the similarity coefficients (Cattell) that were computed for female and male subjects separately as to the concepts *man, woman, leadership, manager* and *businesswoman.* If we look at the similarities in ratings between the five concepts it is obvious that over all bipolar scales, and rather independently of the sex of our subjects, *man, leadership*, and *manager* are concepts that are very similar with respect to most of the attributes used in the differential. The three concepts are rated as highly similar, especially as to the dimensions *hard* versus *soft, active* versus *passive, cold* versus *sentimental*, and *dominant* versus *submissive.* Interestingly enough, female subjects rated the concept *businesswoman* as similar to these concepts: The *businesswoman* is perceived by the female students as belonging semantically with *man, manager*, and *leadership.*

This tendency is not as strong for our male subjects. They also see the term *businesswoman* as more similar to *man* than to *woman* but not as highly similar to *leadership* and to *manager* as the female subjects do. The high similarity between the ratings for *manager* and for *leadership* suggests that these two terms are quasi-synonymous. This finding, taken together with the ratings of the concept *man*, could lead one to argue that *leadership* and *manager* represent a configuration of attributes that is most discriminatory as to the concept of *woman.* To understand these differences on the level of individual attributes more clearly, we made a discriminant analysis with the same data. Figures 11-1 and 11-2 visualize the semantic relations within our set of concepts separated for male and female subjects.

Here we recognize even more precisely that women are conceived as sharing some attributes with men and some with businesswomen, but they do not share any relevant attributes with managers or with leadership. What does this mean? Again, it can be inferred that the real, the prototypical woman is not "leaderlike." She may be "ladylike," however. Moreover, she represents just the opposite of manager- and leadership-relevant traits.

The highly discriminative dimensions between the concepts *woman* and *leadership* are *soft* versus *hard, silent* versus *loud, permissive* versus *strict, talkative* versus *quiet*, and *cold* versus *sentimental.* These are precisely the same dimensions that discriminate between *man* and *woman*, which concepts are, in addition, distinguished by the dimensions *relaxed* versus *tense* and *cowardly* versus *bold.* Whereas the discriminative dimensions between *woman* and *man/leadership* are (factorially) related more to potency versus activity, the dimensions discriminating between *man* and *leadership* are more on the side of evaluation. *Man* is rated as more positive on the *fair–*

Table 11-1. Similarity of Coefficients and Semantic Differential Ratings for the Concepts *Man, Woman, Leadership, Manager,* and *Businesswoman*

	1 Man	2 Woman	3 Leadership	4 Manager	5 Businesswoman	6 Man	7 Woman	8 Leadership	9 Manager
1 m[a] Man									
2 m Woman	-.5								
3 m Leadership	.8	-.5							
4 m Manager	.9	-.4	.9						
5 m Businesswoman	.5	-.1	.7	.7					
6 f Man	.9	-.5	.8	.8	.5				
7 f Woman	-.3	.9	-.2	-.2	.2	-.2			
8 f Leadership	.8	-.6	.9	.9	.7	.7	.2		
9 f Manager	.8	-.6	.9	.9	.7	.8	-.3	.9	
10 f Businesswoman	.7	-.2	.8	.8	.8	.6	.2	.2	.8

[a]m, male subjects (*N* = 50); f, female subjects (*N* = 50).

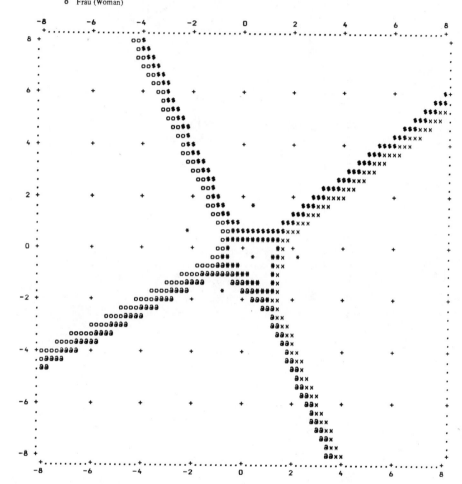

Figure 11-1. Territorial map of the canonical discriminant function (female subjects, *N* = 50) for the concepts Leadership, Manager, Business woman, Man, and Woman.

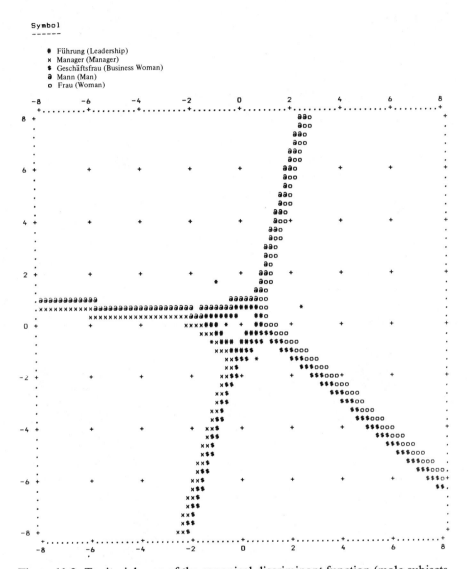

Figure 11-2. Territorial map of the canonical discriminant function (male subjects, $N = 50$) for the concepts Leadership, Manager, Business woman, Man, and Woman.

unfair, the *good–bad*, and the *clear–diffuse* dimensions. Again, *man* and *leader* seem to be thought of as having the same attributes with regard to their activity and potency, but they are differently evaluated. The (social) construction of the concept *woman* is most different from the concepts *manager* and *leadership*, whereas the concept *businesswoman* seems to be something in between, closely related neither to the concept of *woman* nor to the conceptual cluster *man*, *manager*, *leadership*. Whether these findings can already be taken as evidence for the emergence of a new prototype of the career woman, who succeeds in combining previously contradictory roles, will emerge in the future.

Implications of Gender Stereotypes for Leadership Careers of Women

We have been arguing that the existence of gender stereotypes affects the perception, description, and evaluation of women in leadership positions in at least three directions.

1. Leading women are perceived or construed as having manlike qualities, and they perceive and describe themselves in the same way (male-managerial model of leadership).

2. There is a potential conflict between the (female) gender stereotype and the role model for leadership behavior, which may be alleviated in one way or another sometimes by oscillating between two apparently irreconcilable extremes. It does not seem to be really resolved, however. Hence, it gives the woman leader a rather exceptional and almost deviant, or at least conspicuous, status.

3. The position of woman leader is construed and described in quite different terms from those applied to either men or other women, indicating perhaps the emergence of a new prototype of the leading woman.

We shall now broaden the perspective and look for further implications these gender stereotypes have for the description and evaluation of women who prove as competent as men, who are aspiring to a career, who have taken the role of a leader, or who have attained a leadership position. Many empirical studies, mainly those done in the laboratory, demonstrate that women and men performing the same tasks and achieving the same results are valued quite differently (cf. Basow, 1980; Wallston & O'Leary, 1981, for reviews). In the classic study by Goldberg (1968), for example, women who were asked to rate professional articles for their value, persuasiveness, and profundity, and for the writing style and competence of the author, tended to rate articles attributed to a male author as more valuable and the author as more competent than when the identical articles were bearing a woman's name.

Evaluative biases toward a close association between competence or success and maleness have repeatedly been confirmed (Bem & Bem, 1970;

Deaux & Taynor, 1973; Pheterson, Kiesler, & Goldberg, 1971). The fact that competent men were viewed as more competent than competent women may result in discriminatory hiring practices. A study by Fidell (1970) has shown that even psychologists, who should be expected to be aware of the effects of gender stereotyping, are not immune to sex discrimination: Female job applicants described as holding the same credentials (in psychology) as men were basically evaluated in the same way but were offered lower-level jobs (assistant professorships) than their male colleagues (associate professorships).

Further studies, however, have clarified and modified earlier research findings. An important moderator variable has been found to be the sex linkage of the task. Although Goldberg's study of 1968 had already demonstrated that the competence bias favoring male authors only appeared with topics in traditionally masculine-typed (law and city planning) and neutral (linguistics) fields, though not in predominantly feminine ones (elementary education), the importance of sex-typed tasks and occupations has only later been rediscovered. Thus, women who hold jobs or positions typically reserved for men, such as leadership positions, will meet with even stronger prejudices than those who hold gender-congruent positions. Thus, women who are seen as aspiring to status or power in male-dominated fields are negatively evaluated (Denmark, 1979; Mischel, 1974). Women, then, will only get the same recognition for their achievement as men when their performance has already been publicly recognized as exceptional or legitimized through awards (Abramson, Goldberg, Greenberg, & Abramson, 1977; Jacobson & Effertz, 1974; Pheterson et al., 1971; Taynor & Deaux, 1973). A study by Kaschak (1978a, 1978b), reported in Basow (1980), showed, for example, that gender bias in the evaluation of teaching methods of female and male university professors only disappeared when the professors were described as award winners. It is interesting to note, however, that even though male and female professors were seen as equally excellent, they were judged by different standards: whereas female professors (in feminine fields) were rated as more concerned and likable, male professors (in all fields) were rated as more powerful and effective than female professors.

In some situations the gender bias seems to have an inverse effect when women behave outside of a stereotypical role in a masculine mode and achieve unexpected success. Their success then becomes magnified. Abramson et al. (1977) have called this effect the "talking platypus phenomenon," because "after all, it matters little what the platypus says, the wonder is that it can say anything at all" (p. 123). Whether this effect will also be found consistently with men who are successful in feminine-typed tasks (e.g., nursing, homemaking) has not yet been carefully studied (cf. Levinson, 1975). Other researchers, however, have found that unexpected success in gender-inappropriate occupations results in lower ratings of women's and men's competence (cf. Nieva & Gutek, 1980). Evaluations seem to be made in accordance with a model of gender-role congruency rather than with an achievement model.

These findings that women and men are judged and evaluated differently even when actual performance is held constant have led to further research into judgmental processes. There is evidence from many studies that people's naive causal explanations for success or failure in achievement situations are different for men than for women. A man's successful achievement on a task is generally attributed to ability, whereas a woman's success on the same task is explained by luck or effort. However, failure on a task by men is attributed to bad luck, and failure by women to low ability (cf. Deaux & Emswiller, 1974; Feldman-Summers & Kiesler, 1974; Frieze, Fisher, Hanusa, McHugh, & Valle, 1978; Haccoun & Stacy, 1980). Here again, these effects were most pronounced when the task was masculine-typed, that is, one in which men were expected to succeed. It has been argued that most of the tasks used in achievement situations are masculine-typed and are therefore decreasing women's chances to excel (cf. Deaux, 1977; Wallston & O'Leary, 1981).

The importance of the sex linkage of tasks for differential causal judgments and for gender-specific evaluations of the same task as difficult or easy has not only shown in the laboratory. Traditionally, female occupations are often judged as easier and less favorable than male professions. Although these judgments may have some realistic basis, with women being kept at lower-status jobs, it has been shown that female and male occupations of equivalent demands are rated differently. The social prestige of typical male occupations apparently decreases when the percentage of women in this occupation is growing (Touhey, 1974). One could argue that the more male-dominated and prestigious a profession is, the lower is the probability that women find access to and acceptance in the profession's upper ranks.

Studies addressing the special issue of male-female leadership have yielded similar results. Starting from a more contemporary and more complex view of leadership, which emphasizes the interaction of leader characteristics, follower characteristics, the nature of the task, the organizational structure, and the external environment, suggests that there are many different levels, ways, and means for the manifestation of gender biases. Women have been shown to go unrecognized as leaders (in mixed-sex groups), even if a highly indicative nonverbal leadership cue (the head-of-the-table position) is present (Porter & Geis, 1981). On the other hand, even women who had rated themselves as highly dominant (on a person-ality inventory) failed to assert their leadership role when they were paired with low-dominant men in a dyadic situation, whereas dominant men always emerged as the leader when paired with a low-dominant man or with any category of woman (Megargee, 1969). Megargee reported that it was typically the high-dominant woman herself who proposed the follower role for herself. When Carbonell (1984) was interested to find out if the

"Megargee effect"—that gender identity norms would override leaderlike personality characteristics—could be replicated 15 years later and after a feminist movement had gained public attention, the same pattern emerged, but only when the task was masculine in nature. When the task was modified to appear feminine, dominance scores predicted leadership across all groups.

Because women in a leadership position have to deal with other women and/or men in subordinate positions, potential interaction effects of leader sex and follower sex are of interest. As it is still seen as "almost an 'unnatural act' for a male to be subordinate to a female" (Rice, Instone, & Adams, 1984, p. 14) because it may upset the traditional patterns of deference between men and women (cf. Bass, Krusell, & Alexander, 1971), one could expect that subordinate men are particularly biased toward a negative perception of a female leader. Research on attitudes toward women in leading positions has usually demonstrated that such women are thought to have bad effects on employee morale, to upset the traditional balance of power, and to threaten established systems of norms (cf. Riger & Galligan, 1980). Laboratory studies addressing issues of differential evaluations of leadership styles or specific behaviors emitted by female or male leaders and of ratings of leadership success have provided evidence for the effect of leader sex × follower sex interactions (cf. Terborg, 1977).

Jacobson & Effertz (1974), for example, who had male and female students serve as "leaders" or "followers" on a complex task that was finally unsolvable, found evidence for their hypotheses that both male and female followers would rate male leaders lower than female leaders as to their performance (which was about equal for all groups) because men were expected to be more successful than women in solving such problems. On the other hand, both male and female leaders rated female followers more harshly, because they had expected women to be better followers. Thus, the lack of congruence between gender-role expectations and the actual performance of both women and men results in differential evaluations.

Another situation of conflict may arise when a female leader displays specific behaviors, for example, chastising or harshly criticizing an employee, that would be rated as appropriate leader behavior but inappropriate gender-role behavior. Although it is possible that men's behavior also will be judged according to changing role standards, the probability that their leader behavior is in accordance with what is expected from them as males is much higher. For the woman leader, however, be she a congresswoman or a manager in a large corporation, it may remain unpredictable whether her colleagues or followers (fellow congressmen and voters, fellow managers and employees) are applying a job model in one situation and a gender model in another (cf. Feldberg & Glenn, 1979). As a result of these potential role conflicts women leaders may have to give a lot of consideration and effort to role management.

Most of the studies referred to, however, were either laboratory or paper-

and-pencil studies, more often with students as subjects than with people in actual leadership positions. As will be more precisely stated later in this chapter, these particular methodological circumstances are most conducive to invoking gender biases, because the sex of the target variable (the leader woman) may be one of the few discriminatory cues on which a subject may base his or her judgment. Student subjects, on the other hand, asked to act as leader or to rate simulated or verbally reported "leadership" behaviors, may have no other choice than to react on the basis of those gender stereotypes that are most familiar to them. As a result, gender-related differences between female and male leadership may be exaggerated. We therefore have to take a closer look at those field studies that investigate leadership in its everday context.

Do Women and Men Leaders Really Differ?

Since publication of Maccoby and Jacklin's *Psychology of Sex Differences* (1974) it has been widely accepted that evidence for differences between men and women with regard to cognitive skills, personality dispositions, and social behaviors can be found in only a few areas (e.g., verbal ability, mathematical ability, visual-spatial ability, and aggression). Although these conclusions have been criticized from various angles (cf. Block, 1976; Deaux, 1985; Gilligan, 1982; Hurtig & Pichevin, 1985), we might as well accept that variations within each sex group are usually greater than those between them.

On the basis of these arguments, we would expect to find only minimal differences between women and men in leadership positions. This line of inference, is of course, rather simplistic, as it does not take into consideration that women leaders are an exceptional group in exceptional situations. Thus, mean differences found with average subjects in average situations are possibly not to be generalized to such exceptional people.

On the other hand, the existence of a male-managerial model for the woman leader could suggest that differences between male and female leadership styles and outcomes should be minimal. If women have adopted the characteristics and behaviors typically associated with men's leadership role, they might act like a man and be successful like a man. This perspective, however, neglects the essential role of *recognition* by others, who may all be prone to gender-specific perceptual and evaluational biases.

Evidence provided in the preceding section has indicated that women are often regarded as lacking adequate leader characteristics and that such cognitions and stereotypes result in respective expectations of success and failure in specific situations. It was also evident that these stereotypes are part of the women's own self-concept, which may often be characterized by the conflictive interplay between gender-specific and leader-specific roles of expectations. Taken together these factors do not seem to constitute optimal conditions for adequate female leadership.

If we are to develop a new paradigm for the conception and study of female leadership, we have to go beyond the analysis of factors internal to the person or characteristic of the immediate leadership situation and take into account other biographical, social, and institutional factors that contribute to the marginal position of the woman leader and may serve as barriers to her achievement. These factors may be taken as boundary conditions of female leadership situations.

Factors contributing to the marginal status of female leaders or constituting external barriers to women's careers in leadership positions include:

Traditional socialization and education patterns in the family, at school, at the university, which provide role models and affect or block career choices;

Insufficient education and lack of training and specific skills;

Marital and family patterns;

Dual-career conflicts (between homemaking/motherhood and work life);

Discriminatory hiring practices and promotion policies;

Sex segregation of occupations and sex-typed jobs;

Salary differentials;

"Solo" status of women in groups (high visibility, etc., of women in a minority status), the "token women" (cf. Taylor, Fiske, Close, Anderson, & Ruderman, 1977; Kanter, 1977);

Lack of old boys' networks or mentors for informational and emotional support (cf. Apfelbaum & Hadley, this volume);

Lack of a reference group for social comparison;

Distribution of power and restricted access to bases of power (Johnson, 1976; Unger, 1978).

Whereas some of these factors serve as barriers because they are part of the traditional gender-role and -norm system of our society (e.g., occupational segregation), other factors reflect a state of transition (e.g., the solo woman) that may be indicative of social change.

It is beyond the scope of this chapter to deal with these factors in any detail. They have to be mentioned, however, to outline the level of complexity inherent in the problem of female leadership, which demands further analysis. Some of these factors have already been recognized as important issues for studying women in a state of transition and in a changing world (cf. Apfelbaum & Hadley, this volume; Agassi, 1982; Barnett & Baruch, 1978; Basow, 1980; Gullahorn, 1979; Hoiberg, 1982; Riger & Galligan, 1980; Ruble, Frieze, & Parsons, 1976; Sherman & Denmark, 1978; Stewart & Platt, 1982; Terborg, 1977).

Taking together the experimental evidence of the effects of gender auto- and heterostereotyping, the assumptions about the dual role dilemma, and the statements about the special boundary conditions of female leadership, one is led to assume that a woman could never be as successful a leader as a man. However, the studies conducted in field settings generally do not confirm this assumption, and reviewers of leadership research seem to agree that in real-life situations effects of leader sex disappear (e.g, Brown, 1979; Terborg, 1977). For example, Brown's (1979) comparison of leadership studies run with students (business students) with those done with managers in business showed that most student studies reproduced the commonly held gender stereotype that women make bad leaders, whereas practicing managers usually reported that there are no difference between male and female leadership styles and effects. These differences in results may suggest that practicing managers' attitudes toward female leaders and managers may have changed as a result of actual experience with women in leadership roles—a result that is corroborated by findings of less stereotyping by older managers, who have had more exposure to women managers. Most of the leadership studies yielding the data base for Brown's comparison have used a rather simple questionnnaire methodology to assess differences in perceived leadership traits and abilities, or leadership styles and/or efficiency, and/or satisfaction with the leader. Such simple measures that reduce leadership to style, effect, or subordinate satisfaction may not be adequate to reflect the complexity (and variability) of leadership processes. Hence, they might mask approaches and contributions characteristic of women.

Other research, such as Project Athena at West Point, which is studying cadet training programs with male and female senior cadets as leaders (cf. Rice et al., 1984), tries to make up for these deficiencies mentioned above by examining multiple aspects of leaders' success, leadership processes, and various potential interactive effects of leader sex and follower sex. Although the setting was typically masculine (military training) and although the only data source was subjective questionnaire responses by followers (which are more likely to produce perceptual and evaluational gender biases than would be the case with objective measures), the authors concluded that "leader sex seldom has shown strong and replicable effects in operational settings where male and female cadets regularly train for their roles as military leaders" (p. 27), and they are proud to state the significance of the nonsignificant effects. But are the authors aware that female cadets have gone through a process of institutional socialization toward uniformity? The above conclusions are thus far from proving that there are no differences between male and female leadership characteristics.

The Gender Bias in Psychological Research

So far we have tried to describe the female auto- and heterostereotypes and their effects on leadership-related phenomena. Equally important is the somewhat self-critical question of gender biases in social scientific thinking, mainly about leadership. This question can be dealt with from at least three different perspectives: (1) the general conceptual status of gender as a variable in the social sciences and especially with regard to the topic of leadership, (2) the methodology used to analyze interindividual differences, and finally (3) the neglect of specific research areas while accentuating others.

The Conceptual Status of the Gender Variable

When the sex/gender concept appears in empirical studies it is mostly dealt with as an independent variable (Bardwick, 1971). This is true also for leadership studies (Brown, 1979), which analyze the effects of sex/gender in the same way as is done with other person and/or situational variables. Whereas most differential variables in psychology are theoretical constructs, this is not the case with sex and gender. Sex and gender have no explanatory force. Instead, the effects themselves must be explained by other constructs and moderating processes. Accordingly, different types of explanations are being discussed, one of them focusing on different socialization practices for boys and girls (Block, 1978), another emphasizing processes of social stereotyping (Basow, 1980). Both types of explanations imply the assumption that gender as well as the idea of sex are to a great extent social constructions (Goffman, 1979). There remains, however, the idea of a basically biological sex interacting in complex and rather diffuse ways with a psychologically constructed gender (cf. pp. 174–175). These interaction effects of sex and gender keep changing from situation to situation and from task to task. They result in a kind of inconsistency of effects whereby sex- and gender-specific differences may occur in one study but not in another, although both investigate the same performances under slightly changed conditions (Hurtig & Pichevin, 1985). The confusion becomes obvious when data on gender differences may be partly explained by such nonsystematic interaction effects.

The basic problem for an adequate conceptualization of the gender variable arises partly from the fact that the perception of biological sex, as a highly visible and salient feature of a person, leads to different expectations from the side of the perceiver with regard to the psychological implications of this perceptual feature. Whether a person is a man or a woman is a most relevant determinant of impression formation and of social judgment processes (Mayo & Henley, 1981; Deaux, 1984). It is not the biological sex as such that is responsible for such cognitive effects, but the set of attributes that are consensually thought of as typical of women and another set allegedly typical of men. Probably because biological sex is a dichotomous category there is a tendency to dichotomize people also with respect to their abilities, personality characteristics, behavior styles, and so forth, in accordance with these "basic" categories. Is it that we have a simple equation in our cognitive system specifying that what *looks* different must *be* different?

A growing number of psychologists are aware of these sources of errors. They have begun to realize that, contrary to other evidence, in the case of sex/gender, within-group differences (on most psychological dimensions) are usually greater than between-group differences, but like laypersons they are not immune against the tendency to dichotomize. Only recently has research concentrated on these complex interactions between variables that cannot be seen as really independent with regard to the performances under study but that traditionally have been treated as independent (Deaux, 1985; Unger, 1979; Porter & Geis, 1981).

The adequate conceptualization of a mixture of variables that causes specific nonsystematic effects is a difficult enterprise. Nonetheless, this conceptual labor needs be done in order to overcome the prevailing conceptual and theoretical ambiguities.

Gender Biases in Methodology

Gender bias may systematically enter empirical investigation in accordance with certain methodological decisions at different levels of a study, either through the kind of experimental treatment or through the kinds of instruments used to measure individual differences. Probably the most striking evidence for a systematic error of this sort is the inconsistency of sex/gender differences found between laboratory studies and field studies, with gender differences usually being higher in the laboratory setting. A simple phenomenon seems to acount for this: In the restricted laboratory situation where "strangers interact with other strangers or with pencil-and-paper stimulus others, for brief periods of time in contrived settings" (Terborg, 1977, p. 655), surface characteristics that are easily available become salient cues for judgment processes or behavioral reactions, as may be expected from the theory of availability heuristic (Kahneman, Slovic, & Tversky, 1982). In these situations the sex of a person may become a more relevant and predictive cue than would be the case in everyday situations. Hence studies that use undergraduates as subjects to rate behaviors and behavior styles as to their presumed masculine or feminine quality yield higher sex differences than studies that use managers as subjects who have long-term experience with male and female co-workers (Brown, 1979). On the other hand, data from different field studies are often difficult to compare because of their partly uncontrollable context variables.

A second point at which gender biases may enter empirical studies is the tendency to accentuate even small differences as "positive" results (Hurtig & Pichevin, 1985). Too often these differences are either taken to be self-explanatory or they are explained as gender socialization effects. The fact that usually less than 5% of the behavior variance under study can be explained by sex/gender effects may indicate how cautiously interpretations should be offered (cf. Terborg, 1977).

Gender Stereotypes Held by Scientists

There is one other gender bias effect in scientific thinking that seems to be caused by stereotypes on the side of the scientists. The fact that physical attractiveness as a personal characteristic has mostly been studied with female stimulus persons and male subjects exemplifies this special bias (Wallston & O'Leary, 1981). That, as a complement, perceived competence is usually studied with male stimulus persons adds to the stereotype: To be attractive is a socially desired part of the female stereotype; to be competent is the relevant counterpart for a man.

A second manifestation of gender biases with scientists may be seen in the accentuation of certain topics that are taken to be important for a "male-stream" conception of psychology. An appropriate investigation of the particular female identity, including her special situation in a state of transition (cf. Apfelbaum & Hadley, this volume), does not belong to these topics.

One last piece of evidence for gender biases within the scientific community is the tendency of certain authors to interpret gender differences in favor of their own sex group—a practice that is easily understood sociopsychologically (as in-group favoritism) but casts doubts on the objectivity of data processing.

Conclusion

The topic of woman leadership has proven to be a highly complex, multifaceted, and dynamic problem for psychology as well as of psychology. Depending on how we approach it, it reveals a different facet. From traditional research on leadership it is barely visible: leadership seems to be so ingrained with masculine attributes, or rather with characteristics traditionally attributed to men, that female leaders impress as exceptional, good enough for case studies but not for changing our conceptions of leadership. Conversely, if we approach the leadership topic from the changing psychology of women it is a highly visible and central issue. If we concentrate on traits or behavior allegedly associated with efficient leadership, we hardly find differences worth recording unless we use the magnifying glass of the laboratory experiment. If we broaden our view to encompass the woman leader's background and situation, as compared with the male leaders' environment, we find considerable differences due to boundary conditions. If we try to follow a woman's path to a leadership goal we are immediately confronted with the major barrier to and distinctive feature of female leadership: a powerful gender stereotype that is at variance with the leadership schema. If we try to grasp the dynamics of this gender bias we are impressed by its truly protean nature: It can be as outspoken and simple as a "no" to a qualified applicant because of her sex. It can be as indirect and impersonal as a gender-biased battery of aptitude tests. It can, worst of all, hide in the kind of objectivity to which scientific theory and research are committed. Even on the metatheoretical level we have sensed disturbances: Gender is being offered as an *explanans*, in an attempt to hide the fact that it is the central *explanandum* of the social psychology of female leadership.

Finally, for a book dedicated to changing conceptions of leadership the topic of female leadership is both paradigm and challenge: The existence and success of woman leaders, rare as they may be, present a good example of a social change occurring with us and partly, within ourselves. The challenge is to make our conception of leadership change toward an equitable human science.

References

Abramson, P. R., Goldberg, P. A., Greenberg, J. H., & Abramson, L. M. (1977). The talking platypus phenomenon: Competency ratings as a function of sex and professional status. *Psychology of Women Quarterly, 2*, 114–124.

Agassi, J. B. (1982). *Comparing the work attitudes of women and men.* Lexington, MA: Lexington Books.

Ahrons, C. R. (1976). Counselor's perceptions of career images of women. *Journal of Vocational Behavior, 8*, 197–207.

Ashmore, R. D. (1981). Sex stereotypes and implicit personality theory—In D. L. Hamilton (Ed.) *Cognitive processes in stereotyping and intergroup behavior.* Hillsdale, NJ: Erlbaum.

Ashmore, R. D., & Del Boca, F. K. (Eds.) (1984). *The social psychology of female-male relations: A critical analysis of central concepts.* New York: Academic Press.

Bardwick, J. M. (1971). *The psychology of women: A study of biocultural conflicts.* New York: Harper & Row.

Barnett, R., & Baruch, G. K. (1978). *The competent woman. Perspectives on development.* New York: Irvington.

Basow, S. A. (1980). *Sex-role stereotypes. Traditions and alternatives.* Monterey, CA: Brooks/Cole.

Bass, B. M. (1981). *Stogdill's handbook of leadership research.* New York: Free Press.

Bass, B. M., Krusell, J., & Alexander, R. A. (1971). Male managers' attitudes toward working woman. *American Behavioral Scientist, 15*, 221–236.

Bem, S. L., & Bem, D. J. (1970). Case study of a non-conscious ideology: Training the woman to know her place. In D. Bem (Ed.), *Beliefs, attitudes, and human affairs* (pp. 89–99). Monterey, CA: Brooks/Cole.

Block, J. H. (1976). Issues, problems, and pitfalls in assessing sex differences: A critical review of "The Psychology of Sex Differences." *Merrill-Palmer Quarterly, 22*, 283–308.

Block, J. H. (1978). Another look at sex differentiation in the socialization behaviors of mothers and fathers. In J. A. Sherman & F. L. Denmark (Eds.), *The psychology of women: Future directions in research* (pp. 30–87). New York: Psychological Dimensions.

Bock, U., Braszeit, A., & Schmerl, C. (Eds.) (1983). *Frauen an den Universitäten. Zur Situation von Studentinnen und Hochschullehrerinnen in der männlichen Wissenschaftshierarchie.* Frankfurt: Campus.

Brenner, O. C., & Bromer, J. A. (1981). Sex stereotypes and leader behavior as measured by the Agreement Scale for Leadership Behaviors. *Psychological Reports, 48,* 960–962.

Broverman, I. K., Vogel, S. R., Broverman, D. M., Clarkson, F. E., & Rosenkrantz, P. S. (1972) Sex role stereotypes: A current appraisal. *Journal of Social Issues, 28,* 59–78.

Brown, S. M. (1979). Male vs. female leaders: A comparison of empirical studies. *Sex Roles, 5,* 595–611.

Carbonell, J. L. (1984). Sex roles and leadership revisited. *Journal of Applied Psychology, 69,* 44–49.

Chombart de Lauwe, P. H., Chombart de Lauwe, M.-J., Huguet, M., Perroy, E., & Bisseret, N. (1963). *La femme dans la société. Son image dans differents milieux sociaux.* Paris: Editions du Centre National de la Recherche Scientifique.

Darley, S. A. (1976). Big-time careers for the little woman: A dual-role dilemma. *Journal of Social Issues, 32(3),* 85–98.

Deaux, K. (1977). Sex differences. In T. Blass (Ed.), *Personality variables in social behavior* (pp. 357–377. Hillsdale, NJ: Lawrence Erlbaum.

Deaux, K. (1984). From individual differences to social categories. Analysis of a decade's research on gender. *American Psychologist, 39(2),* 105–116.

Deaux, K. (1985). Sex and gender. *Annual Review of Psychology, 36,* 49–81.

Deaux, K., & Emswiller, T. (1974). Explanations of successful performance on sex-linked tasks: What is skill for the male is luck for the female. *Journal of Personality and Social Psychology, 29,* 80–85.

Deaux, K., & Taynor, J. (1973). Evaluation of male and female ability: Bias works two ways. *Psychological Reports, 32,* 261–262.

Denmark, F. (1979). *The outspoken woman: Can she win?* Paper presented at the meeting of the New York Academy of Sciences.

Dixon, R. B. (1976). Measuring equality between the sexes. *Journal of Social Issues, 32,* 19–32.

Feldberg, R., & Glenn, E. N. (1979). Male and female: Job versus gender models in the sociology of work. *Social Problems, 26,* 524–538.

Feldman-Summers, S., & Kiesler, S. B. (1974). Those who are number two try harder: The effect of sex on attributions of causality. *Journal of Personality and Social Psychology, 30,* 846–855.

Fidell, L. (1970) Empirical verification of sex discrimination in hiring practices in psychology. *American Psychologist, 25,* 1094–1098.

Frieze, I. H., Fisher, J. R., Hanusa, B. H., McHugh, M. C., & Valle, V. A. (1978). Attributions of the cause of success and failure as internal and external barriers to achievement. In J. L. Sherman & F. L. Denmark (Eds.), *The psychology of women. Future directions in research* (pp. 519–552). New York: Psychological Dimensions.

Gibb, C. A. (1969). Leadership. In E. Aronson & G. Lindzey (Eds.), *Handbook of social psychology* (pp. 205–282). Reading, MA: Addison-Wesley.

Gilligan, C. (1982). *In a different voice.* Cambridge, MA: Harvard University Press.

Goldberg, P. A. (1968). Are women prejudiced against women? *Transaction, 5,* 28–30.

Goffman, E. (1979). *Gender Advertisements.* New York: Harper & Row.

Gullahorn, J. F. (1979). *Psychology and women: In transition.* New York: Wiley.

Haccoun, D. M., & Stacy, S. (1980). Perceptions of male and female success or failure in relation to spouse encouragement and sex-association of occupation. *Sex Roles, 6,* 819–831.

Hamilton, D. L. (Ed.) (1981). *Cognitive processes in stereotyping and intergroup behaviors.* Hillsdale, NJ: Lawrence Erlbaum.

Hennig, M., & Jardim, A. (1977). *The managerial woman.* New York: Doubleday.

Hoiberg, A. (Ed.) (1982). *Women and the world of work.* New York: Plenum.

Hollander, E. P. (1985). Leadership and power. In G. Lindzey & E. Aronson (Eds.), *Handbook of social psychology* (3rd ed., pp. 485–537. New York: Random House.

Hollander, E. P., & Yoder, J. (1980). Some issues in comparing women and men as leaders. *Basic and Applied Social Psychology, 1,* 267–280.

Horner, M. S. (1972). Toward an understanding of achievement-related conflicts in women. *Journal of Social Issues, 28,* 157–175.

Hurtig, M. C., & Pichevin, M. F. (1985). Le variable sexe en psychologie: Donné ou construct? *Cahiers de Psychologie Cognitive, 5(2),* 187–228.

Jacobson, M. B., & Effertz, J. (1974). Sex role and leadership perceptions of the leaders and the led. *Organizational Behavior and Human Performance, 12,* 383–396.

Johnson, P. (1976). Women and power: Toward a theory of effectiveness. *Journal of Social Issues, 32(3),* 99–110.

Kahneman, D., Slovic, P., & Tversky, A. (1982). *Judgment under uncertainty: Heuristics and biases.* Cambridge, England: Cambridge University Press.

Kanter, R. M. (1977). *Men and women of the corporation.* New York: Basic Books.

Kaschak, E. (1978a). Sex bias in student evaluation of college professors. *Psychology of Women Quarterly, 3,* 235–243.

Kaschak, E. (1978b, April) *Another look at sex bias in students, evaluation of professors: Do winners get the recognition that they have been given?* Paper presented at the Western Psychological Association Convention, San Francisco.

Levinson, R. M. (1975). Sex discrimination and employment practices: An experiment with unconventional job inquiries. *Social Problems, 22,* 533–543.

Maccoby, E. E., & Jacklin, C. N. (1974). *The psychology of sex differences.* Stanford, CA: Stanford University Press.

Mayo, C. & Henley, N.M. (Eds.) (1981). *Gender and non-verbal behavior.* New York: Springer-Verlag.

Megargee, E. E. (1969). Influence of sex roles on the manifestation of leadership. *Journal of Applied Psychology, 53,* 377–382.

Mischel, H. (1974). Sex bias in the evaluation of professional achievements. *Journal of Educational Psychology, 66,* 157–166.

Moscovici, S. (1961). *La psychanalyse, son image et son public.* Paris: Presses Universitaires de Paris.

Moscovici, S. (1981). On social representations. In J. P. Forgas (Ed.), *Social cognition. Perspectives on everyday understanding* (pp. 181–209). New York: Academic Press.

Nieva, V. F., & Gutek, B. A. (1980). Sex effects on evaluation. *Academy of Management Review, 5,* 267–276.

Nieva, V. F., & Gutek, B. A. (1981). *Women and work: A psychological perspective.* New York: Praeger.

Pheterson, G. I., Kiesler, S., & Goldberg, P. A. (1971). Evaluation of women as a function of their sex, achievement, and personal history. *Journal of Personality and Social Psychology, 19,* 114–118.

Porter, N., & Geis, F. (1981). Women and nonverbal leadership cues: When seeing is not believing. In C. Mayo & N. M. Henley (Eds.), *Gender and nonverbal behavior* (pp. 39–61). New York: Springer-Verlag.

Rice, R. W., Instone, D., & Adams, J. (1984). Leader, sex, leader success, and leadership process: Two field studies. *Journal of Applied Psychology, 69,* 12–31.

Riger, S., & Galligan, P. (1980). Women in management. An exploration of competing paradigms. *American Psychologist, 35,* 902–910.

Rosenkrantz, P., Vogel, S., Bee, H., Broverman, I. K., & Broverman, D. M. (1968). Sex role stereotypes and self-concepts in college-students. *Journal of Consulting and Clinical Psychology, 32*, 287–295.

Ruble, D. N., Frieze, I. H., & Parsons, J. (1976). Sex roles: Persistence and change. *Journal of Social Issues, 32(3)* (special issue).

Schein, V. E. (1973). The relationship between sex role stereotypes and requisite management characteristics. *Journal of Applied Psychology, 57*, 95–100.

Schein, V. E. (1975). Relationships between sex role stereotypes and requisite management characteristics among female managers. *Journal of Applied Psychology, 60*, 340–344.

Schein, V. E. (1976). Think manager—think male. *Atlanta Economic Review, 26(2)*, 21–24.

Sherif, C. (1982). Needed concepts in the study of gender identity. *Psychology of Women Quarterly, 6*, 375–398.

Sherman, J. A., & Denmark, F. L. (1978). *The psychology of women: Future directions in research*. New York: Psychological Dimensions.

Siltanen, J., & Stanworth, M. (1984). The politics of private woman and public man. *Theory and Society, 13*, 69–90.

Stewart, A. J., & Platt, M. B. (1982). Studying women in a changing world. *Journal of Social Issues, 38(1)* (special issue).

Stogdill, R. M. (1974). *Handbook of leadership*. New York: Free Press.

Taylor, S. E., Fiske, S. T., Close, M., Anderson, C., & Ruderman, A. (1977). *Solo status as a psychological variable. The power of being distinctive*. Unpublished manuscript, Harvard University, Cambridge, MA.

Taynor, J., & Deaux, K. (1973). When women are more deserving than men: Equity, attribution and perceived sex differences. *Journal of Personality and Social Psychology, 28*, 360–367.

Terborg, J. (1977). Women in management: A research review. *Journal of Applied Psychology, 62*, 647–664.

Touhey, J. (1974). Effects of additional women professionals on ratings of occupational prestige and desirability. *Journal of Personality and Social Psychology, 29*, 86–89.

Unger, R. K. (1978). The politics of gender. In J. A. Sherman & F. L. Denmark (Eds.), *The psychology of women: Future directions in research* (pp. 461–518). New York: Psychological Dimensions.

Unger, R. K. (1979). Toward a redefinition of sex and gender. *American Psychologist, 34*, 1085–1094.

Wallston, B. S., & O'Leary, V. E. (1981). Sex makes a difference: Differential perceptions of women and men. In L. Wheeler (Ed.), *Review of Personality and Social Psychology* (Vol. 2, pp. 9–41). Beverly Hills: Sage.

Wintermantel, M., & Christmann, U. (1983). Person description: Some empirical findings concerning the production and reproduction of a specific text type. In G. Rickheit & M. Bock (Eds.), *Psycholinguistic studies in language processing* (pp. 138–151). Berlin: de Gruyter.

Zellman, G. L. (1976). The role of structural factors in limiting women's institutional participation. *Journal of Social Issues, 32*, 33–46.

Chapter 12

Leadership Ms.-Qualified: II. Reflections on and Initial Case Study Investigation of Contemporary Women Leaders

Erika Apfelbaum and Martha Hadley

Several years ago, when Simone Veil was Health Minister of France and was rated among the most popular French political figures, she appeared on a television program, which had also invited as a guest that day Brigitte Bardot. In an interview following the show, Veil was asked to describe her feelings about meeting the famous actress. Smiling, she replied:

> I was very intimidated. Women, when asked, will tell you that they dream of being a movie star, not a minister of health; a man dreams of being President of the Republic, and not Alain Delon (Bothorel, 1977).

Veil's humorous and good-natured response pointedly reminds us that we have been socialized within a societal context that neither provides ready-made leadership role models for women nor kindles within them the desire to attain leadership positions.

However, there is much more involved when we begin to analyze the situation of women currently holding leadership positions. In this chapter, we shall consider certain prevailing approaches to the study of leadership as well as sketch some of our preliminary findings from interviews with contemporary women leaders. In doing this, two interrelated directions will be followed. The first suggests that, although women have not typically been socialized to develop what are conventionally thought of as leaderlike characteristics, there are many practices or *functions* associated with leadership positions that do, in fact, have parallels in women's traditional roles. These functions, practices, or skills are employed in the service of women's roles and values, but they may be transferable to more publicly acknowledged leadership roles. The second perspective highlights the patterns in the perceptions, experiences, and developments of women who, across different sectors of society and in two different countries, have attained acknowledged, public leadership positions in the present socio-historical context.

The growing trend in recent years for women—even those with small children—to enter the work force is now in the process of creating a changing social reality, as more than two thirds of working-age American women now hold jobs (Higbee, 1985). Despite their increasing participation, however, the proportion of working women in the upper echelons has not kept pace; disproportionately few women reach prominent high-level management positions, join the boards of directors of their corporations, or occupy the various leadership positions available in private enterprises or in academia. The situation in the public sector and in the political arena is proportionately even more imbalanced. This may be a historical consequence of the fact that in most societies women were granted the right to work long before the right to vote. In any case, their long-term general exclusion from the political process has resulted in the current situation, in which it is an extremely rare occurence to find women as prominent political figures.

Of course, there are exceptions to this rule, and these may be subsumed under several categories:

1. For *charismatic* leadership, Joan of Arc was probably a rather unique case and has become over the years a quasi-mythical figure. Less well publicized historical instances exist where women's names have been attached to the social movements they initiated and/or led, for example Ulrike Meinhof, Rosa Luxemburg, Emma Goldman, or Betty Friedan.

2. Women who become heads of family businesses or queens by succeeding to monarchs assume *inherited* leadership positions. In such cases, the legitimacy and entitlement of the woman occupying a leadership position is purely a function of legal inheritance, and is not being constantly evaluated or challenged on the basis of a demonstration of personal aptitudes or skillful leadership capability, as is the case for other leadership categories. Because of this essential difference, women born into leadership positions may not represent realistic role models for other women, whose pathways to leadership lack the instantaneous validation that accompanies an entrance to the top of a hierarchy through inheritance.

3. There are also some well-known examples of women who have *achieved professional eminence*, becoming leading figures in their disciplines because of their professional and/or scientific achievements. Thus Margaret Mead, Marie Curie, and others may be cited to demonstrate that women are not excluded from leadership in the worlds of science and academia. Some of these cases may require a closer look, paying particular attention to the special obstacles that these women who have "made it" have had to overcome en route. Thus Françoise Giroud (1981) stressed how reluctant contemporaries were in acknowledging Marie Curie's achievements as *hers* rather than her husband's. Social comparison theory (Festinger, 1954) suggests that such exceptional women may appear too different from the average woman, or at least from the perceptions most women have of themselves, to serve as comparison or reference points. When such talented

women are made to appear as token leaders, whatever excellence and uniqueness they possess disappears from view, and perhaps because of the perceived exceptionality of their leadership, they again cease to operate as realistic "comparison others" or role models for other women.

4. Finally, in recent years there has been a growing number of women who are *selected leaders*, being elected, appointed, or nominated to such important public offices as prime minister (Indira Gandhi, Golda Meir, Margaret Thatcher), president (Isabel Peron, Simone Veil), governor-general (Jeanne Sauvé), senator (Margaret Chase Smith), congresswoman, (Geraldine Ferraro), United Nations ambassador (Jeane Kirkpatrick), mayor (Jane Byrne), Supreme Court justice (Sandra Day O'Connor), and others.

Altogether, however, the women who have reached prominent and visible leadership positions by virtue of charisma, inheritance, professional eminence, or selection remain in people's perceptions and imagination as exceptions rather than as potential role models. A systematic study of the way media portray these women, we predict, would show that such presentations may actually discourage rather than promote any role identification by stressing the exceptionality of their capabilities, their personalities, or their leadership situation. Media presentations of women leaders, in other terms, are rarely neutral; rather, they insist on, and perhaps mystify, the exceptionality of such cases. As a result, visible women leaders may be limited in the extent to which they may become assimilated as realistic role models providing inspiration for a new generation of women.

However, the media notwithstanding, the situation might in fact be slowly changing; increased upward mobility for women and their growing number in upper echelons as well as in selected leadership positions are probably joint consequences of both their increasing power in the electorate and legislative changes (largely as a result of the actions of recent feminist movements) aimed at correcting social inequities facing women. These changes affect the overall social status of women, their work, and their patterns of professional promotion. These changes in behavior should ultimately lead to specific changes in women's sense of personal and political power and to more general changes in both men's and women's mentalities, their consciousness, and their day-to-day perceptions of and interactions with each other.

At present, however, the social environment is in a period of historical, cultural, and normative transition and is characterized by a wide variability in attitudes and readiness to accept the changing roles of women, especially in visible leadership positions. During these last few decades, the social-ization of women has become increasingly diversified. At one pole of this continuum we find a subculture of women socialized under the old traditional norms, where little girls grow up to become wives, mothers, cooks, and housekeepers. At the opposite end, one finds those raised under norms that stress increased autonomy in work or life-style beyond the traditional role constraints and career goals. Side by side, these variously socialized women are increasingly entering the male-led world of work. The range of this continuum sets the stage for confrontations of norms, values, attitudes, and aspirations with those commonly found in the traditional culture of work.

Because of this current dynamic situation of confronting belief systems, it is particularly interesting and relevant to study the case histories of women who have blazed new leadership trails and have become "pioneers," in the sense of having been the first to occupy acknowledged leadership positions traditionally held by men. Within such a context of social change, our study necessarily involves time-bound, transitory phenomena, yet it will at the same time present a unique opportunity to observe firsthand some aspects of leadership generally overlooked by leadership researchers. The pioneer women we wish to study have successfully negotiated the corridors of power in the male-dominated work world, but they started from a different socialization base and often proceeded along different career pathways. This puts them in a status of *double marginality*: on the one hand, their exceptional status as leaders differentiates them from most women, whereas their differential socialization and career advancement pattern in the professional world set them aside from the male leadership reference group. We hypothesize that such marginality as it exists at present should have some effect on how these women cope with their leadership positions and on their interactions with those around them (male leaders, subordinates, partners, etc.) as adjustments are made to the novelty and/or marginality of the situation of having a woman in a leadership position.

Toward an Expanding Conceptualization of Leadership

Unlike those theoretical discussions of leadership that seek to delimit general laws and provide more universalistic explanations, in this study we focus attention on the contextual specificities surrounding leadership, which include the sociological and structural aspects of the environment and the dynamics of social change, as they are reflected in norms, aspirations, and the development of career pathways. Such components are central to an understanding of the paths to power and/or leadership styles, even though these broader contextual features have been generally overlooked or neglected in current leadership research; we suggest that they be stressed as much as personal qualities or the strategic presentation of leaders (cf. Kennan & Hadley, this volume). In this way, we can go beyond current conceptualizations of leadership, which have been constrained within rather narrow boundaries and have examined a limited set of variables.

Upon closer examination of the current literature on leadership, it seems to us that the range of phenomena subsumed under the label "leadership" remains broad and imprecise; in fact, the notion of leader is often indiscriminately used without clear specification or reflection on whether it refers to someone with a constituency or followers, to someone who is innovative in a scientific or artistic field, or to someone with managerial functions. Furthermore, as part of this definitional problem, social science theories of leadership seem to have adopted, rather uncritically, popular notions of leadership and given them scientific status without further specification. Thus many studies focus on charismatic leadership (Weber, 1925) or on managerial leadership (Fiedler & Chemers, 1974). In the area of managerial leadership studies, for example, we can see clearly one of the common restrictions on leadership research: exclusive consideration is given to situations where men have been in the majority, if not the exclusive, role in filling leadership functions. It might be more accurate to label this research area as "male management."

There are of course areas where women have traditionally exercised managerial functions and where they have to assume responsibilities for various decisions. However, neither social scientists nor the lay public consider, for example, the skills required in running a family and in the teaching and socializing work done in various educational institutions as constituting arenas for the wielding of power and the demonstration of leadership functions. Therefore, the range of skills developed and used in these social contexts by women are not for the most part acknowledged as leadership skills. They therefore have not been taken into account in current research; this we see as another indication of the restricted range of leadership research and a reflection of the static view of a traditional social reality.

Yet these behaviors, and a variety of other accumulated skills exercised daily by women within the realm of their traditional roles, seem very similar to those that men utilize in various managerial positions. In other words, most contemporary research on leadership "perhaps reflecting the realities of the times. . . . has been concerned largely with men leading other men, and occasionally with men leading women" (Nieva & Gutek, 1981, p. 83). Recently, because of the increasing numbers of women joining the work force as well as the growing interest in research in women's studies, a certain number of projects have begun to deal specifically with the issue of women and leadership. According to Nieva and Gutek's review of the topic (1981, chapter 7), the research in this area can be categorized along three main lines: (a) an approach that focuses on the *personalities* of the leader, trying to discover whether women possess the proper personality traits that entitle them to apply for such positions; (b) an approach that questions the adequacy of women's *leadership styles*; and (c) an approach that considers the question of *leadership as power* and thus focuses on the differences between men's and women's use of power.

All three approaches share an overarching concern with a basic question of how both men and women leaders can be evaluated and distinguished against the traditional models and criteria of (male) leadership. No consideration is given to the evaluation of those managerial and leadership skills wielded primarily by women.

In Table 12.1 we have sketched some of the basic *savoir faire* skills (ability to handle things), which women have been traditionally trained and socialized to exercise quite competently and which are therefore part of their social and cultural heritage. We have juxtaposed this list of activities against what we hypothesize to be equivalent activities exercised by men in managerial leadership. The data remain to be gathered about the extent of the accuracy of this proposed matching. However, should such correlations be supported, totally or partially, what, we might then ask, would be the implications of such results for leadership theory in general? For the moment, we can only point to the total absence in contemporary accounts of

Table 12-1. Socialized Leadership Functions: Women's Heritage and *Savoir Faire*

Activities Associated with Conventional Roles of Women	Implied Leadership Functions
Running a home, classroom, or office; raising children, supporting, nurturing others	Management: maintaining relations, organization, and operations
	Initiating action and relations
	Taking responsibility for others and for activities
	Providing direction and ground for individual improvement
Negotiating and facilitating relations with others in the family as well as others in local settings	Negotiation and diplomacy leading to utilization and resolution of conflict
Teaching within and outside of the family group	Interpretation of and communication about events, circumstances, organizing principles, etc., to others
Recognizing and attending to the spiritual needs of self and others in everyday life	Sustaining morale and providing a larger, more transcendent world view
Maintaining and at times being the conscience of the family or community	Representing and providing a means of identification with legitimacy, honor, moral order

theories of leadership of discussion of leadership functions as they are exercised within the realm of women's traditional roles.

The comparison in Table 12-1 between women's *savoir faire* and men's skills seems to indicate that although the activities are equivalent, they do not imply the same type of contexts. Women, in their daily activities in the traditional roles of housewives and educators, tend to exercise leadership functions in interpersonal actions. They make decisions for, have influence over, and take responsibility for identifiable individuals and their well-being. Such individuals constitute their immediate surroundings or environment. In contrast, what is usually studied under the label "leadership functions" implies less personal domains of action: Traditional leadership functions are exercised in larger social and institutional domains, where the consequences of the decisions often fall impersonally and remotely on distant individuals, as is the case in large organizations or in politics.

Interviewing Women Leaders: A Pilot Study

Women's leadership today must therefore be examined against a structurally changing social environment. Our study begins by acknowledging the givens of current sociohistorical reality, which has generally left women in the margins when it comes to public leadership positions and roles. We have begun to explore how contemporary women ascend to leadership positions while coping with the constraints associated with their occupation of positions as acknowledged leaders—positions that would normally or traditionally be held by men. We examine the different reactions to their leadership praxis and the different paths they have taken toward leadership. We look at patterns in the motives, perceptions, and experiences of women who have attained acknowledged leadership positions in public or private arenas.

To develop some initial hypotheses, we interviewed 15 women who have reached prominent leadership positions in a variety of sectors of society both in France and in the United States; they are all highly visible and competent women who work in politics, finance, business, enterprise, journalism, and the judicial system.

Our objective in exploring these issues with contemporary women leaders includes a desire to better understand how the specific sociohistorical context in which these women's leadership is inescapably entrenched has influenced their evolution as leaders, shaped their roles, and determined the circumstances surrounding how, where, and when they attain such positions. We furthermore wanted to get some initial sense of the connection between their heritage and identity as women and their positional and structural identity as leaders: How have they been able to reconcile or separate, combine or ignore what traditionally have been two antagonistic identities, namely, being a woman and being a leader?

Through the life histories that we gathered from these women, we were trying (a) to explore the dynamics of how they have constructed their leadership roles; (b) to describe their experience of being in a minority as women leaders; and (c) to note how the awareness of this marginality, uniqueness, or "differentness" shaped the various steps and behaviors associated with their leadership functions. We thus tried to explore the phenomenon called leadership in a way that takes into account (1) the development of the individual's perceptions of self; (2) the adjustment to and interaction of that self with unique life situations during the development of the career; and (3) the dynamic contextual effects of a transitional sociohistorical reorganization of such institutions as work and traditional sex roles. We tend to think that leadership cannot be explained solely in terms of personal qualification—for example, valued personality traits or appropriate styles—nor solely in terms of situational demands, without taking into account additional contextual and developmental factors. By exploring the phenomenon of women's leadership and examining atypical cases and marginal occurrences, we hoped to uncover some of the contextual factors that are usually ignored or considered as extraneous variables by leadership researchers; in this way we hoped to contribute to a broadened analysis of leadership.

Our data gathering for this pilot study included the 15 interviews we have undertaken so far as a pilot study which would provide us with a preliminary reconnoitring of the terrain; on the basis of these women's discourse we hoped to develop a more systematic set of hypotheses. In the selection of respondents, we were at once faced with the question, "Who is a leader?"—a question implicating the theoretical problem of defining the range of issues covered under such a label. For our purposes, we decided to interview women who currently are, or have very recently been, in the public sphere in highly visible governmental or corporate structures, in positions traditionally held by men in any given institution.

The interviews were conducted by the authors, and each lasted about an hour and a half. Tape recordings were made for later analysis, and the respondents were assured that their names would not be revealed nor would any quotes used be directly attributed to them. The general outline for the interviews was designed by both authors and was systematically applied across all interviews. In line with the exploratory, case history approach of this initial study, the preliminary analysis reported below will be thematic or qualitative in nature, and a selection of quotes and examples will serve as illustrations of particular themes and concepts to be discussed. The transcripts generated by these 15 interviews as well as from other projected interviews will eventually be submitted to more systematic content analysis procedures.

Given the limited sample on which the following account is based, we must keep in mind that our findings may partially be the vagaries of a small, selective sampling and of random individual differences, as well as being in part linked to the recently changing attitudinal set in society, which, if it does not encourage, at least tolerates women who develop aspirations radically different from the traditionally socialized notions of "women's place."

Pathways to Leadership: The Activation of Women Leaders

Given the sociohistorical reality of the paucity of women leaders, it is not surprising to learn that, in most cases, the women who today hold acknowledged leadership positions did not plan at the outset to have career patterns explicitly orienting themselves toward leadership positions. Among the women interviewed to date, relatively few expressed the idea that from the beginning things were always clear to them and that they were determined, or concerned about, *doing* something and leaving some imprint on society. Those few women who were more future-oriented toward achievement were either of a younger generation or from exceptional families in which other women had already paved the way by becoming public figures. However, in reviewing these women's life histories, we were struck by the fact that, for many, there had been somewhere along the line a key event that broke their ties with a conventional life-style and life evolution. This might have been the personal impact of a war, of some major social unrest, or of some more private disruption such as the death of a close and significant family member. These events not only forced these women to change their personal agendas, but led them to redefine their reality—psychological and social—such that they would no longer remain passive onlookers or victims of events; instead they actively began to reposition themselves in life.

For example, an accomplished woman leader recollected that, when her husband died unexpectedly and she was left alone, she suddenly recognized that it would be exclusively up to her if either she or her child were ever to "be someone." They could not rely on her husband's identity and achievement to define a place for them in society. This repositioning of herself as a potential achiever (as if she implicitly gave herself permission to switch roles and become someone else) and as a maker of a name, in conjunction with her need to find a way to make sense of her husband's death, set her going along her radically changed life path.

This is just one example of the responses these women have made to adversity: responses they have referred to more or less explicitly and of which they may be more or less conscious. In any event, when these disruptions occur in their lives, these women become diverted from following the traditional pathways of other women like themselves. Thus, adverse external circumstances have (a) differentiated these women and perhaps marginalized them from other women, although the traditional others remain a strong, active reference group for them; (b) brought out in them certain qualities or attitudinal sets such as strong determination; and (c) contributed toward breeding certain strong values. We shall see that determination and values are instrumental in guiding these women through the unknown labyrinth of career pathways and the byways of power, and provide strong tools for coping and innovating when faced with novel situations requiring responses for which no precedent exists.

Another variation on this pattern of life disruption leading to career change is provided by cases of women who fulfilled traditional women's roles until life circumstances changed their paths and led them to reevaluate their own incentives. Consider the cases of women who begin by working for and serving male leaders in traditional roles as their secretaries, wives, "girls Friday," and the like. Then at some point they find themselves at a turning point, often stimulated by an exceptional and unpredictable circumstance, when they shift gears and begin to strive actively toward becoming leaders themselves. Such a change is accompanied by correlated shifts in self-concept and expectations of self.

A final pattern for some women (the minority in our sample) involves following relatively undisrupted trajectories along a career path. These women's careers are closer to those of men who patiently climb the ladder of leadership rather than being parachuted in from a network, club, elite academy, or *grande école*. Such women begin as supporters of men who are or were leaders; these men continue to act as mentors for the women assistants until, over time, these women emerge as leaders in their own right.

Generalizing from the majority of cases, however, some unique situation has often been responsible for changing their career path and consequently their perception of themselves. All have an unusual career pattern as compared to their contemporaries, both men and women, and follow unconventional roads to leadership and power as compared to men in similar positions. Their careers can be described as a gradual personal development of the necessary skills and self-conceptualization enabling them to engage in their current prominent roles.

Most of the time these women do not have the background or heritage of socialization shared by the men who have reached similar positions. In particular, these women have usually not gone through the same institutional training channels, because (a) these simply were not open to them at the time of their professional training, (b) access to certain steps of the hierarchy was blocked for them; or (c) they did not have at the outset clear enough conceptions of their careers which would lead them into leadership-oriented pathways. As a consequence, although they are highly visible, the interviewees generally expressed the sense that they are not as fully entitled to their leadership positions as men would be in comparable situations.

This perceived lack of entitlement is totally independent of their perceived job competence, which is never in question in the interviewee's mind.

Consequences of the Particular Pathways: Network Support, Interchangeability, Entitlement, and the Protégé System

The disruptions that ultimately led these women into pathways to power at the same time put them on different social tracks from those followed by the average women of their own cohort, and also from those followed by male leaders. Although in the end they became eligible for positions usually reserved for men, their different route upward has given them the sense, in their own minds, that they were not fully interchangeable with their male counterparts. They did not have the same background, nor therefore did they possess equivalent support systems.

Network Support

In particular, most of the women interviewed did not benefit in the same way men did from participation in the growing male networks of supporters, rivals, or friends that are generally part of the leadership apprenticeship in corporate, political, and academic arenas, These informal networks usually form in professional schools, such as the French *grandes écoles*, or through common membership in social clubs, masonic lodges, and other organizations, and come into play in various negotiations and stages of career advancement. Most of the women did not share such a traditional "old boys' network," which can be highly useful for future appointments, hirings, promotions, and the formation of an organizational "royal court." Women leaders therefore are often on their own, and the women in the interviews recognized such isolation. They then have to create alternatives to substitute for some of the functions these informal networks accomplish. It is predicted that a study following up, for example, the women who have gone through the *grandes écoles* in France would show that, at least until very recent times, they still are not treated equivalently, despite identical pathways, and do not benefit from the leadership network systems. There are variations in the degree to which the women we interviewed are aware that they lack such affiliations or are conscious of the ways they have used— or are able to use—such networks, albeit indirectly, through their mentors. Generally, however, we find that they do not share with their male counterparts an equal sense of network support.

One woman political leader presented an interesting variation on this theme. She had clearly been mentored by her male predecessor and was tolerated, although resented, by the network of men around this powerful man. In fact she views herself as having been elected in spite of them, attributing her victory to her sense of closeness with her electoral constituency rather than with the political machine. Once she had been elected to office, she consciously attempted to rebuild some new networks of influence but claimed to have given up because it did not prove, for her, to be an effective way of getting things accomplished. These are examples of some of the contributing social realities that give women the sense of lack of entitlement in their leadership positions.

The Protégé System

Another consequence of the lack of traditional pathways and professional training for at least some women in our sample from the older generation was the fact that their rise to power or their upward mobility pattern relied more frequently, as well as more exclusively, on a protégé system (cf. Nieva & Gutek, 1981). Many of the women we interviewed acknowledged that their apprenticeship had been the result of a mentor who taught them the basics and helped them through early critical experiences. This system also exists among male leaders, often as a potential promotion pattern, but in protégé systems a woman's past will haunt her more than a man's. This extra vulnerability about her entitlement and the lack of an equivalent male-style support network are a double burden for the woman.

In another scenario, which we have frequently encountered in our interviews, women have come to power and into positions such as governmental offices by the will of a superior authority—*le fait du prince.* "I am a token woman," claims a currently highly popular political figure. "If I have come to this position, it is because I am a woman and because it was the prince's doing."

Some women acknowledge that they have been qualified for leadership by a superior's decisions for reasons that seem to be partly independent of their intrinsic qualities, and women are deeply conscious of this paradox when their competence is not necessarily the main reason for their appointment. Rather, their leadership may be dependent on the fact that they were eligible for leadership precisely at a time when it was appropriate to promote women. This situation makes these women remain constantly aware of the precariousness of their positions, as they are at the mercy of the prince's will for their promotions or demotions. Simultaneously, however, being nominated by the prince gives them a status of unchallengeable legitimacy, which is a facilitating factor in their daily leadership praxis. Thus, for example, in cases where a woman has been appointed to a position of high public office by the highest authority in a given hierarchy, *her* exercising of authority is generally viewed by others as sufficiently legitimized by the high authority's nomination, and thereupon her authority is less likely to be questioned.

The protégé system and the superior authority's nomination as leadership pathways are probably equally likely to occur for men as for women, especially in the political arena, but one might predict that a comparative study would show that the attribution pattern and the justification systems in accounting for these promotions are probably very different for men and women, in the eyes of both the leaders themselves and their entourage.

Lack of Interchangeability and Entitlement

On a more social perceptual level, the women we interviewed—at least those of an older generation—are aware that they are not interchangeable with men in all circumstances despite the similarity of their positions and their equivalent recognized competence. In the eyes of the public, they do not have the same entitlement, and therefore certain actions they take will not have the same impact as when they are initiated by men. The interviewees have an acute awareness of this inequality. For example, one woman we interviewed worked for a leading weekly magazine expressing the views of the political opposition. However, when she was appointed by the male editor to replace him during his absence, she felt obliged to sign her strong editorial denouncing the Algerian war with the name of the magazine, rather than with her own name, in order to give full credibility to the statement. This clearly illustrates how women in leadership positions may at times be hampered by the social ecology in which they evolve. They still are *social anomalies* in the eyes of others—men and women—and have to take this into account when they take action.

The experience of some women leaders who are not part of an established network often involves the difficulties of integrating themselves into a long-established exclusive hierarchy, and they are acutely aware of how others perceive them. Many described their first situation as the only woman in a meeting, acting as if they belonged but often feeling others did not accept their right to be there, as if they had usurped power and as if others challenged the entitlement of their position. In various ways, their experiences are akin to those faced by an innovative scientist whose data and ideas provide anomalies for the leading paradigm and thus meet firm and sometimes blindly irrational resistance from the entrenched scientific community. The established scientists may resist new ideas and changes in practices that could lead to a paradigm shift and thus threaten their own self-representations as leaders (Lubek & Apfelbaum, 1979). After all, an old boys' network is an old boy's network—in science as in business or in politics.

The Anomalies of Women's Leadership Praxis: Coping With Issues of Authority

By whatever ways women presently come to power positions, they must constantly overcome feelings about lack of entitlement. They have internalized what they feel is the general sense of those surrounding them in their social environment concerning their entitlement. They maintain a sense of full confidence in their competence. This confidence is, for women, an absolute must—an *a priori* condition that cannot be bypassed in any attempt to rise to high leadership positions. Despite this competence, there is a general sense of being neither completely comparable nor inter-changeable with men in identical positions. This increases their sense of tokenism, precariousness, and vulnerability, each of these being ever-present elements of the social ecology in which women's daily leadership praxis occurs. Coping with this situation, even when it is not always explicitly perceptible or acknowledged, is described as requiring constant efforts, adjustments, and innovative strategies.

The area in which all these factors become particularly problematic and where the denial of entitlement from the entourage creates constant frictions concerns the question of authority. Things are fairly clear, women claim, when a high authority has nominated or appointed the woman (as in cases of appointments to ministerial offices). In these cases, the decisions the woman takes are all legitimized by the nomination itself. In contrast, when the leadership position is obtained by climbing the ladder of the pro-fessional hierarchy, there are greater risks of challenges of authority as well as of competence. Women claim that they constantly have to reassess the legitimacy of their decisions and that their power base is constantly being challenged, often with arguments involving personal innuendo. To cope with these adverse conditions they have to demonstrate constantly their total competence. They cannot afford to make mistakes because the consequences of such a mistake for the legitimacy of their power position are disproportionate to the fault.

A number of women have mentioned, in one form or another, that it was crucial in various work settings to maintain the belief in front of male colleagues and partners that no matter how high up their own positions might have been, they acknowledged in one way or another their male partner's superiority. One way of avoiding the role conflict situation due to the perceived anomaly of a woman in authority, in a normative context still clinging to traditional norms of male supremacy, was described by one interviewee. She talked about playing "momma leader" (a metaphoric representation of the late Prime Minister Golda Meir's image of leadership style); here the leader avoids crudely imposing her authority, decisions, and personal power by intermingling them, consciously or unconsciously, with the behavior of nurturant motherhood. As one political figure remarked, "It is is when you want to break away from this momma leader model that the problems start."

Another political figure recalled that her most difficult and stressful experience was when she became the first head of a new international agency. This body was composed of some of the highest authorities representing their respective countries, who were unequally prepared to face a woman as their leader. "At times," she said, "it was an unbearable and constant challenge to my integrity."

Although constantly reminded of their gender by their entourage, many of the interviewees were simultaneously called upon to suppress, minimize, or conceal their womanhood, unless they could use it in a maternal way that allowed the entourage to fall back into familiar patterns of responses. Women leaders are therefore, so to speak, social anomalies who have to negotiate the base for their leadership and construct their strategies, constantly keeping in mind the limits and constraints of the social ecology in which their position is entrenched.

Constructing the Functions, Praxis, and Social Ecology of Leadership

Because of these various limitations and because most of these women are not willing to put aside the values associated with their conventional women's socialization and heritage, they have had to develop a leadership philosophy and practice that encompasses their difference as women and that includes recognition both of their specificity and of their own personal concern with integrating these differences. As a consequence, the development of leadership activities (patterns, strategies) seems at times to be a highly personalized, creative process. Women construct their leadership style based on their different personal, social, and institutional experiences without much cultural reference (models, precedents) or cultural imagination concerning leadership as practiced by women. This need to construct an identity as a leader often results in different interpretations of leadership functions; thus to a certain extent women construct a personalized and novel leadership praxis. As one woman put it, "I had to be myself; to try and do it following the men who had done this before would have made me less credible and uncomfortable, like I was acting the part rather than living it."

In this partly innovative process of constructing their own strategies, modes of behaviors, and philosophy of leadership, the women we interviewed relied more or less explicitly on values originating in the family: "Women have a touch, they attend to details and people in a way that makes a difference." More generally speaking, however, most of the women interviewed stressed their will and determination to maintain intact values relating to family, nurturance, and children. Thus, a woman who directs some 400 persons at an advertising agency said, "If my children were to convince me that what I am after now is wrong, I would consider quitting."

Because of this strong bond and sense of fidelity to women's values and because of the pioneering status of their position, several women expressed a feeling of great responsibility that extends beyond their roles as leaders to the fact that they are women who somehow represent all women. They feel the burden of providing proof that a woman can do that job and do it well. Some justify some of the general political stances they take on issues as acts of faithfulness to their fellow women.

In addition, all these women expressed strong identification with certain basic values that are deeply internalized and serve as guidelines for their professional activities. Women in politics, for example, rather than identifying solely with party lines, are often guided by more basic, ethical principles and values that shape to a certain extent the way they evaluate the situation and make decisions. They may then rely on these values to identify with their leadership role when they may not feel justified or entitled to attain, claim, or assume leadership themselves.

Belief in certain personal values appears to have enabled many women to create and/or rationalize to themselves their own motivation and pursuits in the face of tremendous adversity or odds. For example, the leader of a financial institution in New York believes that the development of capital in a country or for a group that is trying to get established is a strong political act, one with more impact than sending CARE packages or even, at times, passing legislation. Being able to see and do things in unconventional ways perhaps represents certain free-spirit attitudes available to non-traditionally-socialized leaders which can serve as an instrumental element for the construction of their leadership strategy. Their identification and connection with critical values is sometimes facilitated by being in the right place at the right time in their lives. Thus, a black woman lawyer who left law school as the civil rights movement began to peak was carried by her role in the movement to a point where she can now identify herself with her current position as a pioneering black woman in the federal judicial system; she can now define herself in relation to the fulfillment of the ideals of that movement.

Most of these women recognize the nonpragmatic nature of these values with which they are so strongly identified; they are aware that these values are not often instrumental in achieving political goals in a traditional way. In fact, some admitted avoiding or losing political battles because of their own unwillingness to fight or compete directly in situations where values and issues important to them are either put aside or used for the sake of winning the game (even if only temporarily). Refusals of such compromises have been described by a number of women in our sample, although the strategies for compensating such refusals vary from one to another. For the sample of women who accepted participation in these interviews, we would claim that they have not completely accepted, nor have they totally identified with, the power games (and their rules) inevitably present in the social context in which they must operate.

One interesting transcultural difference sharply emerged in our sample. American women, in contrast to French women, when reflecting upon themselves emphasized more, or at least referred more explicitly to, the importance of personal values and the influence of these values on their leadership practice and style. However, it is still too early, given the vagaries of a limited sample, to try to draw general conclusions about cultural differences involved in constructing leadership strategies and in later reflections upon, and rationalizations about, these itineraries.

Given the anomalies of women's leadership praxis and pathways, a further question presents itself: "How do women perform their tasks and leadership functions, and more precisely, how do they view themselves in their daily practice?" Although all our respondents recognized the importance of individual styles and variations in the conceptions of the leadership functions, they also all agreed that, at rock bottom, leadership is a matter of accomplishment, in the sense of doing what needs to be done. Their definition of leadership in terms of getting the job done, as well as their self-definition as participatory leaders, expressed their focus on the accomplishment of results as well as the sense of caring and responsibility that motivates their actions. Several women contrasted their approach to leadership with styles that entail a great deal of pontificating or theorizing about the conceptualization of issues or ideology. They preferred down-to-earth actions addressing actual problem solutions: a more pragmatic and achievement-oriented leadership praxis. These women indicated that their approach to leadership praxis is regarded with a mix of admiration, devotion, and defensiveness by others in comparable situations who are more inclined to leave the "how" of leadership—the overseeing of the day-to-day operations—to others whom they appoint. The women in our sample reported that they tend to roll up their sleeves, literally, and "get their hands dirty" in the basic, groundbreaking work of a job, to the point that some claimed to lose track, at times, of how they are viewed by others, because of their focus on getting specific things done.

These women not only actively do what has to be done, but follow up on what others do at all levels; this contrasted with the more traditional style of first stating that certain things need to be done and then passing orders for actions to a person or group, who in turn passes the orders to successive levels in the hierarchy. This participatory style is closely linked to the way these women delegate authority or responsibility, always keeping contact with all levels of the hierarchy of which they are in charge. Recall from Table 12-1 that maintaining these direct interpersonal bonds is very similar to the ways of leading and managing smaller institutions, such as households.

Furthermore, the women in our sample stressed the importance of developing relations with others at all points in the hierarchy, as part of the task of identifying needs, strengths, and so forth within the organization. (This at times verges on the maternal, momma leader style—"They know I'll listen.") In so doing, they introduce a very personalized managerial style. Thus, despite the sense of lack of entitlement expressed above, these women clearly feel that the legitimacy of their power is contingent upon relations with others and on their ability to act on behalf of others.

In brief, the women in our sample claimed that their leadership starts with a concrete base of experience, care, and responsibility rather than from abstract principles, and once a problem has been identified, they insist on participatory supervision, concentrating more on the practical, end-efficient means of getting things done. Whether or not they are explicitly aware of it, the women interviewed described their leadership praxis as being different, in that it is more down-to-earth and more reality-bound and realistic. (In a way, they express some doubts about men's praxis, in much the same way that men express doubts about women's ability to be efficient on the job.) The interviewees, whether consciously or not, transfer into a situation requiring them to construct and carry out leadership functions their *savoir faire* skills, based on what we have identified above (see Table 12-1) as traditional women's leadership functions. They reported that these skills, which generations of women have been socialized to develop, produce a caring type of management. They adapt and use these skills to accomplish current leadership tasks and contribute to their own sense of legitimacy, thus getting the job done "on their own terms."

Creating an Alternative Ecology

In our sample, it was the French women who consistently stressed their sense of intense social isolation, experienced when they, as women, moved into leadership positions. Unlike the American women, they all described how they sought and established friendships with other women, which could be at any level of the organization's hierarchy. These ties involved some kind of unspoken, implicit mutual understanding and *entente* (or *connivence*). The relation thus established with these women cut across assigned statuses and roles and, by bringing more familiarity into the environment, provided the woman leader with a greater sense of security. One woman who owns and runs a nationwide business explained that she never used to have women friends until she became president of her company, but that now shc could hardly do without these workplace friendships. It appears as if these women are attempting to develop an idiosyncratic social ecology within the workplace, as a means to help counteract the constant stress of their position and to cope with day-to-day unexpected contingencies. It almost seems as if they had to construct, without willful effort, an alternative support system that might provide them with some of the equivalent functions that an old boys' network provides for men leaders.

These same women spontaneously evoke, with nostalgia and emotion, the recurrent concerns expressed to them by support service workers such as the building concierge or the chauffeur about their late working hours, going home alone, and so forth. When this concern by nonfamily members comes from someone at the workplace, it is generally from someone low enough in the organizational hierarchy that the devotion, admiration, and acts of kindness remain unambiguously divorced from competitive power considerations such as career advancement. These acts of kindness generally occur in a neutral context, for example, during an intermission or between the workplace and the home, as the woman switches from one locus of power into another. The very fact that, in the interviews, the women felt the need to insist on these tokens or expressions of emotional support offers us a clue as to the importance they attach to such gestures. It hints to us that here they may find partial compensation both for the sense of insularity that comes with their prominent positions and for the general lack of emotional support they encounter in the professional setting (and sometimes in their family environment as well).

These women also reported that they may seek out younger women as collaborators. Sometimes as they guide them and help them orient their future development, they themselves tend to become mentors for a younger generation. If this is the case, then we may be witnessing a period of radical change where the mechanisms for self-regeneration of women's leadership are progressively being established. We interpret these events as attempts to create an alternative ecology in which women can find the adequate elements of a support base—available to men in other settings—which will aid in the balanced exercise of the various leadership functions.

At first it may seem somewhat puzzling to find similar needs mentioned only rarely in the interviews with American women. In fact, it is likely that there are some very basic cultural differences between the two countries, involving radically different social norms and regulations involving self-disclosure, professional demeanor, interactions with psychologist interviewers, and the like. As another example of such differences in interview discourse, we noted that the French women, without being asked, all spoke freely about, and in some cases even were insistent about emphasizing, certain issues belonging to the private spheres of their lives, for example, their concerns about the difficulties of maintaining a balanced relation with their spouses. Rarely did the American women mention similar preoccupations. It may well be for them that the spheres of the personal and the professional are more sharply demarcated, with little overlap. Therefore, when interviewed about leadership, issues involving work become totally dissociated from the personal sphere of their lives, and hence a different discourse is offered.

The Public and the Private: The Double Standard for Women Leaders, a Further Ms.-Qualification

To paraphrase a zen koan, a woman leader remains a woman remains a woman, no matter how well she may duplicate the functions of a male leadership role. No matter how hard she tries, she cannot escape being perceived and judged as a *woman* leader. Her gender is always in the way of any evaluation and acts as a filter for evaluating all her activities. All the women, but particularly those in positions of political leadership, indicated how conscious they are of the interpretations they receive from others *vis-à-vis* their characteristics as women; they are caught in a situation where the private and the public are inescapably intermingled.

For men leaders, reference to the private domain, such as the family, usually emerges under exceptional circumstances and often is portrayed as a special bonus, in addition to all the professional accomplishments. The classic example occurred in the 1950s when Richard Nixon appeared about to lose the vice-presidential nomination because of charges of campaign improprieties. He addressed a large television audience, accompanied by his smiling wife, and made a plea for public support. Much of the speech dealt with his family and its organization and financing; for example, his wife chose, instead of furs, a "sensible Republican cloth coat." In fact, the only wrongdoing admitted to during the broadcast was in accepting a gift for his children, a dog named Checkers. This speech may well have saved Nixon's political career.

For women, on the contrary, the juxtaposition of public and private domains seems to be the rule. This provides a regular source of conflict which cannot be ignored but must be given constant attention: The women need to construct their strategies around this question of the overlap of public and private spheres. They feel, for example, that their expression of emotion, hairstyle, clothing, and interactive style with others are always being observed, interpreted, judged, and commented upon. They know that the fashionableness of their dress or hairstyle or their relations with their husband or children will always be a target for public discussion. They are all too aware that what belongs to the private domain can at any time be made public and can be used against them to tarnish their leadership image. Articles that discuss how women leaders prepare their own or their family's dinner may simultaneously serve the function of putting these women back into the kitchen, thereby putting them back into their traditional "place," and thus putting them down. For these women, the private cannot remain neutral. In a recent article it was argued that "young girls" in Britain, in having Prime Minister Thatcher as a role model, did not have an honorary man:

> In Mrs. Thatcher they see not only a hard-line Tory but a woman who cries when her son is lost in the desert, who manages to look good when nearly 60 and who will not fire a minister who gets into a sex scandal, because she is loyal to him. (Maddox, 1984).

Consequently there is a permanent focus and an ever-present concern to keep the proper balance between the public and the private image. Although the problem seems to be universal, the coping strategies for the women in our sample were quite varied. Some tend to keep the two worlds as separate as possible, in an attempt to overcome the conflict caused by the overlapping roles defined by gender and profession. They spend much energy avoiding situations that might generate a statement such as, "Sure she is the president, but she still is a good mother." Others try to integrate, more or less consciously, their private life and image with their projected public image. On certain occasions, this can serve the positive function of facilitating acceptance of them as leaders, when the acknowledgment of their traditional role makes them seem a less threatening figure (e.g., a momma leader). The older women are relieved that their age prevents, or at least diminishes, the constant need to cope with such interfering issues as the necessity of keeping male partner at a proper distance, in a proper interpersonal relationship. The younger women are aware of the constant burden of having to set the rules for interactions and communications, and the need to reassess one's positions with respect to the interlocutor. Thus, the necessity of balancing public and private images, given the perceptions of both the public and the press, becomes a focal point for the construction of their specific leadership modalities. Here women leaders are treated noticeably differently from men.

Future Perspectives

Our conclusions thus far remain largely impressionistic, given the sample's limited size and unsystematic selection. The preliminary analysis of our interviews must also eventually give way to more systematic content analysis techniques. Nonetheless, despite these limitations, at least three variables emerged which, we feel, will require further systematic study on a larger sample. For the *age cohort* or generation variable, our limited sample did not permit sufficient differentiation of career pathways; yet we feel there is more to be studied concerning differences in personal and training pathways and the internalized sense of entitlement. For the younger, up-and-coming generation, it may well turn out that the different pathways to leadership for men and women have begun to converge and are becoming more similar (cf. the recent trend toward forming women's business networks). Another important variable to take into consideration in future research is the distinction between women leaders in *political versus management* arenas. To what extent are there differences in situations involving nominations through the "will of a prince" or mentor, and to what extent are they linked to factors involving differential stability and permanence of power hierarchies in business and political institutions? The third factor concerns the *transcultural* aspects of leadership, and it has been at once heuristically stimulating and somewhat frustrating to see various differences emerge between the French and American subsamples. The women's grasp of issues and the way these are conceptualized and then expressed in interviews are somewhat culture-bound; a concept such as "power" had different connotations on either side of the Atlantic. Obviously, more systematic study is needed to separate out these cross-cultural differences.

The cross-cultural variable also touches the very dynamics of the data-gathering process—the interview situation. Even if the research design were to include counterbalancing to control for interviewer differences between the two authors—one American, one French—there are still important cultural differences in the meaning attributed to a one-and-a-half-hour interaction between strangers that has been mutually labeled an "interview." Each response to our interview questions is formulated within a given sociocultural context that sets the norms and limits, both about what belongs to the subject under investigation and what can be divulged in such a setting.

We have relied on the interviews as a means of extracting those portions of the discourse that are accurate reports of the actions, feelings, and motives of leadership praxis. We realize, however, that the way in which people speak about themselves in their verbal reports not only reflects their real-world actions but is colored as well by certain social representations, as the interviewee rethinks, reevaluates, reconstructs, and reports her praxis in the light of her own particular socialization and cultural background. Also, the interviewees did not always report retrospectively all the social and contextual constraints that had surrounded their praxis at the time they implemented their leadership functions. The limiting effects of the expectations that others have of their leadership—which often become internalized—always hover in the background of these interviews and require further probing and analysis. These interviews thus provide data on leadership praxis, the filtered social representations of leadership, and even the stereotypes of leadership externally imposed by others and internalized by the women themselves.

It is our contention that leadership should not be currently viewed solely in static, universalist terms such as style, personalities, or power, but needs in addition to reflect changing historical, cultural, normative, contextual, and developmental factors. We therefore suggest that a far broader conceptual analysis of leadership than is presently available is needed, because the social phenomenon of women's leadership continues to grow against a changing social ecology. How will the transitions now under way in men's and women's respective social statuses affect the praxis of up-and-coming generations of leaders and how will such changes in the social ecology filter down through the prestigious training institutions (such as the Harvard Business School or France's École National d'Administration) and affect the socialization of future leaders? In any event, as we have attempted to show in this study, the phenomenon of *women's leadership* can no longer be treated as just a minor, exceptional anomaly; within the study of leadership in the social sciences, it now has distinctive enough characteristics that it can no longer be ignored or misqualified.

Acknowledgments. The assistance of Ian Lubek at various stages during the writing of this manuscript is gratefully acknowledged.

References

Bothorel, J. (1977, December 6). Simone Veil: Femme . . . mais surtout ministre. *Le Matin*, p. 12.

Festinger, L. (1954). A theory of social comparison processes. *Human Relations, 7*, 117–140.

Fiedler, F. E., & Chemers, M. M. (1974). *Leadership and effective management.* Glenview, IL: Scott, Foresman.

Giroud, F. (1981). *Une femme honorable.* Paris: Fayard.

Higbee, A. (1985, February 2). American topics. *International Herald Tribune*, p. 3.

Lubek, I., & Apfelbaum, E. (1979). Analyse psycho-sociologique et historique de l'emprise d'un paradigme: L'apprentissage S-R, l'hypothèse frustration-agression et l'effet Garcia. *Recherches de psychologie sociale 1*, 123–149.

Maddox, B. (1984, January 13). A reply: No, women aren't better off in America. *International Herald Tribune*, p. 4.

Nieva, V., & Gutek, B. (1981). Women and work: A psychological perspective. New York: Praeger 1981.

Weber, M. (1925). *Wirtschaft und Gesellschaft.* Tübingen: J.C.B. Mohr.

Chapter 13

Scientific Leadership

Joseph Agassi

In this chapter I shall begin by rejecting the two traditional views of leadership, of the Enlightenment and of Romanticism. The Enlightenment is often known as the eighteenth century philosophy, but erroneously so, as it includes John Stuart Mill, Bertrand Russell, and even Karl Popper. Likewise, Romanticism is often known as the nineteenth century philosophy, but erroneously so, as it includes Martin Heidegger, Michael Polanyi, and even Thomas S. Kuhn. They offered unacceptable ideas—especially unacceptable when applied to any leadership, scientific or political. Leadership is both unavoidable and possibly desirable. Examination of both the positive and the negative role leaders play reveals that even within the scientific community there is no way to escape leadership. Ignoring the role of leaders in science does not help us control them democratically and is therefore harmful, or at least it reduces the benefit from their activities. Only by discussing the function of leaders can we force them to fulfill their function tolerably well. The first part of this chapter is a discussion of the general issue of leadership and after that some conclusions from the discussion are applied to the specific issue of scientific leadership. Only then will it be possible to discuss the urgent matter of the function of scientific leadership and how best it can be exercised.

The Need For Leadership

The western democratic tradition differs from all other known traditions in many respects, no less in its attitude toward leadership than in any other. Broadly speaking, democracy limits the power of leaders by democratic checks and balances and by direct democratic controls. The ideological expression of this attitude is the rejection of the cult of personality. The democratic individual finds it incredible that so many political leaders in ancient Egypt and ancient Rome were considered divine, that comrade Stalin was considered all-knowing and above reproach or criticism, that the Nazis pledged blind obedience to their leaders. This rejection of the cult of personality was rooted in the theory of the autonomy of the individual. According to this theory rational individuals make their own rules, follow their own understanding and conscience, and therefore owe allegiance to no one and follow no one but themselves.

All this sounds commonplace and will cause no raised eyebrows when said in almost any democratic company, whether a political or social gathering or an intellectual seminar or study group. This is an empirical fact. Those puzzled by these statements will either be puzzled about the need to utter them since they seem so obvious, or will be provoked to explain their dissent, thus risking being accused of antidemocratic or authoritarian tendencies.

A view may seem so obviously democratic, however, yet be far from obvious. Thus, the traditional democratic view of political leadership is blatantly false and even clearly inconsistent. The inconsistency is between the democratic control of leadership and the democratic rejection of it. To continue my empirical observation, people confronted with this inconsistency declare it a mere matter of formulation. Challenged to remove the contradiction, they discover that the task is much harder than it looked initially.

The way to remove the contradiction is this: The autonomy of individuals is not impaired by their electing a representative and delegating authority to that representative. (A representative is the same as a delegate in this context, although in general when we delegate authority we allow our representative to surmise our wish on some specified sort of occasion.) Democratic control, then, is the process by which individuals ensure that their representative acts according to instructions. This does remove the contradiction, but it runs contrary to all known facts. Everyone familiar with the political process knows the difference between a representative and a leader and even between a representative's action as a delegate and his or her action as a leader. Nor are all actions of the representative as a leader unconstitutional in character, needing to be prevented by tight controls.

This criticism can be made more theoretically, by reference to more abstract political facts. It is generally agreed that democratic control is not the same as the elimination of the representative's errors, that when a whole constituency errs, it may very well require that its representative follow its instruction all the same: To limit democratic representation to demonstrated views precludes democratic dissent and debate; the requirement for democratic disagreement amounts to permission for a constituency to send in good faith a representative sharing most of the opinions of most of its members—even though they may be in error. This, however, is not to say that democracy permits any error at all to be espoused by an elected representative or leader. We usually distinguish errors made in good faith despite all reasonable precaution, from errors that are irresponsible. It is against irresponsible error that democratic control is directed.

Traditional democratic theory of leadership representation declares individuals autonomous and so responsible only to themselves. Responsibility is thus the direct outcome of autonomy; hence, clearly, the representative's responsibility is voluntarily delegated and voluntarily accepted. This theory is false. Leadership older than democracy may be commendable or condemnable: Responsible leadership is certainly superior to irresponsible leadership even in a predemocratic society. Can traditional democratic theory make sense of this preference? No. A valiant effort was made recently by Ronald Dworkin to make sense of it by declaring every society tacitly a democracy and every constitution implicitly upholding the principles of human rights. This sounds odd, because most constitutions notoriously reject democracy and violate universal human rights. This, however, is a technicality: Constitutions are often inconsistent, and as the United States Supreme Court repeatedly illustrates, many laws on the statute books there were unconstitutional nonetheless. The reason that this theory that all constitutions are democratic is so objectionable is that responsible leadership of an undemocratic state must act undemocratically quite regularly, yet they at times act responsibly, and at times not. Nor is all democratic action responsible; even the democratic act of holding a referendum need not be responsible. It is, indeed, the accepted view of many historians that the frequent use of the obviously democratic institution of ostracism weakened and finally destroyed Athenian democracy. True or false, this is but an instance of the failure of the democratic leadership to act responsibly and adequately, with the result that there can arise tyranny by popular demand. If individuals are responsible only to themselves, then clearly action by popular demand is largely responsible action. The consequent of this obvious conditional statement is false; therefore, so is its antecedent. For we do recognize the relinquishing of political responsibility as different from the relinquishing of personal autonomy: Becoming a slave is morally objectionable in a different way then supporting a tyranny, and moral apathy is different from political apathy. Presumably, perhaps, in normal circumstances the political apathy of an ordinary citizen is not really reprehensible or problematic, whereas moral apathy is always both reprehensible and an urgent problem for the political and moral leadership.

We conclude that responsible leadership is not limited to democracy, nor is irresponsible leadership absent there; responsibility cannot then be reduced to individual autonomy. Once we conclude that there is not only such a thing as responsible leadership but also responsible citizenry, we can see how remote from being satisfactory is the classical democratic reduction of responsibility to individual autonomy.

The traditional antidemocratic theory of politics need not be given much critical attention. It calls for strong political leadership responsible not to the people but to itself and to the national destiny to which it alone has a privileged access. Irresponsibility is then discoverable only as the result of failure, if at all. Failure may be charged to sheer unforseeable bad luck, such as stationing one's troops on ground where a large-scale natural disaster strikes. This theory is most questionable, and sounds convincing only because its traditional democratic alternative is erroneous. For, democratic autonomy is no foundation for the authority of responsible government. Now this fact is not sufficient foundation for the rejection of democratic autonomy, even if autonomy should prove to be irrelevant to the question, how shall we establish responsible government? Thus traditional anti-democrats reject autonomy and democracy on the excuse that the one is an insufficient ground for the other. Yet all those who wish to retain democracy, and all those who wish to boost democratic autonomy and responsibility, will do well to express an unqualified preference to democracy over non-democracy.

However, once we opt for democracy first and thus relinquish un-democratic leadership, it is not sufficient to demand that democratic leadership be responsible: The responsibility of the democratic leadership must be defined vis-à-vis its expected function. In particular, if it has no vital function we may raise the question of the desirability of doing away with leadership altogether. It is a curious fact that the support of a tyrannical government advocated by Thomas Hobbes and the support of a minimal government advocated by John Locke differ mainly on this very point. Hobbes argued that government is required to prevent civil war on the assumption that man to man is wolf, whereas Locke taught the opposite on the assumption of man's natural goodness. (This is why Hobbes counts as inherently a liberal despite his frank advocacy of tyranny.) The assumption of the radical right, as it is called, is no longer the natural goodness of man, but the mere corollary to it: that society can best be regulated by the market mechanism on condition that government intervene minimally with the market and act (as Locke recommended) only as the keeper of the civil order and the enforcer of freely undertaken contracts. That the radical right's position as articulated here is impossible to implement is obvious: Suffice it to observe that society cannot be governed without some policy toward neighboring nations, and that this policy of necessity constitutes a gross intervention in the market. Yet this criticism of the radical right is less significant than the praise it deserves for its description of the role of government which thus lays certain responsibilities at its door. Yet even on the assumption of the doctrine of the radical right concerning the role of government, the government's responsibilities are not thereby fully de-scribed. The government of a democratic society in which not all citizens belong to the radical right must have some additional responsibilities which are somehow related to public opinion. (This explains why the demo-cratically oriented radical right repeatedly exhibits antidemocratic traits.)

It is a remarkable fact that, despite the long tradition of democracy which preceded the work of John Stuart Mill, he was the first (together with Alexis de Tocqueville) to say that in some other cases the majority has to rule even if the majority is in error, whereas in some cases it is contrary to the spirit of democracy to allow the majority to rule, even if the majority is in the right. Such things as minority rights and the citizens' right to their own convictions regardless of the majority view must be respected and protected in a democracy with (almost) no qualifications, he taught. This is admirable, of course, yet it is only the thin edge of the wedge. We face now a very broad and significant question: How much authority does the majority opinion carry? This is a very complicated matter, pertaining, as it does, to an extremely broad range of possible situations.

The picture is complicated by the existence of levels of activity which invite leadership. The lowest level is that of facing concrete situations which call for public action or for mass action that invites coordination. Thus, when it is more important to act together than to choose the best way to act, what is contemptuously known as herd mentality is the proper mentality: Contempt for this kind of action does not make it wrong. Acting like a herd does not make people a herd, whereas not acting like a herd when it is imperative to do so is taking an unnecessary risk and so is irresponsible. (It is a risk either to life or to the outcome of the leader's responsible action). The refusal to act responsibly by displaying obedience produces the typical alienation of ever so many Western intellectuals who wish to, but cannot, be politically active. In a military action, when the leader—be he the lieutenant or the minister of defense—gives a mistaken order, it may be a risk to one's life to strike out on one's own, for example. It is a very serious and painful question to face when one must, as the leader of a minority maltreated by an irresponsible majority, decide whether to maintain unity or to break away. The thinkers who declare such problems rooted in herd mentality are profoundly inadequate as social animals to the point of becoming a demoralizing and a depoliticizing influence in their society.

The injustice of contempt for herd behavior can best be seen in the magnificent and democratic manifestation of herd behavior in democratic countries like the United States, and to a much greater extent in undemocratic countries like Poland, where anonymous participation is undertaken at the risk of life and at least of personal liberty, such as it is. There is little doubt that the inability to organize opposition to the regime, in Nazi Germany or in Stalinist Russia, makes it quite impossible to assess the potential of that opposition were it possible to lead it one way or another in a concerted fashion.

On a somewhat more abstract level, when unity is threatened it is the task of the leadership to see how it can be maintained, if at all, and to maintain it, if the cost is not too high. Here one cannot judge the degree of responsibility of an unsuccessful leadership without knowing what effort it has made to seek a solution, and whether it did find an adequate solution. (Here R. G. Collingwood is partly right: although we can reconstruct and assess responsible error, it is at times easier to have an adequate picture of a successful action than of a failure to act or of a failed action.) There is no doubt, for example, that in a country where highway accidents are intolerably common, as is the case almost everywhere in the industrialized world, the almost universal irresponsibility of the political and public leadership there rests in its very failure to raise high on the agenda the question of how to handle the situation.

On a still more abstract level, the leadership, to be democratic, has to cater to differences of conditions, values, and opinion and to conflicting interests within sectors of the public (cf. John Stuart Mill). Nor are these two roles unconnected. One of the most vicious and demoralizing influences on democracy is the reactionary theory (regrettably endorsed by Marx and through him by many who erroneously consider themselves progressive) that all political views are mere reflections or rationalizations of interest, whether political or economic. The role of leadership is to raise the level of public responsibility and to cater to the general or public interest rather than the narrow group interest. One can easily sink into the mire of moralizing and denounce every act taken on the basis of personal interest and call for disinterested, morally correct behavior. Such moves are neither morally nor politically serious but are rooted in a profound confusion (and were justly ridiculed by Marx and Engels in the *Communist Manifesto*).

The situation is extremely problematic and is known in the literature as the conflict between immediate and deferred gratification, short-term and long-term interest, local and global considerations, and so on. We do not know when it is wiser to utilize our resources at once, and when to keep them for an emergency. We do not know how much we should spend on essentials and how much on luxuries, or how much we should invest in creating good will and how much we should utilize it. On most of these matters, vague socially and politically accepted standards are applied through vague deliberations. When unusual circumstances happen, this procedure is not good enough, and quite often it is the role of the leadership to present the situation clearly enough so as to amass consensus. If we consider the consensus on the application of vaguely accepted vague standards as common sense, then the leadership often exhibits the paradoxical quality of exceptional common sense in such cases: the solution is exceptional, yet it achieves immediate consensus. Because of the vagueness of all this, we can also observe the opposite case of irresponsible leadership who may often sound commonsensical, especially after the leadership represses, rather than encourages, critical debates. Cannons instead of butter! Heavy industry instead of light industry! Hard science instead of mere metaphysics, literary talk, and broad outlines!

The Scientific Leadership

The leadership of the scientific community is a test case for all discussions of leadership, as nowhere is autonomy more valued than in science, and nowhere is there less need for any organized political or quasi- or semipolitical group action. Indeed, throughout the golden age of classical science—from the mid-seventeenth century to the end of the nineteenth— there was no social organization of science except in the scientific societies, most of which sprang into being in the early nineteenth century. The universities were indifferent to science until France instituted scientifically oriented secular universities in the wake of the French Revolution and Prussia responded somewhat later. In England things went more slowly: the granting of honorary doctorates at Oxford to John Dalton and Michael Faraday was quite controversial, yet at the same time, toward the mid-nineteenth century, something like scientific education began there with the improvement of mathematical teaching and the offering of a mathematical specialization. The first scientific laboratory in an English university was instituted in 1870 at Cambridge. Except for the Royal Observatory and the Royal Institute, which together housed no more than a dozen researchers, there were no researchers institutions in England prior to World War I, and university professors there seldom did scientific research.

With a scientific community so amorphous as to be considered a club of sorts, one wonders if it had any place for leadership. That depends on how science in general is viewed. The most popular view of science today is one devised by Michael Polanyi and popularized by Thomas S. Kuhn. They describe the scientific community as one free from external pressure yet subject to internal pressure from its own leadership. The leadership, says Polanyi, is intellectual: It makes mainly intellectual proposals that are accepted by the scientific community, or else it loses its place at the helm. Kuhn elaborates and sees-observes that pressure is applied both in the intensive professional training and in the imposition of new paradigms for researchers to emulate. The means of pressure, says Kuhn, are linked to the financial and prestige benefits of the scientific community. The people who invent a new paradigm, then, control the means of livelihood of any potential deviant. How, then, is the decision made whether to endorse a new paradigm or to overthrow the leadership? Assume that the majority vote is the effeactive unanimous vote (namely, that the minority is forced to toe the line or leave), and take it as what decides matters. How, then, do individuals vote? Polanyi says, and Kuhn agrees, that scientists use tacit personal knowledge: each of them decides privately and unanimity is reached by means of the force of the tacit, ineffable, but uniform tradition they share.

Polanyi, then, explains the united scientific front by reference to tradition. Kuhn also refers to more mundane social factors, such as scientific jobs, to explain the same fact. The tradition is maintained because society at large accepts the authority of the scientific leadership, then. What, then, holds society at large? Kuhn has not spoken to this question. Polanyi, at least, has strongly expressed his adherence to the values of liberal democracy. This difference may or may not reflect the difference in time and place, with Polanyi as a central European, politically committed scientist from early in this century and Kuhn as a midcentury, American Ivy Leauge, politically indifferent professor. Be that as it may, Polanyi views the leader as limited by tradition and as dependent on it, whereas Kuhn's view is anchored in the social situation of science as a profession and so allows for a more dynamic, less tradition-bound scientific community. Yet both consider science with no leadership unthinkable.

Whatever happened to the classical ideology of science, the philosophy of the Enlightenment, and its appeal to the autonomy of the individual and its view of legitimate leadership as the mere representation of autonomous individuals?

The political philosophy of the Enlightenment movement led to the American and French Revolutions. The former succeeded; the latter failed. The philosophers of the Romantic reaction saw this failure as a refutation of Enlightenment ideas and argued that we must replace autonomism with traditionalism. Autonomy was to be granted only to the lone hero: be he an artist, a religious reformer, or a political leader. The Reaction thus replaced universalism with particularism, not to say parochialism and xenophobia. Its ideology was not fit for the scientific community, which (with the exception of Nazi science) always remained universalist and international. The scientific community, then, stuck to its ideology, but withdrew from the political arena almost exclusively, although some of its pioneers, such as John Stuart Mill, reinvaded the social sciences. The majority of the scientific community hid behind specialization and avoided voicing liberalism outside science, and some, even some important thinkers, were followers of the Enlightenment within science but of the Reaction within politics. This was disastrous, and sooner or later scientists could not avoid voicing liberalism in general. Even scientists who had had reactionary, almost Nazi sympathies had to voice liberal opinions after World War II. Werner Heisenberg is the most conspicuous example.

This development was not a mere reversal to the philosophy of the Enlightenment. The universalism and liberalism scientists now preached was no longer of the radical sort; rather, commonsense made them recognize the political leadership of the liberal democratic states. They likewise recognized science as a community, as a social substratum or class, a social elite of the sort that modern liberal democratic states allowed to thrive, not necessarily in agreement with the classical egalitarianism of the Enlightenment. Science thus came after World War II to be recognized as authoritative, its authority deemed interlarded with the authority of its leadership. The authority of the scientific leadership was thus considered rational—albeit commonsensically and with no clear-cut theory of rationality to replace the one preached by the great traditional thinkers of the

Enlightenment. When Kuhn gave expression to all this in the United States, most scientists and practically all scientific leaders said that he had well-articulated exactly what they had felt all along, and thus they embraced his doctrines without hesitation.

Two important innovations stand behind Kuhn's scheme, which were allowed neither by the Englightenment nor by the Romantic movement. They are the Manhattan Project and the practice of specialization. The Manhattan Project, and a number of similar organizations which succeeded it, including NASA, AEC, and CERN, are politically important organizations manned by people with scientific degrees working on very specific and frankly technological problems. Their sociology and research fit Kuhn's description well enough and make one overlook the pathetic failure of the leaders of the Manhattan Project to participate in major political and military decisions. It was their right and duty to think about their participation well in advance, yet they did not, and then they were caught quite unprepared. Specialization, however, now obliterates this failure and makes the sad precedent into a norm: Scientists now claim leadership at most only within the scientific community and eschew responsibility for anything else. This way the role of scientists as leaders in national and international politics is entirely ignored in this context, and so they play this role on the basis of unexamined commonsense, not on the basis of any well articulated theory. We may ignore here the role of scientists as leaders outside science, and notice that the more specialized science is, the more important the role of leaders becomes in determining and in coordinating all of its specializations and subspecializations: With most scientists specialized, they now need coordination and guidance more than ever. When scientists were individual club members, coordination and united front were hardly necessary. Now they are essential. Let us look at the new problem situation and its call for a leadership.

The specialized scientists can overlook politics, and the arts and much of the sciences, but they cannot ignore all the sciences outside their domains of specialization: domains of specialization have the awkward habit of overlapping in some unexpected ways. When they do, someone ought to know and some specialized knowledge must be transferred. Here a new situation occurs which is not permitted by the classical canons of science: one scientist has to trust another. Perhaps this was always so. The Enlightenment tradition of science, however, refused to recognize this and demanded that scientists trust only their own intellect and senses, and give their assent to nothing they have not personally examined. This is the Enlightenment doctrine of autonomy and of openmindedness, the theory of rational assent. And the theory of rational assent describes the facts of classical science better than those of modern science: Though few researchers were in possession of the mathematical skill required to examine Newton's calculations, they all could understand enough of Newton's theory to seem to have examined it personally and endorsed it deliberately and to have given their assent to it quite rationally, with no influence from peers. In the modern world, this description obviously does not even approximate the facts. Today scientists frankly admit to accept on faith many claims made by peers in neighbouring specialties. This way the problem became pressing: How can we rationally trust the opinions of others?

This problem is still repeatedly and systematically masked by most philosophers of science, most of whom still endorse the theory of rational assent, now better known by the name of inductive logic. They thereby stick to the philosophy of the Enlightenment and seek criteria for each person's choice of the right theory—criteria for inductive rational belief—as if everyone could apply these criteria and make the right choice of theory for oneself on the basis of logic and empirical evidence alone, quite regardless of what the world thinks. It is obvious that even if such an inductive formula were possible and could be discovered, the only individuals who could apply it to a given field of expertise would be at most the acknowledged experts in that field. If psychiatrists think psychotherapists are superstitious and vice versa, the inductive formula could hardly straighten matters out: No one would apply the formula to mental illness except expert psychiatrists and expert psychotherapists, and they will use the formula to intensify their disagreement. This is a very well known fact. It was amply stressed by Sir Francis Bacon, the father of the modern theory of induction. The inductive method, he said, is only useful when used by openminded individuals; when used by others, who approach matters with preconceived opinions, induction only strengthens prejudices. This is why Sir Francis Bacon demanded that we give up our prejudices as the very first step. Does anyone hope that the inductive formula will decide that psychiatrists are right and psychotherapists prejudiced, or vice versa? On the contrary, the very inductive philosophers who seek the formula wish the formula to confirm science and repudiate prejudice by itself: they never discuss the question, what is and what is not science, and they dare not go into case studies with their proposed formulas.

The problem is not, How can I judge who is right? For it matters little if I side with one party or another in a scientific dispute to which I am no party. Nor is the problem one of inductive policy, so-called, namely, How should I act? For as far as the application of advanced science and of advanced technology is concerned, matters are not given to the decision of the individual, or even to the whole scientific and technological community, but rather the behavior of scientific experts is constrained and governed by the laws of industrially advanced society. It is not that the experts and the laws are good, for the scientific leadership is still not brought under sufficient democratic control (think of the deplorable conduct of Glenn Seaborg and the Atomic Energy Commission), and no scientific leadership at all considers itself responsible in the area of technological legislation—after all, this area requires legal, political, sociological, and technological expertise. Most of the people involved are not even aware of the enormities of the problems, and those aware of them tend to advertise and propagate prophecies of doom—exaggerated or not—which include no viable solution. The problem of which party in a scientific dispute has credibility may indeed impinge on the area of research concerning the interface between the scientific community and society at large. This problem impinges on all cross-field researchers. This is why the solution which presently rules is quite ineffective. The solution now current—and justified by Kuhn—is the idea that each field must be divided into subspecialties and that in each subspeciality the debate must go on fiercely until consensus is reached. Why will this not do? It leads to the result that all cross-specialty study benefits from endorsing the lowest common denominator. It leads to the expulsion of dissenters and so of persistent critics, thus putting a limit to tolerated criticism from within and placing critics in democratic society in the position of outsiders. (In societies not constrained by democratic niceties they end up in Siberia, as noted by Joseph Stalin in the opening of his famous essay on linguistics.)

The situation is getting to a critical stage, as is well-known, but there is no responsible leadership to bring the scientific community out of the crisis. Were the crisis a threat only to the scientific community, then a responsible leadership could arise, could declare the battle lost, and could try to lead out of the crowd the scientists sold to the fleshpots of Egypt a new, small, dedicated, truly scientific voluntary community. In the present ecological and nuclear crisis this kind of move would, I propose, be downright irresponsible. So we are in a fix. Of course, it is quite conceivable that the crisis is not very desperate, since the scientific community includes many concerned individuals who perform very high quality work, who may rise to positions of responsibility and effect leadership, and who may successfully reform the customs and traditions of the scientific community. One way or another, however, it is not for responsible members of the scientific community to sit and wait for such an escape. If one hopes for such an escape or any other, then one should attempt to discuss it with colleagues, to say the very least.

It is clear that the structure of the scientific community is linked to national and international systems: educational, military, industrial, political, and others. Even the publishing empires on the trade market turn the situation to an advantage for inefficient large corporations, thereby affecting the life of the scientific community most profoundly, with their hyperconservative textbooks and the dependence on them of the most distinguished members of the scientific community when acting as authors, due to publication pressure, money needs, the need to maintain one's position as a leader, and so on. The learned world has been radically transformed in recent decades with almost no one having minimally planned or attempted to satisfactorily assess the changes.

Now both research and organization (especially innovative research and organizational reforms) are quite impossible except in workshops, and workshops are usually organized on traditional lines. Thus, we are almost trapped in an almost vicious circle. In particular, the requirement that the intellectual and the organizational leadership be identical and that ex-researchers-turned-administrators must pretend to stay in their positions as researchers, forces them to produce utterly worthless papers and, what is worse, to pretend to be co-authors of papers written by individuals who depend on their administrative help, even when this help is not at all a personal favor. (This was reported by Karin Knorr-Cetina.) It is unreasonable to expect people who behave so irresponsibly to become responsible leaders. It is therefore advisable that they be obliged to write papers on their experiences as science administrators rather than on progress in the field they administer in. (*Physics Today* censored my proposal to that effect by silently omitting a paragraph from a note of mine, and even threats of law-suits did not help.) Yet science administrators have usually neither the training nor the channels to produce research regarding their positions of leadership. Things look almost hopeless. They simply cannot even report scientifically their experiences as administrators.

What is required is to establish a legitimate specialization of cross-specialization studies and a specialization of the study of leadership, political and/or scientific. These proposals are dangerous, since they will necessarily be the refuge of the inept and of the power-hungry. What is therefore required is the study of the inept and the power-hungry and the role of these proposed disciplines and the possibility of preventing the inept and the power-hungry from preying on the students of leadership to the point of making the whole proposal useless.

The Functions of Scientific Leadership

Administrative studies describe organizational functions as maintainance and adjustment, and it is generally assumed that conflicts between these two functions are as easily discernable as their complementarity is obvious: A system not maintained does not survive to be adjusted, and a system not adjusted does not survive to be maintained. The conflict is due to the fact that adjustment mechanisms comptete with maintenance mechanisms. They are thus complementary to each other. It is at any rate beyond dispute that a major role of responsible leadership is to consider to some extent not only the day-to-day interests but also the long-term interests of the system they lead, and this includes consideration of improving efficiency. It is well known that Stalin's irresponsibility was not confined to his brutality, but expressed itself everywhere in his administration in his clear-cut preference for maintenance over adjustment; for example, in his preference for inept administrators, who depended on him and so could more easily be trusted, over competent ones, who could afford to be autonomous. The poor adjustability thus attained led to the near-collapse of the Soviet Union under the attack of Nazi Germany, when, in haste, adjustment was made—temporarily—a higher priority than maintenance.

The maintenance and adjustment of the scientific community seem utterly unproblematic (and by comparison perhaps they are), and in the period of classical science it was assumed that no one need attend to them. In particular, it was taken for granted that recruitment and training of new members of the commonwealth of learning should remain unproblematic: The learned press was assumed to be open to all interested literate individuals. Today it is assumed that leading scientists play the role of the scientific leadership and cater to the needs of the members of their specialty. This is an obvious error, and hiding behind it shows the depth of depravity of political responsibility within the scientific community, leaders and members alike, concerning national politics and the politics of science. The fact is all too obvious and is regularly implied in the standard complaints—complaints which are expressions of helplessness, and due to the absence of a responsible political leadership—concerning the control exercized by the national government, by university administrations, and by administrations of certain professional exclusive clubs, mainly medical, legal, and accounting, but also the Ivy League, the Nobel Committee, and more; implied in similar complaints about the awkwardness of the information transmission system of the learned world; implied in similar complaints about the petrification of our scientific education system, in high schools, colleges, and graduate schools. We can easily see how constrained is the leadership of the learned community by the very fact that its role is not clearly discussed, that many still stick to the Enlightenment movement's fiction that scientists are autonomous and so have no use for leadership, that others admit the need for leadership and so deny that intellectuals can or should be morally autonomous.

The situation is as ludicrous as that of any person in authority, whether in charge of a firm, a workshop, or a household, who complains about the conduct of those under his or her charge. By myth scientists are autonomous, yet by myth they are bound by administrators and leaders to their unpleasant positions. But autonomy is the coping with circumstances.

The question of what role the learned community should assign to its leadership begins with the sheer size of the learned community, even within one discipline. The problem of communication transfer is insoluble today, even within a given subdiscipline, unless some people are engaged in information sifting, and sifting is the act of a person in a powerful role—a leadership position, in fact. When Michael Ventriss was engaged in the deciphering of Linear B but a few decades ago, he could mail his own newsletter to all concerned—about 100 individuals—yet today, were he alive, he could not keep his communication on a private basis. Editors decide what to publish. They should decide by assessing the interest of their readers. That they do not is an obvious fact, and anyone who contests it should consult people with experience. It is also a most pernicious fact. (I have already mentioned the fact that editors of prestigious periodicals act as censors at times.)

Two very strong reasons exist for the pernicious conduct of editors: cowardice and conflict of interest. Cowardice is a psychological characteristic, and so it does not suffice to explain a social phenomenon. When the role of a brave person is filled by a coward, the coward may very well be quickly replaced. If not, the reason may be that all those who should see to it that the coward be replaced are likewise cowards. This makes cowardice a social psychological phenomenon, inviting a sociological explanation for its prevalence within a stratum or a subculture. Another reason for the non-removal of a coward from the position of a brave person may be that there exist institutional arrangements which prevent the needed replacement. This, too, is a sociological explanation. It is quite generally agreed that, whatever the arrangements are, they usually serve to maintain the system and preserve its stability. Otherwise the system risks destruction, rapidly regresses, or disappears. Indeed, the cowardice of the one in charge is itself a maintenance factor: colleagues elect such a person in the hope of boosting the prudence required for the maintenance of the system. Perhaps they elect a coward because, being cowards themselves, they fear the idea of appointing a brave person to a position of power. Then, however, the question is not only how a coward gets elected, but also why most electors are cowards. Hence, cowardice is not the point; prudent conduct is. Moreover, we know that when a society is on the brink of destruction, only a very brave and imaginative policy may save it. At times a suitable leader does appear and saves the system, at times not. At times the prudent leadership actively prevents the possibility of a brave and imaginative leadership. This calls for an explanation, and one is readily available: The system is geared to normal conditions, in which prudence is advisable, and is not flexible enough to adjust to stress conditions, and so it regresses or even vanishes entirely.

Recently a study of the minutes of the Nobel Prize Committee was published which shows how its membership is often swayed by the one or two really conservative scientists among them. The injustice they showed toward one daring scientist or another has been condemned by some young, thoughtless, impetuous historians of science. Yet the committee had its reasons: It could not afford to reward too often scientists whose work later turned out to be utterly insignificant. Now they regularly do so nonetheless, because in the wish to be safe they prefer to reward obvious contributions, however small, to doubtful ones, howerver big. Science and prudence, as Karl Popper has observed, simply do not mix.

This is one major item on the hidden agenda of the leadership of the learned community: When should we declare a member of the avant-garde an established thinker? If we cannot, how can we incorporate that individual's ideas without too much injustice yet without admitting too much? (Most scientists, being very poor sociologists, are convinced that full admission makes the establishment look silly, that an establishment which looks silly is a destabilizing factor, and that an unstable system is not one scientists can live in. Each of those claims, however, is quite obviously false and empirically refuted.) For example, Michael Faraday was rewarded and recognized for his experiments, and his ideas were diffused and entered the mainstream through many inlets, but not through his own writings (Agassi, 1971). Even now, over a century after Faraday's death, the establishment has not admitted the point. The reviews of my book flagrantly distorted it to the point of outright concealment of the point made here in one sentence. The review of my book in *Science* set the tone: It claimed that my book only repearts what another, pro-establishment book has said; the author of that book has also reviewed my book and declared it as distortion or a work of fiction.

The fact that the establishment of science has an official ideology which officially is not criticized, that it behaves in a manner it officially cannot endorse—the existence, in short, of a double standard in the community of science—makes this community akin to many others, even though it is somewhat less dishonest than the others. Yet its very dishonesty imposes on it a more or less hidden agenda.

The problem the hidden agenda has to solve, of course, has to do with the balance between maintenance and adjustment. For the scientific community to adapt, the scientific establishment has to know what are the best ideas available in the scientific marketplace. To maintain its stability however, it must introduce these slowly, while keeping it moving on its proper course. The time lag between the production of an idea and its reception by or blessing from the establishment becomes ever longer and forces some items off the agenda altogether as too short-lived for their survival over the time lag. This is highly unacceptable. Yet the deeper question is, Why do we need all this maintenance and, if we do need it, can it be better achieved by an open agenda than by a hidden one?

Why then maintenance? Because of the need to balance conflicting interests against each other. Were the only interest of the scientific community the advancement of learning there would be not much of a problem to begin with. As long as this was the overriding interest, indeed, there was much less of a problem than the scientific community faces nowadays, since World War II or so.

We know from Georg Simmel's theory of the web of affiliation (now that at last the sociolgical establishment is slowly coming around to admitting the greatest sociolgist of the turn of the century to some place in its pantheon) that conflict avoidance is neither possible nor desirable. The existence of science is linked to education, to technology, and to politics, not to mention the means of livelihood of scientists and the prestige of leading scientists and of leaders of the scientific community. It is also clear that Max Weber's moralizing (and hence, to repeat, reactionary) call for scientists to be so dedicated as to place the cause of truth above all other interests is futile. At least it must stay so until we known when dedication to research is laudable and when it is but an excuse—a manifestation of irresponsibility to family and to peers. Weber himself had, at times, to leave his research and participate in academic political activity. One can declare Weber's sermon correct and consequently condemn Weber's own neglect of learning, for however brief a spell, as the neglect of the highest cause he should have remained committed to, and hence one can declare Weber's own political activity irresponsible. If, however we wish to insist, as common sense seems to commend, that Weber's political activity was responsible, then one must declare Weber's sermon as quite inadequate as an answer to the question, how much effort should one devote to the politics of the scientific community, and under what conditions? There is no doubt that, as such, Weber's activity was a laudable, perhaps even a necessary activity: His fight was meant to maintain academic freedom and dedication to research.

The question of how much of the scientist's time need be devoted to ensuring proper research conditions and how much to the research itself is but a variant of the problem of the division of resources to long-term and short-term ends. It is in general an insoluble problem. Yet we can do much without solving the general problem. We can admit, to begin with, that the scientific leadership exists and that it does not always comprise the leading scientists, much less the best around. We can also decide to make our hidden agenda open and improve the means of handling it.

If we agree to make the hidden agenda of the scientific community open, then we can also agree to begin with the discussion, as the very first item on the open agenda, of the question, What are the interests of the scientific community and of each sector and subsector of it? We therefore need not discuss the list of these interests except in order to argue that they do invite an agenda. Once we agree that we need an agenda to discuss the diverse interests of the scientific community, then arguments in favor of having it openly discussed are quite general: arguments in favor of democracy and of democratic control. Now, if we agree that the scientific community has some general disinterested concerns, such as the search for the truth and for the urgent means of keeping the human race from destroying itself, perhaps also helping the race to improve living conditions on earth, then already we have to discuss the relative merit of these concerns. We can also, and quite easily, admit the existence of some unspecified selfish interests of the scientific community, and at least one mixed interest: that of finding some candidates for recruitment into the scientific community and finding the financial means required for their training. This agenda, much too short, already invites a debate on relative priorities which democratic leadership will insist that it be as open as can be.

In particular, if we admit that we want both autonomy and civic responsibility for each member of the scientific community and that then we may try to erect a responsible leadership of the scientific comunity, and if we admit that the maintenance of the community may conflict with its adaptation but that we seek for minimal stability for it and the optimal ways to maintain it while maximising its adaptation, then at once a few matters will be cleared up. We will then easily perceive that not conviction but information is what the autonomous researcher wishes to have from the literature—from texts for undergraduates to up-to-date research data—and that neither disagreements nor difficulties need be masked in name of the maintenance of the learned community. Problems will then be open to discussion in public forums, and if these are organized by responsible leaders—administrators, moderators, and others—and run by concerned scientists of all sorts, then changes to the good may be expected to follow without too long a delay.

References

Agassi, J. (1971). *Faraday as a Natural Philosopher*. Chicago: University of Chicago Press.

Agassi, J. (1981). *Science and Society*. Dordrecht: Reidel.

Agassi, J. (1985). *Technology*. Dordrecht: Reidel.

Chapter 14
Epilogue

Serge Moscovici

I must admit that I have certain reservations about every leader, great or small. I sniff at him from afar, and quickly move away. As far as the doctrine of good and evil is concerned, if I do not agree with the majority opinion, I make an effort to hold no opinion at all. However, I do not easily let myself be drawn into conversations grappling with the question, "Is he good? Is he evil?" He *is*, and that suffices to determine my reactions. To which some who do not know me might say that I am a nihilist. They are in fact mistaken. I find it easy to obey a leader—though my opinion is not asked—if he does not force me to admire or respect him for that. I feel this is quite simple. I have begun with these confessions, because the subject of this conference was not an easy one to deal with, and I suspect, without having verified it, that the majority of the participants shared my feelings. Thus, we felt a certain hesitation to broach this subject and to deal with it thoroughly. Is this the only reason? Certainly not. We met in Germany, and no one would forget the havoc the leadership principle wreaked in Germany's history and in ours. When we Europeans say leader, we think, as if by conditioned reflex, of Hitler. Mistakenly, undoubtedly, but that is the way it is, and this name for everyone present was heavy with memories and terror. The majority had seen him in the flesh. This contributed to the atmosphere in which we discussed certain texts which have become chapters in this book.

One cannot speak dispassionately of leadership during this fin de siécle. But what, you ask, is to become of scholarship? Quite simply, one brings it back to those moments in history when this passion was kindled. But perhaps we should use a different word instead of *passion* we should use *paradox* or even *taboo*. Why? One need only look around and think of the evolution that has taken place. Everyone agrees on the principle of democracy. Therefore every modern nation tries to govern itself by means of exchanges, decisions, and consensuses reached among equals. The individual exercising a function is merely a representative, a mediator, or a secretary. The sovereign people choose among forces and talents, organize and reach decisions as the last authority. It is a fact that the various social movements pointed to such an evolution, and we worked within this framework. In general, contemporary society should no longer be subjected to or driven by a leader. The times when history became confused with the biography of famous men or when politics was the exclusive realm of such men should be over. The decline of leaders is considered an accomplished and inevitable fact. Yet if there is an institution in the world today that is flourishing once again, it is leadership. The examples are obvious. Stalin and Castro, Mao Tse-Tung and de Gaulle, John Paul II and Roosevelt were and are great men. They were great men from the beginning of their power. Regular and solemn summit meetings confer recognition on this institution of leadership, and it is significant that some leaders are in the process of establishing dynasties. Think, for instance, of Ceaucescu in Roumania or of Kim Il Sung in North Korea. Even in India, the largest democracy in the world, the name Gandhi perpetuates itself. Without mincing words, let us say that in too many countries universal suffrage by vote or acclamation is suppressing itself. We have much feared the tyranny of the majority, but there has been much suffering from the moment the pendulum tipped toward a tyranny directed against the majority. Stendhal, who foresaw this development, spoke a terrible truth. He summarized his epoch with the words, "The nation is drunk with glory; farewell to liberty."

In short, everything seems to indicate that leadership is an unintended and undesirable consequence of democracy, or a "perverse effect" as we say in France. It is from this perspective that we consider leadership to be an object of analysis for the social sciences. In the words of Popper, "The characteristic problems of social sciences arise only out of our wish to know the *unintended consequences*, and more especially the *unwanted consequences* which may arise if we do certain things." Professor Groh, as usual, served as our guide and as our historical conscience. In a very compact communication, of which his chapter gives witness, he retraced the steps from the peasant revolts to contemporary rebellions, in particular those in which the German socialist movement participated. Considering the role that movement played within the workers' movement in general, one understands the significance of this example. It appears that between the sixteenth and the nineteenth centuries numerous uprisings were fought without leaders. In contrast, the workers' movement, which as a matter of principle always distrusted great men and intended to put an end to their reign, was under their thumb from the beginning. It is not necessary to mention names or to pass judgment on the personal value of a Lassalle or a Liebknecht. It is the tendency they exemplify that counts. This much is without doubt: the workers' party had an effect contrary to its members' intentions. They gave themselves leaders, although it was their principle to end the institution of leadership. Thus, the famous iron law of the oligarchy is reconfirmed from a different perspective—but not quite, since Dieter

Groh demonstrates the paradox in collective action. And then this: It is the characteristic of the socialist movement to give itself leaders without leadership. That is to say, they accept the leaders' authority without having established a principle that legitimizes their power. This has resulted in a permanent debate, the ideological consequences of which are known. It became necessary to justify what was unintended and considered undesirable.

Of course, one can observe the same paradox outside of workers' movements. It is contained in this enigmatic word *charisma* which has become so popular. Everyone uses it, although few understand its exact meaning. This fuzziness is probably the reason for its success, as everyone attributes the meaning he or she wants to it. Charisma means an extraordinary and personal leadership. For half a century it has spread like a forest fire. Professor Cavalli has devoted two outstanding volumes to it. Naturally, in his chapter he takes up again and refines the ideas presented in these volumes, ideas that are not yet as well known as they deserve to be. He presents an analysis of the relationship between modern dictatorship and mass democracy. Indeed, charismatic domination establishes the link between the principle of authority within a society in crisis and the principle of equality during the crisis of a society which cannot arrive at a definition of a legitimate form of power. What is astonishing about this? Is this not happening before our very eyes? His presentation is pertinent concerning the spread of the totalitarian order under both fascism and Nazism. It was a new order establishing itself to respond to these crises without resolving them. In the wake of its leaders, notably of Hitler, people let themselves be led into a consenting and loyal submission. It was by means of charisma that these leaders came to power, and through popular acclamation that their power was recognized. In one sense, everything is within these means, the use of which Professor Cavalli has explained in depth.

Professor Lepsius deals with the same subject. His erudition evokes admiration when he places the notion of charismatic leadership within the framework of Weber's theory. Certainly, this notion has been vulgarized and muddled with other ideas, reducing its originality. This has caused some confusion. We must always return to the fundamental ideas. Professor Lepsius does just that in reminding us that charisma is an exceptional trait and takes on revolutionary meaning within a society governed by tradition. He also reminds us that charismatic domination works outside of all hierarchies and is based upon a direct emotional link with the collectivity. At the same time, however, this leadership originates in a crisis of this same collectivity. Expressing himself very clearly, he demonstates the logic of this, applying it then to a particular case: Hitler and Germany. In my opinion, the two chapters complete each other. Admittedly they express a personal experience and a perception that would not be the same for a political scientist or sociologist. Together, they show the meaning of a "hot" leadership exercised upon masses *in statu nascendi*, to use Weber's expression, or in a "state of effervescence," to use Durkheim's phrase. We are on the threshold of a new mass psychology which inspired and preoccupied these two founders of modern social science.

With Professor Grauman's chapter we change our perspective and our level. By presenting the ideas of Lewin to us, he deals directly with the question of power. Undoubtedly, social psychology has been marked by these ideas and by the method used to confirm them, but perhaps one has forgotten how these ideas are connected with the field theory. This theory, by emphasizing analogies from physics, makes it possible to define power with precision as a form of interdependence. It is the capacity of one person to evoke forces that act upon another person within a more or less organized context. Thus, that person potentially can exert influence and create a common social reality. But the power fits into the framework of the group. Professor Graumann explains very clerly the meaning that the idea of the "group as a whole" takes on here, and how one is to approach it practically. I do not emphasize his historical analysis, but it has the merit of dealing with the essential and showing that the path begun by Lewin has not yet been followed to its end. One thing is certain: Reading this rich chapter familiarizes us with the data, allowing us to pick up once again an interrupted task—interrupted, on the one hand, by Lewin's death, but also by the individualistic tendency that dominates in social psychology today.

However, Professor Fiedler's study shows that if the study of leadership has been interrupted, it has not been totally abandoned. We know Professor Fiedler's work and the repercussions of his theory. He knows what he is talking about when he emphasizes the contrast between the "large" and the "small" theories of leadership. The former conjecture abundantly though they are lacking in facts, whereas the latter are plentiful in details but form few conjectures. This remark, I believe, applies not only to the study of leadership. At any rate, Professor Fiedler proposes a model, the cognitive resource theory, and a series of studies intended to validate it. Using a henceforth traditional method he shows how the performance of the leader depends on his or her intellectual capacity. This, of course, has been debated by numerous authors. These intellectual capacities turn out to be necessary and effective only when the leader is commanding, and when he or she benefits from the faith and support of the group. One is nonetheless surprised to note that these capacities will weaken the leader's performance if he or she is not commanding, meaning, perhaps, if his style is "laissez-faire" or "democratic," to use Lewin's terms. I say "perhaps" because this has not been studied, and it would be important to do so. The question of the importance of the qualities of the leader, so often neglected, is posed once again in these studies.

A leader is necessary during any cooperation among several parties, and this leader must be competent, meaning that he or she possesses the necessary information to ensure such cooperation. When 20 men lift a plate of concrete they obey a foreman. If they were to consult among themselves while the action is taking place they would risk dropping the concrete. A captain, once he sets foot on board, is the master, directly under God. So it seems that a leader is a necessary part of any group action. Professor von Cranach examines the reasons for such a necessity. Starting with his well-known theory of goal-oriented action concerning individuals, he extends it to apply to the group. This enriches our understanding of how information is treated and used by a collective system. This exemplifies the function of the leader, who at once mobilizes the energy of the group, changes the direction of its behavior, and resolves conflicts between means and ends. Thus, this model is at the opposite end of the spectrum from Lewin's.

Professor von Cranach's synthesizing ability is remarkable, however, at least where his capacity to relate heretofore disparate elements is concerned, and in the interpretation he gives of charisma, for example. Certainly, notions of motivation and emotion are evoked in these three chapters, as well as individual qualities. In general, however, one has the impression that one is dealing with a "cold" leadership, impersonal and mechanical. This leadership fits within a hierarchy and an organization that allows the adaptation of the group to reality. So, paradoxically, it seems that political scientists and sociologists are placing greater emphasis on subjectivity and the affective relationship to leadership. It is they who insist on the crisis situation and on the direct link between the leader and the masses, outside of all organization. In short, they insist on the psychological aspects of this kind of social power. The psychosociologists, on the other had, deemphasize the role played by subjectivity and affectivity. They place greater importance on the functions and objective justifications of leadership. Whenever possible, they attempt to associate leadership with that other form of social power, the existence of a hierarchy and of collective organization. In short, the former focus on those who command, the latter on those who are commanded. The element of constraint, which seems obvious to the first, is of secondary importance to the latter. I am stating here a general impression that is contradicted by many a detail. I am perfectly aware of this. If there is nonetheless a contrast, what are the reasons for it? One reason, at least I believe, is self-evident: politics. One can focus on many an aspect of the evolution of social psychology, but one must mention its depoliticization. The attention given to political phenomena and problems is progressively decreasing. Lewin represents a turning point: He still defines leadership in political terms, but, as Professor Graumann has shown, after him this approach has been more or less abandoned. The phenomena and problems of power are only studied in the context of relationships between individuals or between individuals and groups. The framework is an organization or a company, or any other small group whose members have a common goal. This question, however, calls for a much profound debate, which has been, in fact, initiated during our conference.

Leadership, by its nature, presupposes the use of symbols in order to act, and the creation of social representations in order to exist. Every leader must be an artist of communication, and a work of art to communicate. The leader's reality is, in large part, made up of images and words. We may not like this, but it is a fact nonetheless—a fact all the more important in a democracry and a society of communication such as ours. The subject is, of course, quite vast. This book broaches it in two chapters nonetheless, and in a very original fashion. First, the chapter by Professors Katz and Dayan examines media events in television programming. It is characteristic of these episodes to deviate from news and regular broadcasting. They use figurative language, striking circumlocutions, and condensations of images. Three media events in particular focus on a leader: contests, conquests, and coronations. Together they form a kind of symbolic basis, fed on memories and archetypes. The exceptional individual, the heroic individual above the rest, is set off against this background. I am surely summarizing the gist of their theory poorly, but as far as I can understand, the theory shows to what extent television feeds a representation that contrasts the one and the many. The qualities of the one resemble charisma, and so the scene of domination, its fantasy or its model, stands out in its cultural context. Then the actual actors can come into play to realize this fantasy or model. The theory is more subtle, however; the desire that leads to communication and the forms of this desire remain undetermined. Contests, conquests, and coronations are thus the expression of a desire for both conflict and reconciliation with authority. These are the rites of a modern celebration of very archaic impulses. We have come very close to a modern anthropology of leadership, the concrete and practical significance of which is obvious to everyone.

With the chapters by Drs. Kennan and Hadley we plunge in completely. We are fascinated, for they take us back to an elementary observation: In our societies the candidate for political leadership is a consumer product like any other. The practical question then poses itself: What must be the qualities of this product so that the consumers choose it above all the rest? I would not dare summarize the authors' at once rigorous and detailed analysis of product and consumer. I am unqualified to reach a judgment on this analysis. I admit, however, that I noted a certain ambivalence, which I will summarize as follows: On the one hand, the analysis fully rehabilitates the place of social psychology in this domain. The theorists may well reject it, but the practitioners are obliged to use it. It shows us to what extent the phenomenon of leadership is indeed what Marcel Mauss called the total social phenomenon. In leadership, subjective and objective, irrational and rational, symbolic and real elements are combined. It is banal to say it, but not to do it. Kennan and Hadley succeed with talent and I admire them. On the other hand, I feel a bit uneasy with this "secularization" of political practice. This is undoubtedly another facet of that unintended and unwanted consequence of which I spoke above. Sometimes one tends to avoid thinking about this, but the transformation of the right to vote, and of public opinion in the process, is of ethical even more than of political significance. In any case, this desacralization which we can observe going on around us cannot be without effect on its very existence. These two chapters establish a connection between the "hot" and "cold" leadership of which we spoke earlier. They demonstrate, at least partially, its symbolic function.

Not all leaders are men, although it is men who make up the majority in conferences and have held the levers of power for millenia. I know *leader* is for some synonymous with *male*, and that it will still take some time before we can get beyond that synonymy. Even if we do smile at the statement by Schopenhauer: "Even the idea of seeing women governing in the place of men makes one burst into laughter, but the sisters of charity are not inferior to the brothers of mercy."

One day I hope the two chapters on women and leadership contained in this book will be counted among the contributions towards a change in the meaning of that synonymy. Is it better to be led by a man or a woman? If you were to ask me, I would say that I have no idea, for history does not permit me to answer such a question. Is leadership by a man different from leadership by a woman? I would answer that I doubt it, for no theory exists that asserts such a difference. The difficulty of the study of leadership by women is patent, because such questions obviously cannot be answered, even if everyone does ask them. However, the authors of the two chapters devoted to this subject have explored with great astuteness the paths by which women have gained access to positions of leadership. I must note that we had the idea to do these studies during the conference, and that the studies were done later.

Leadership for Professor Kruse and Dr. Wintermantel is both showing leadership behavior and being recognized as a leader. It is this dual conception that makes woman leadership an ambivalent and conflict-ridden topic if at all. For the topic of women in leadership positions is so far only rarely approached in leadership research and certainly not accounted for in leadership theory. The ambivalent and conflictive situation of women aspiring to attain and hold leading positions originates in the existence of conflicting, almost mutually exclusive, social norms: those contained in the gender stereotype and those of a social representation of leadership that is predominantly masculine. The tension resulting from such conflict becomes manifest psychologically in states of uncertainty and oscillation, and socially in tendencies to over- or underrate the achievement of women in leadership positions. One could add that, sociologically speaking, the situation of women leaders is closer to states of *anomie* than to social normalcy. It definitely is a state of transition with almost all the characteristics of the "marginality" and of social change. Evidence from the leadership literature as well as from two studies in psychological semantics substantiates the challenge to leadership theory to change from implicit gender bias to explicit gender equity.

Professor Apfelbaum and Dr. Hadley initially gathered some fascinating evidence. Their analysis of this material is no less fascinating: One observes a sort of rupture at the outset of the careers of the women interviewed, which thrust them onto the public scene. These women then acquired the necessary capacities to assert themselves in a milieu that was at once strange and hostile to them. Their study shows clearly how in this respect they were often denied titles due to them, and to what extent they needed a close-knit support group. The authors argue that the women whom they interviewed were not completely identified with the strategies and rules of power. It would be important to understand why.

Following their reasoning closely, one becomes aware to what extent values and social representations determine at once the actions of these women and the reactions to them. Undoubtedly, they cannot forget for a single instant that they are women leaders, no more than a Jewish leader, a Catholic in a Protestant country, a black in a white nation, or a Georgian in a Russian state can forget their minority status. I give these examples not to argue that women's situation is just one among many, but for precisely the opposite purpose. I want to show that the content of these chapters has a much more general significance, and that they focus on a too often neglected dimension of the phenomenon we are studying. One remark, however: I feel that we should take the role of the *Zeitgeist* more rigorously into account. The climate of opinion can hasten the opening of new opportunities to a group that had heretofore been denied access. However, the climate of opinion can also create the illusion that the problems have been solved and that the obstacles have been overcome. In this way the climate of opinion can hide to what extent such an emancipation can be artificial and fragile. This, I believe, is true today for women, but not only for them.

When we repeat into the wind that man is a social animal we should emphasize *animal* and not *social*. The chapter by Professor Crook takes us back to the evolution and the biological roots of the species. With his accustomed refinement and astuteness he points out the oddness that biologists feel when dealing with the notion of leadership. Wary of anthropomorphism, they are obliged to give in as much to the facts as to the social model itself. The analogies are too obvious to do without. We follow Professor Crook in his examination of these analogies with all the more fascination since they resemble a fairy tale or fable. Descriptions of what goes on in the animal world always makes one feel a little like a child listening to a beautiful story. The story in this chapter is as beautiful as it is instructive. I am persuaded that it teaches us something about us, and about the human world, but our discussions with ethologists must be held on a more profound level and on a more long-term basis for us to grasp exactly what we are learning. In any case the points of orientation have been set, and that is the most important.

I remember suggesting that our conference should include a study on scientific leadership. I, for one, do not understand how so much can have been written about scientific societies without seriously alluding to scientific leadership. All too often scientists are presented as one happy family—this is where the expression "scientific community," copying the expression "business community" I suppose, comes from—or scientists are portrayed as working within a free and direct democracy. Consequently, one thinks of relations among scientists, of their common language and work, in these terms. However, one need only examine one's personal experience to recognize the omnipresence of leadership. Descartes, the recluse, could well say that we need not obey any authority. He did not, however, include scientific authority in his list. Perhaps you will argue that scientific authority is without importance or impact. Then the burden of proof lies on you. The fact is that charismatic leaders have existed in science, from Durkheim to Freud, from Einstein to Bohr, from Delbrück to Monod, to be brief. There are many others, but we need not break down open doors. Scientific leadership might seem a contradiction in terms. Professor Agassi convinces us of the contrary. A reputable philosopher of science, he shows to what extent leaders are present in scientific groups. They control the input and output of information. Simply showing that they are as inevitable and as undesirable as in society at large constitutes a discovery in itself. He is not sure that one can control them any more effectively than leaders in general, nor is it evident that a free flow of information can exist within science any more than elsewhere. Can the fear of plagiarism and the quest for originality permit it? To suppose, on the other hand, that democracy could institute such a free flow is to speak without rigor and to engage in wishful thinking. One would be in for disappointments and futile moral upheavals. Science would be in this eventuality one of these social machines in perpetual flux that one studies all too often in the sciences of man. It is time to stop examining them, just as the physical sciences no longer examine perpetual motion machines. That is not to say that another condition of society is not possible or desirable. This only excludes an impossible condition.

What seems clear to me, in reading all these chapters, is that we have succeeded in delimiting a phenomenon and in discovering its different aspects. There is, as we can see, a gap between the importance of leadership in the political and historical reality of our time and the kind of disinterest researchers show for this phenomenon. In short, leadership is a totem in society and a taboo in science. Consequently, it is obscured and deformed. It is almost as if after having focused too much attention on leadership in the past—and Professor Graumann explains why in the preface—one felt one could reestablish the balance by not paying enough attention to it now, or by paying no attention to it at all. This book contains sufficient arguments and new ideas to promote a new growth of interest. It also shows that only an interdisciplinary approach will lead to a growth of knowledge in this domain.

Acknowledgments. To Kathy Stuart for translating this article from French into English.

Author Index

Subject Index

Springer Series in Social Psychology

Attention and Self-Regulation: A Control-Theory Approach to Human Behavior
Charles S. Carver/Michael F. Scheier

Gender and Nonverbal Behavior
Clara Mayo/Nancy M. Henley (Editors)

Personality, Roles, and Social Behavior
William Ickes/Eric S. Knowles (Editors)

Toward Transformation in Social Knowledge
Kenneth J. Gergen

The Ethics of Social Research: Surveys and Experiments
Joan E. Sieber (Editor)

The Ethics of Social Research: Fieldwork, Regulation, and Publication
Joan E. Sieber (Editor)

Anger and Aggression: An Essay on Emotion
James R. Averill

The Social Psychology of Creativity
Teresa M. Amabile

Sports Violence
Jeffrey H. Goldstein (Editor)

Nonverbal Behavior: A Functional Perspective
Miles L. Patterson

Basic Group Processes
Paul B. Paulus (Editor)

Attitudinal Judgment
J. Richard Eiser (Editor)

Social Psychology of Aggression: From Individual Behavior to Social Interaction
Amélie Mummendey (Editor)

Directions in Soviet Social Psychology
Lloyd H. Strickland (Editor)

Sociophysiology
William M. Waid (Editor)

Compatible and Incompatible Relationships
William Ickes (Editor)

Facet Theory: Approaches to Social Research
David Canter (Editor)

Action Control: From Cognition to Behavior
Julius Kuhl/Jürgen Beckmann (Editors)

Springer Series in Social Psychology